Praise for *Learning TensorFlow.js*

What Gant has done with this book is to cut to the chase, and teach you the important
stuff you need to know while keeping you firmly within the
web developer role, using JavaScript and the Browser.

—*Laurence Moroney, Lead AI Advocate, Google*

Machine learning has the potential to influence every industry out there. This book
enables you to take your first steps with TensorFlow.js, allowing any JavaScript developer
to gain superpowers in their next web application and beyond. This book is a great
introduction to machine learning using TensorFlow.js that also applies what you learn
with real world examples that are easy to digest.

—*Jason Mayes, Senior Developer Relations Engineer for
TensorFlow.js at Google*

Gant's ability to navigate explaining the complexities of machine learning while avoiding
the pitfalls of complicated mathematics is uncanny, and you'd be hard-pressed to find a
better introduction to data science using JavaScript.

—*Lee Warrick, Fullstack JavaScript Developer*

I'm delighted to have read *Learning TensorFlow.js*. It is without doubt a good way to get
out of my comfort zone of backend engineering and try out building some exciting
frontend applications, leveraging the power of the book's content about Tensorflow.js as
the go-to framework for ML web applications.

—*Laura Uzcátegui, Software Engineer, Microsoft*

This book serves as the right introduction to building small deep learning models fit for web and mobile based applications. The examples in the book along with the detailed explanation will make your learning smooth and fun.

—*Vishwesh Ravi Shrimali, Engineer, Mercedes Benz R&D India*

I wish that I'd had this book myself to learn neural networks and TensorFlow.js in the past! Astonishingly simple and beautifully written, it goes from zero to doing a full capstone project in 12 short chapters. A must-have in every library.

—*Axel Sirota, Machine Learning Research Engineer*

This is a much-needed introduction to TensorFlow.js, with great examples, amazing illustrations, and insightful quotes at the beginning of each chapter. A must-read for anyone who's serious about doing AI with JavaScript.

—*Alexey Grigorev, Founder of DataTalks.Club*

Machine learning for the web is still in its infancy, and books such as the one you're holding right now are super important. As a machine learning engineer working on ML tools for the JavaScript environment, my top recommendation for web developers seeking to add ML to their projects is definitely *LearningTensorFlow.js*.

—*Rising Odegua, Cocreator of Danfo.js*

Learning TensorFlow.js
Powerful Machine Learning in JavaScript

Gant Laborde

Beijing · Boston · Farnham · Sebastopol · Tokyo

Learning TensorFlow.js

by Gant Laborde

Published by O'Reilly Media, Inc., 1005 Gravenstein Highway North, Sebastopol, CA 95472.

O'Reilly books may be purchased for educational, business, or sales promotional use. Online editions are also available for most titles (*http://oreilly.com*). For more information, contact our corporate/institutional sales department: 800-998-9938 or *corporate@oreilly.com*.

Acquisitions Editor: Jennifer Pollock	**Indexer:** Ellen Troutman-Zaig
Development Editor: Michele Cronin	**Interior Designer:** David Futato
Production Editor: Caitlin Ghegan	**Cover Designer:** Karen Montgomery
Copyeditor: Kim Wimpsett	**Illustrator:** Kate Dullea
Proofreader: JM Olejarz	

May 2021:   First Edition

Revision History for the First Edition
2021-05-07:   First Release

See *http://oreilly.com/catalog/errata.csp?isbn=9781492090793* for release details.

978-1-492-09079-3

[LSI]

This book is   dedicated
to the most infectious & gentle smile.
To the irrepressible spark & endless
joy of my heart. To my loving
daughter, I love you,
Mila.

Table of Contents

Foreword

AI and machine learning are revolutionary technologies that can change the world, but they can only do that if there are developers using good APIs to take advantage of the advancements these technologies bring.

One such advancement is the ability to run machine learning models in the browser, empowering applications that act intelligently.

The rise of TensorFlow.js tells me that AI has arrived. It's no longer exclusively in the realm of data scientists with supercomputers; it's now accessible to the millions of developers who code in JavaScript daily. But there's a gap. The tools and techniques for building models are still very much in the hands of those who know the mysteries of Python, NumPy, graphics processing units (GPUs), data science, feature modeling, supervised learning, tensors, and many more weird and wonderful terms that you probably aren't familiar with!

What Gant has done with this book is to cut to the chase, teaching you the important stuff you need to know while keeping you firmly within the web developer role, using JavaScript and the browser. He'll introduce you to the concepts of AI and machine learning with a clear focus on how they can be used in the platform you care about.

Often, I hear developers ask, when wanting to use machine learning, "Where can I find stuff that I can reuse? I don't want to learn to be an ML engineer just to figure out if this stuff will work for me!"

Gant answers that question in this book. You'll discover premade models that you can take lock, stock, and barrel from TensorFlow Hub. You will also learn how to stand on the shoulders of giants by taking selected portions of models built using millions of items of data and many thousands of hours of training, and see how you can transfer learn from them to your own model. Then, just drop it into your page and have Java-Script do the rest!

Developers ask, "How can I use machine learning on the platform I care about without extensive retraining?"

This book goes deeply into that—showing you how to bridge the gap between Java-Script and models that were trained using TensorFlow. From data conversion between primitives and tensors to parsing output probabilities into text, this book guides you through the steps to integrate tightly with your site.

Developers ask me, "I want to go beyond other people's work and simple prototypes. Can I do that as a web developer?"

Again, yes. By the time you've finished this book, not only will you be familiar with using models, but Gant will give you all the details you need to create them yourself. You'll learn how to train complex models such as convolutional neural networks to recognize the contents of images, and you'll do it all in JavaScript.

A survey in October 2020 showed that there were 12.4 million JavaScript developers in the world. Other surveys showed that there are about 300,000 AI practitioners globally. With the technology of TensorFlow.js and the skills in this book, you, dear JavaScript developer, can be a part of making AI matter. And this book is a wonderful, wonderful place to start.

Enjoy the journey!

— Laurence Moroney
March 2021

Preface

"If you choose not to decide, you still have made a choice."

—Geddy Lee (Rush)

Let's Do This

Hindsight is always 20/20. "I should have bought some bitcoin when it was at X" or "If only I had applied at startup Y before they became famous." The world is replete with moments that define us for better or worse. Time never goes backward, but it echoes the lessons of our younger choices as we go forward. You're lucky enough to have this book and this moment to decide.

The foundations of the software industry are changing due to artificial intelligence. The changes will ultimately be decided by those who grab hold and shape the world into what it will be tomorrow. Machine learning is an adventure into new possibilities, and when it is unified with the broad exposure of JavaScript, the limits drift away.

As I like to tell my audience in my talks on AI, "You didn't come this far in creating software only to come this far." So let's get started and see where our imagination takes us.

Why TensorFlow.js?

TensorFlow is one of the most popular machine learning frameworks on the market. It's supported by Google's top minds and is responsible for powering many of the world's most influential companies. TensorFlow.js is the indomitable JavaScript framework of TensorFlow and is better than all the competitors. In short, if you want the power of a framework in JavaScript, there's only one choice that can do it all.

Who Should Read This Book?

Two primary demographics will enjoy and benefit from the contents of this book:

The JavaScript developer

If you're familiar with JavaScript, but you've never touched machine learning before, this book will be your guide. It leans into the framework to keep you active in pragmatic and exciting creations. You'll comprehend the basics of machine learning with hands-on experience through the construction of all kinds of projects. While we won't shy away from math or deeper concepts, we also won't overly complicate the experience with them. Read this book if you're building websites in JavaScript and want to gain a new superpower.

The AI specialist

If you're familiar with TensorFlow or even the fundamental principles of linear algebra, this book will supply you with countless examples of how to bring your skills to JavaScript. Here, you'll find various core concepts illustrated, displayed, and portrayed in the TensorFlow.js framework. This will allow you to apply your vast knowledge to a medium that can exist efficiently on edge devices like client browsers or the Internet of Things (IoT). Read this book and learn how to bring your creations to countless devices with rich interactive experiences.

This book requires a moderate amount of comfort in reading and understanding modern JavaScript.

Book Overview

When outlining this book, I realized I'd have to make a choice. Either I could create a whirlwind adventure into a variety of applications of machine learning and touch on each with small, tangible examples, or I could choose a single path that tells an ever-growing story of the concepts. After polling my friends and followers, it was clear that the latter was needed. To keep this book sane and under a thousand pages, I chose to remove any JavaScript frameworks and to focus on a singular pragmatic journey into the visual aspects of AI.

Each chapter ends with questions and a particular challenge for you to test your resolve. The Chapter Challenge sections have been carefully constructed to solidify lessons into your TensorFlow.js muscle memory.

The Chapters

Chapters 1 and 2 begin with core concepts and a concrete example. This yin-and-yang approach reflects the teaching style of the book. Each chapter builds on the lessons, vocabulary, and functions mentioned in previous chapters.

Chapters 3 through 7 give you the vision to understand and implement existing AI tools and data. You'll be able to create impressive libraries as well as employ models in projects that were created by scores of data scientists.

Chapters 8 through 11 begin giving you the power of creation in TensorFlow.js. You'll be able to train models in JavaScript, and I firmly believe this is one of the most fun and exciting sections of the entire book.

Chapter 12 is the final challenge. The final chapter presents a capstone project that empowers you to take everything the book has to offer and express it using your own faculty.

The Takeaway

After reading this book, regardless of your previous experience, you'll be able to find, implement, adjust, and create machine learning models in TensorFlow.js. You'll have the ability to identify an application of machine learning in a website and then follow through with fulfilling that implementation.

Conventions Used in This Book

The following typographical conventions are used in this book:

Italic
> Indicates new terms, URLs, email addresses, filenames, and file extensions.

`Constant width`
> Used for program listings, as well as within paragraphs to refer to program elements such as variable or function names, databases, data types, environment variables, statements, and keywords.

`Constant width bold`
> Shows commands or other text that should be typed literally by the user.

`Constant width italic`
> Shows text that should be replaced with user-supplied values or by values determined by context.

 This element signifies a tip or suggestion.

This element signifies a general note.

 This element indicates a warning or caution.

Using Code Examples

Supplemental materials (code examples, exercises, etc.) are available for download at *https://github.com/GantMan/learn-tfjs*.

If you have a technical question or a problem using the code examples, please send an email to *bookquestions@oreilly.com*.

This book is here to help you get your job done. In general, if example code is offered with this book, you may use it in your programs and documentation. You do not need to contact us for permission unless you're reproducing a significant portion of the code. For example, writing a program that uses several chunks of code from this book does not require permission. Selling or distributing examples from O'Reilly books does require permission. Answering a question by citing this book and quoting example code does not require permission. Incorporating a significant amount of example code from this book into your product's documentation does require permission.

We appreciate, but generally do not require, attribution. An attribution usually includes the title, author, publisher, and ISBN. For example: "*Learning TensorFlow.js* by Gant Laborde (O'Reilly). Copyright 2021 Gant Laborde, 978-1-492-09079-3."

If you feel your use of code examples falls outside fair use or the permission given above, feel free to contact us at *permissions@oreilly.com*.

O'Reilly Online Learning

 For more than 40 years, *O'Reilly Media* has provided technology and business training, knowledge, and insight to help companies succeed.

Our unique network of experts and innovators share their knowledge and expertise through books, articles, and our online learning platform. O'Reilly's online learning platform gives you on-demand access to live training courses, in-depth learning paths, interactive coding environments, and a vast collection of text and video from O'Reilly and 200+ other publishers. For more information, visit *http://oreilly.com*.

How to Contact Us

Please address comments and questions concerning this book to the publisher:

O'Reilly Media, Inc.
1005 Gravenstein Highway North
Sebastopol, CA 95472
800-998-9938 (in the United States or Canada)
707-829-0515 (international or local)
707-829-0104 (fax)

We have a web page for this book, where we list errata, examples, and any additional information. You can access this page at *https://oreil.ly/learning-tensorflow-js*.

Email *bookquestions@oreilly.com* to comment or ask technical questions about this book.

For news and information about our books and courses, visit *http://oreilly.com*.

Find us on Facebook: *http://facebook.com/oreilly*

Follow us on Twitter: *http://twitter.com/oreillymedia*

Watch us on YouTube: *http://youtube.com/oreillymedia*

Acknowledgments

I want to say thanks to the editors, production staff, and employees of O'Reilly, who have been a delight to work with while writing this book.

Of course, thank you to the preeminent Laurence Moroney, the author of this book's foreword. You've been an icon and an inspiration in my growth. I've learned so much from you, and I'll continue to thrive in the wake of your machine learning lessons and achievements.

The tech reviewers for this book were some of the friendliest and most thorough people I've had the pleasure of working with.

Laura Uzcátegui

> Your kind and inspirational feedback was enchanting to read. Your intuition helped make this book feel right.

Vishwesh Ravi Shrimali

> You caught all my jokes. You're obviously a smart and friendly person, and in that way, you pushed me to be better. I appreciated all of your advice and wisdom.

Jason Mayes

> I knew you before you were selected as a technical editor for this book, so I think of you as a friend as much as a teammate in making this book the best it can be. Your feedback was meticulous, intelligent, and irreplaceable. Thank you sincerely.

Axel Damian Sirota

> I can feel the high personal support in every bit of feedback you gave. You took the time to be smart and kind. Your artistry was a gift to this book.

Lee Warrick

> You continue to review and challenge me to be better in all my works. This book is the latest example of my accomplishments prospering from your insight.

Michele Cronin

> I enjoyed every meeting we had. You are a sustained delight! Thank you for being you. You made this book effortless. How you did it, I'll never know.

Special thanks to Frank von Hoven III, who asked all the right questions and handed me pages upon pages of handwritten notes of feedback (Figure P-1). Your flair and honesty kept me guided in delivering a strong and inspirational message.

Figure P-1. Awesome support and feedback by Frank

Lastly, thanks to my loving family, who avoided interrupting me as much as possible but also knew when I needed a good interruption. Alicia, my love, you know me better than I know myself. You surprised me with invigorating coffee when I needed to push forward and a stiff drink when it was time to stop and repose. Every day, the best of me is because of you.

## CHAPTER 1

AI Is Magic

"Any sufficiently advanced technology is indistinguishable from magic."

—Arthur C. Clarke

OK, AI is not actual magic. The truth is AI is a step above and beyond other technology to the point that it *feels* like magic. It's easy enough to explain an effective sorting algorithm, but digging into intelligence itself touches the third rail and zaps us all into a whole new level of technological power. That exponential power-up is made possible through the wisdom and aptitude of TensorFlow.js.

For more than half a century scientists and engineers have re-created the metaphorical wheel in AI and fine-tuned the mechanics that control it. When we dig into AI in this book, we'll grasp those concepts with the flexible yet durable framework of TensorFlow.js and, with it, bring our ideas to fruition in the expanding domain of JavaScript. Yes, JavaScript, the world's most popular programming language.[1]

The concepts and definitions provided here will equip you with tech-ray vision. You'll cut through acronyms and buzzwords to see and understand the AI infrastructure that's been emerging in every field around us. AI and machine learning concepts will become clear, and the definitions from this chapter can serve as a reference for identifying core principles that will fuel our academic blastoff into TensorFlow.js illumination.

---

1 Programming language stats: *https://octoverse.github.com*

We will:

- Clarify the domain of AI and intelligence
- Discuss the types of machine learning
- Review and define common terminology
- Cross-examine concepts through the lens of TensorFlow.js

Let's begin!

 If you're already familiar with TensorFlow.js and machine learning terminology, philosophy, and fundamental applications, you may want to skip directly to Chapter 2.

The Path of AI in JavaScript

TensorFlow.js, to put it in the most mundane definition possible, is a framework for handling specific AI concepts in JavaScript. That's all. Luckily for you, you're in the right book at the right time in history. The AI industrial revolution has only just begun.

When computers came into being, a person armed with a computer could do and nearly impossible tasks at significant scale. They could crack codes, instantly recall information from mountains of data, and even play games as if they were playing another human. What *was* impossible for one person to do became not only possible but customary. Since the dawn of that key digital invention, our goal has been to empower computers to simply "do more." As singular human beings, we are capable of anything, but not everything. Computers expanded our limitations in ways that gave us all newfound power. Many of us spend our lives honing a few skills, and among those, even fewer become our specialties. We all build a lifetime's worth of achievements, and some of us rise to the best in the world at one thing, a skill that could only be earned with luck, information, and thousands of days of effort...until now.

AI enables us to skip to the front of the line; to boldly build that which has never been built before. Daily we're seeing companies and researchers take that computational leap over and over again. We're standing at the entrance of a new industry that invites us to play a part in how the world will change.

You're in the driver's seat, headed to the next big thing, and this book is your steering wheel. Our journey in learning the magic of AI will be limited only by the extent of your imagination. Armed with JavaScript-enabled machine learning, you're able to tap into with cameras, microphones, instant updates, locations, and other physical sensors, services, and devices!

I'm sure you're asking, "But why hasn't AI been doing this before? Why is this important now?" To appreciate that, you'll need to take a trip into humanity's search for reproduced intelligence.

What Is Intelligence?

Books upon books can be written on the concepts of thought and especially the path toward machine intelligence. And as with all philosophical endeavors, each concrete statement on intelligence can be argued along the way. You don't need to know everything with certainty, but we need to understand the domain of AI so we can understand how we landed in a book on TensorFlow.js.

Poets and mathematicians throughout the centuries waxed that human thought was nothing more than the combination of preexisting concepts. The appearance of life was considered a machination of god-like design; we all are simply "made" from the elements. Stories from Greek mythology had the god of invention, Hephaestus, create automated bronze robots that walked and acted as soldiers. Basically, these were the first robots. The concept of robots and intelligence has rooted itself in our foundation as an ultimate and divine craft from this ancient lore. Talos (*https://oreil.ly/L8Ng2*), the gigantic animated warrior, was famously programmed to guard the island of Crete. While there was no actual bronze robot, the story served as fuel for mechanical aspiration. For hundreds of years, animatronic antiquity was always considered a path to what would seem like human "intelligence," and centuries later, we're starting to see life imitate art. As a child, I remember going to my local Chuck E. Cheese, a popular restaurant in the United States with animatronic musical performances for children. I remember believing, just for a moment, that the puppet-powered electric concert that ran every day was real. I was inspired by the same spark that's driven scientists to chase intelligence. This spark has always been there, passed through stories, entertainment, and now science.

As the concepts of machines that can work autonomously and intelligently grew through history, we strived to define these conceptual entities. Scholars continued to research inference and learning with published works, all the while keeping their terminology in the realm of "machine" and "robot." The imitation of intelligence from machinery was always held back by the lack of speed and electricity.

The concept of intelligence stayed fixed in human minds and far out of the reach of mechanical structures for hundreds of years, until the creation of the ultimate machine, computers. Computing was born like most machines—with a single purpose for the entire device. With the advent of computing, a new term emerged to illustrate a growing advancement in intelligence that significantly mirrors human intellect. The term AI stands for artificial intelligence and wasn't coined until the 1950s.[2] As computers grew to become general-purpose, the philosophies and disciplines began to combine. The concept of imitating intelligence leaped from mythology into a scientific field of study. Each electronic measuring device for humankind became a new sensory organ for computers and an exciting opportunity for electronic and intelligent science.

In a relatively short time, we have computers interfacing with humans and emulating human actions. The imitation of human-like activity provided a form of what we're willing to call "intelligence." *Artificial intelligence* is that blanket term for these strategic actions, regardless of the level of sophistication or technique. A computer that can play tic-tac-toe doesn't have to win to be categorized as AI. AI is a low bar and shouldn't be confused with the general intelligence of a person. The smallest bit of simplistic code can be legitimate AI, and the apocalyptic uprise of sentient machines from Hollywood is also AI.

When the term AI is used, it's an umbrella term for intelligence that comes from an inert and generally nonbiological device. Regardless of the minimal threshold for the term, mankind, armed with a field of study and an ever-growing practical use, has a unifying term and straightforward goal. All that is measured is managed, and so humankind began measuring, improving, and racing to greater AI.

The History of AI

Frameworks for AI started by being terribly specific, but that's not the case today. As you may or may not know, the concepts of TensorFlow.js as a framework can apply to music, video, images, statistics, and whatever data we can amass. But it wasn't always that way. Implementations of AI started as domain-specific code that lacked any kind of dynamic capability.

There are a few jokes floating around on the internet that AI is just a collection of IF/THEN statements, and in my opinion, they're not 100% wrong. As we've already mentioned, AI is a blanket term for all kinds of imitation of natural intelligence. Even beginning programmers are taught programming by solving simple AI in exercises like Ruby Warrior (*https://oreil.ly/ze9mi*). These programming exercises teach fundamentals of algorithms, and require relatively little code. The cost for this simplicity is that while it's still AI, it's stuck mimicking the intelligence of a programmer.

For a long time, the prominent method of enacting AI was dependent on the skills and philosophies of a person who programs an AI are directly translated into code so that a computer can enact the instructions. The digital logic is carrying out the

---

2 *Artificial intelligence* was coined by John McCarthy in 1956 at the first academic conference on the subject.

human logic of the people who communicated to make the program. This is, of course, the largest delay in creating AI. You need a person who knows how to make a machine that knows, and we're limited by their understanding and ability to translate that understanding. AIs that are hardcoded are unable to infer beyond their instructions. This is likely the biggest blocker to translating any human intelligence into artificial intelligence. If you're looking to teach a machine how to play chess, how do you teach it chess theory? If you want to tell a program the difference between cats and dogs, something that's trivial for toddlers, would you even know where to start with an algorithm?

At the end of the '50s and beginning of the '60s, the idea of the teacher shifted from humans to algorithms that could read raw data. Arthur Samuel coined the term *machine learning* (ML) in an event that unhinged the AI from the practical limitations of the creators. A program could grow to fit the data and grasp concepts that the programmers of that program either couldn't translate into code or themselves never understood.

The concept of using data to train the application or function of a program was an exciting ambition. Still, in an age where computers required entire rooms and data was anything but digital, it was also an insurmountable request. Decades passed before computers reached the critical tipping point to emulate human like capabilities of information and architecture.

In the 2000s, ML researchers began using the graphics processing unit (GPU) to get around the "lone channel between the CPU and memory," known as the *von Neumann bottleneck*. In 2006, Geoffrey Hinton et al. leveraged data and neural networks (a concept that we will cover in our next section) to understand the patterns and have a computer read handwritten digits. This was a feat that was previously too volatile and imperfect for common computing. *Deep learning* was capable of reading and adapting to the randomness of handwriting to correctly identify characters at a state-of-the-art level of over 98%. In these published papers, the idea of data as a training agent jumps from the published works of academia into reality.

While Hinton was stuck crafting a ground-up academic proof that neural networks work, the "What number is this?" problem became a stalwart for machine learning practitioners. The problem has become one of the key trivial examples for machine learning frameworks. TensorFlow.js has a demo (*https://oreil.ly/vsANx*) that solves this problem directly in your browser in less than two minutes. With the benefits of TensorFlow.js we can easily construct advanced learning algorithms that work seamlessly on websites, servers, and devices. But what are these frameworks actually doing?

The greatest goal of AI was always to approach or even outperform human-like capabilities in a single task, and 98% accuracy on handwriting did just that. Hinton's research kindled a focus on these productive machine learning methods and coined industry terms like *deep neural networks*. We'll elaborate on why in the next section, but this was the start of applied machine learning, which began to flourish and eventually find its way into machine learning frameworks like TensorFlow.js. While new machine-based learning algorithms are created left and right, one source of inspiration and terminology becomes quite clear. We can emulate our internal biological systems to create something advanced. Historically, we used ourselves and our cerebral cortex (a layer of our brains) as the muse for structured training and intelligence.

The Neural Network

The idea of deep neural networks was always inspired by our human bodies. The digital nodes (sometimes called a *perceptron network*) simulate neurons in our own brains and activate like our own synapses to create a balanced mechanism of thought. This is why a neural network is called *neural*, because it emulates our brain's biochemical structure. Many data scientists abhor the analogy to the human brain, yet it often fits. By connecting millions of nodes, we can build deep neural networks that are elegant digital machines for making decisions.

By increasing the neural pathways with more and more layers, we arrive at the term *deep learning*. Deep learning is a vastly layered (or deep) connection of hidden layers of nodes. You'll hear these nodes called *neurons, artificial neurons, units,* and even *perceptrons.* The diversity of terminology is a testament to the wide array of scientists who have contributed to machine learning.

This entire field of learning is just part of AI. If you've been following along, artificial intelligence has a subset or branch that is called machine learning, and inside that set, we have the idea of deep learning. Deep learning is primarily a class of algorithms that fuel machine learning, but it's not the only one. See Figure 1-1 for a visual representation of these primary terms.

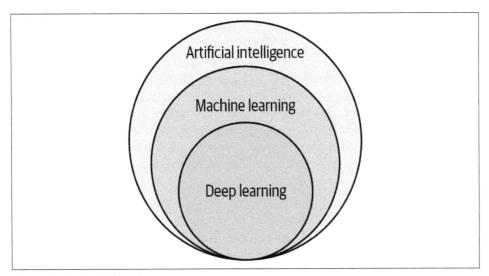

Figure 1-1. AI subdomains

Just like a human, an iteration of teaching or "training" is used to properly balance and build out the neurons based on examples and data. At first, these neural networks are often wrong and random, but as they see example after example of data, their predictive power "learns."

But our brains don't perceive the world directly. Much like a computer, we depend on electrical signals that have been organized into coherent data to be sent to our brain. For computers, these electrical signals are analogous to a *tensor*, but we'll cover that a bit more in Chapter 3. TensorFlow.js embodies all these advancements that research and scientists have confirmed. All these techniques that help human bodies perform can be wrapped up in an optimized framework so that we can leverage decades of research that have been inspired by the human body.

For instance, our visual system, which starts in our retinas, uses ganglions to relay photoreceptive information to our brain to activate these neurons. As some of you remember from children's biology, we have missing spots in our vision, and technically we see everything upside down. The signal isn't sent to our brains "as is." This visual system has technology built into it that we leverage in today's software.

While we're all excited to get our 8K resolution TV, you might believe our brains and vision are still beyond modern computing capabilities, but that's not always the case. The wire connecting visual signals from our eyes to our brain has only about 10 Mb of bandwidth. That's comparable to LAN connections in the early 1980s. Even a streaming broadband connection demands more bandwidth than that. But we perceive everything instantly and quickly, right? So what's the trick? How are we getting superior signals over this surpassed hardware? The answer is that our retinas compress and "featurize" the data before sending it to our deeply connected neural network. So that's what we started doing with computers.

Convolutional neural networks (CNNs) work on visual data the same way our eyes and brains work together to compress and activate our neural pathways. You'll further understand and write your own CNN in Chapter 10. We're learning more about how we work every day, and we're applying those millions of years of evolution directly to our software. While it's great for you to understand how these CNNs work, it's far too academic to write them ourselves. TensorFlow.js comes with the convolutional layers you'll need to process images. This is the fundamental benefit of leveraging a machine learning framework.

You can spend years reading and researching all the unique tricks and hacks that make computer vision, neural networks, and human beings function effectively. But we're in an era where these roots have had time to grow, branch, and finally produce fruit: these advanced concepts are accessible and built into services and devices all around us.

Today's AI

Today we use these best practices with AI to empower machine learning. Convolutions for edge detection, attention to some regions more than others, and even multi-camera inputs for a singular item have given us a prechewed gold mine of data over a fiber-optic server farm of cloud machines training AI.

In 2015 AI algorithms began outperforming humans in some visual tasks. As you might have heard in the news, AI has surpassed humans in cancer detection (*https://oreil.ly/ZCz0B*) and even outperformed the US's top lawyers in identifying legal flaws (*https://oreil.ly/9dW3S*). As always with digital information, AI has done this in seconds, not hours. The "magic" of AI is awe-inspiring.

People have been finding new and interesting ways to apply AI to their projects and even create completely new industries.

AI has been applied to:

- Generating new content in writing, music, and visuals
- Recommending useful content
- Replacing simple statistics models
- Deducing laws from data
- Visualizing classifiers and identifiers

All of these breakthroughs have been aspects of deep learning. Today we have the necessary hardware, software, and data to enable groundbreaking changes with deep machine learning networks. Each day, community and *Fortune* 500 companies alike release new datasets, services, and architectural breakthroughs in the field of AI.

With the tools at your disposal and the knowledge in this book, you can easily create things that have never been seen before and bring them to the web. Be it for pleasure, science, or fortune, you can create a scalable, intelligent solution for any real-world problem or business.

If anything, the current problem with machine learning is that it's a new superpower, and the world is vast. We don't have enough examples to understand the full benefits of having AI in JavaScript. When batteries made a significant improvement in life span, they enabled a whole new world of devices, from more powerful phones to cameras that could last for months on a single charge. This single breakthrough brought countless new products to the market in only a few years. Machine learning makes breakthroughs constantly, leaving a whirl of advancement in new technology that we can't even clarify or recognize because the deluge has exponentially accelerated. This book will focus on concrete *and* abstract examples in proper measure, so you can apply pragmatic solutions with TensorFlow.js.

Why TensorFlow.js?

You have options. You could write your own machine learning model from scratch or choose from any existing framework in a variety of programming languages. Even in the realm of JavaScript, there are already competing frameworks, examples, and options. What makes TensorFlow.js capable of handling and carrying today's AI?

Significant Support

TensorFlow.js is created and maintained by Google. We'll cover more about this in Chapter 2, but it's worth noting that some of the best developers in the world have come together to make TensorFlow.js happen. This also means, without any effort by the community, TensorFlow.js is capable of working with the latest and greatest groundbreaking developments.

Unlike other JavaScript-based implementations of machine learning libraries and frameworks, TensorFlow.js supports optimized and tested GPU-accelerated code. This optimization is passed on to you and your machine learning projects.

Online Ready

Most machine learning solutions are confined to a machine that is extremely customized. If you wanted to make a website to share your breakthrough technology, the AI is commonly locked behind an API. While this is completely doable with TensorFlow.js running in Node.js, it's also doable with TensorFlow.js running directly in the browser. This no-install experience is rare in the world of machine learning, which gives you the ability to share your creations without barriers. You're able to version and access a world of interactivity.

Offline Ready

Another benefit of JavaScript is that it runs everywhere. The code can be saved to the user's device like a progressive web app (PWA), Electron, or React Native application, and then it can function consistently without any internet connection. It goes without saying that this also provides a significant speed and cost boost compared to hosted AI solutions. In this book, you'll uncover countless examples that exist entirely on browsers that save you and your users from latency delays and hosting costs.

Privacy

AI can help users identify diseases, tax anomalies, and other personal information. Sending sensitive data across the internet can be dangerous. On-device results stay on-device. You can even train an AI and store the results on the user's machine with zero information ever leaving the safety of the browser.

Diversity

Applied TensorFlow.js has a powerful and broad stroke across the machine learning domain and platforms. TensorFlow.js can take advantage of running Web Assembly for CPUs or GPUs for beefier machines. The spectrum of AI with machine learning today is a significant and vast world of new terminology and complexity for newcomers. Having a framework that works with a variety of data is useful as it keeps your options open.

Mastery of TensorFlow.js allows you to apply your skills to a wide variety of platforms that support JavaScript (see Figure 1-2).

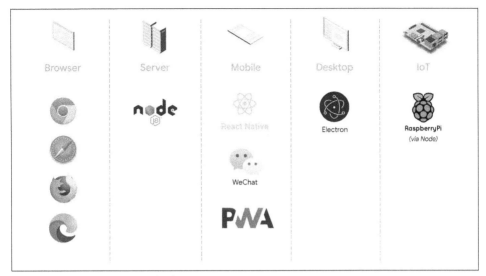

Figure 1-2. TensorFlow.js platforms

With TensorFlow.js you're free to choose, prototype, and deploy your skills to a variety of fields. To take full advantage of your machine learning freedom, you'll need to get your footing with some terms that can help you launch into machine learning.

Types of Machine Learning

Lots of people break machine learning into three categories, but I believe we need to look at all of ML as four significant elements:

- Supervised
- Unsupervised
- Semisupervised
- Reinforcement

Each of these elements deserves books upon books. The short definitions that follow are simple references to familiarize you with the terms you'll hear in the field.

Quick Definition: Supervised Learning

In this book, we'll focus on the most common category of machine learning, *supervised machine learning* (sometimes called *supervised learning* or just *supervised* for short). Supervised ML simply means that we have an answer key for every question we're using to train our machine. That is to say, our data is labeled. So if we're trying to teach a machine to distinguish if a photo contains a bird, we can immediately grade the AI on whether it was right or wrong. Like a Scantron, we have the answer key. But unlike a Scantron and because it's probability math, we can also identify how wrong the answer was.

If an AI is 90% sure a photo of a bird is a bird, while it got the answer right, it could improve by 10%. This illuminates the "training" aspect of the AI with immediate data-driven gratification.

 Don't worry if you don't have hundreds of ready-to-go labeled questions and answers. In this book, we'll either provide you with labeled data or show you how to generate it yourself.

Quick Definition: Unsupervised Learning

Unsupervised learning doesn't require us to have an answer key. We only need questions. Unsupervised machine learning would be ideal, as most information in the world does not come with labels. This category of machine learning focuses on what a machine could learn and report from unlabeled data. While this subject might seem a bit confusing, humans perform it every day! For instance, if I gave you a photo of my garden and asked you how many different types of plants I own, you could tell me the answer, and you don't have to know the genus and species of each plant. It's a bit of how we make sense of our own worlds. A lot of unsupervised learning is focused on categorizing large amounts of data for use.

Quick Definition: Semisupervised Learning

Most of the time, we don't live with 100% unlabeled data. To bring back the garden example from earlier, you don't know the genus and species of each plant, but you're also not completely unable to classify the plants as As and Bs. You might tell me I have ten plants made up of three flowers and seven herbs. Having a small number of known labels goes a long way, and research today is on fire with semisupervised breakthroughs!

You might have heard the term *generative networks* or *generative adversarial networks* (GANs). These popular AI constructs are mentioned in numerous AI news articles and are derived from semisupervised learning tactics. Generative networks are trained on examples of what we would like the network to create, and through a semisupervised method, new examples are constructed. Generative networks are excellent at creating new content from a small subset of labeled data. Popular examples of GANs often get their own websites, like *https://thispersondoesnotexist.com* are growing in popularity, and creatives are having a field day with semisupervised output.

GANs have been significant in generating new content. While popular GANs are semisupervised, the deeper concept of a GAN is not limited to semisupervised networks. People have adapted GANs to work on every type of learning we've defined.

Quick Definition: Reinforcement Learning

The simplest way to explain reinforcement learning is to show that it's needed by handling a more real-world activity, versus the hypothetical constructs from earlier.

For instance, if we're playing chess and I start my game by moving a pawn, was that a good move or a bad move? Or if I want a robot to kick a ball through a hoop, and it starts by taking a step, is that good or bad? Just like with a human, the answer depends on the results. It's a collection of moves for maximum reward, and there's not always a singular action that produces a singular result. Training a robot to step first or look first matters, but probably not as much as what it does during other critical moments. And those critical moments are all powered by rewards as reinforcement.

If I were teaching an AI to play *Super Mario Bros.*, do I want a high score or a speedy victory? The rewards teach the AI what combination of moves is optimal to maximize the goal. Reinforcement learning (RL) is an expanding field and has often been combined with other forms of AI to cultivate the maximum result.

Information Overload

It's OK to be surprised by how many applications of machine learning were just mentioned. In a way, that's why we're in need of a framework like TensorFlow.js. We can't even comprehend all the uses of these fantastic systems and their effects for decades to come! While we wrap our heads around this, the age of AI and ML is here, and we're going to be part of it. Supervised learning is a great first step into all the benefits of AI.

We'll cover some of the most exciting yet practical uses of machine learning together. In some aspects, we'll only scratch the surface, while in others, we'll dive deep into the heart of how they work. Here are some of the broad categories we'll cover. These are all supervised learning concepts:

- Image categorization
- Natural language processing (NLP)
- Image segmentation

One of the main goals of this book is that while you can understand the concepts of the categories, you won't be limited by them. We'll lean into experimentation and practical science. Some problems can be solved by overengineering, and others can be solved by data engineering. Thinking in AI and machine learning is the key to seeing, identifying, and creating new tools with TensorFlow.js.

AI Is Everywhere

We're entering a world where AI is creeping into everything. Our phones are now accelerated into deep learning hardware. Cameras are applying real-time AI detection, and at the time of this writing, some cars are driving around our streets without a human being.

In the past year, I've even noticed my emails have started writing themselves with a "tab to complete" option for finishing my sentences. This feature, more often than I'd like to admit, is clearer and more concise than anything I would have originally written. It's a significant visible achievement that overshadows the forgotten machine learning AI that's been protecting us from spam in that same inbox for years.

As each of these plans for machine learning unfurl, new platforms become in demand. We're pushing models further and further on edge devices like phones, browsers, and hardware. It makes sense that we're looking for new languages to carry the torch. It was only a matter of time before the search would end with the obvious option of JavaScript.

A Tour of What Frameworks Provide

What does machine learning look like? Here's an accurate description that will make Ph.D. students cringe with its succinct simplicity.

With normal code, a human writes the code directly, and a computer reads and interprets that code, or some derivative of it. Now we're in a world where a human doesn't write the algorithm, so what actually happens? Where does the algorithm come from?

It's simply one extra step. A human writes the algorithm's trainer. Assisted by a framework, or even from scratch, a human outlines in code the parameters of the problem, the desired structure, and the location of the data to learn from. Now the machine runs this program-training program, which continuously writes an ever-improving algorithm as the solution to that problem. At some point, you stop this program and take the latest algorithm result out and use it.

That's it!

The algorithm is much smaller than the data that was used to create it. Gigabytes of movies and images can be used to train a machine learning solution for weeks, all just to create a few megabytes of data to solve a very specific problem.

The resulting algorithm is essentially a collection of numbers that balance the outlined structure identified by the human programmer. The collection of numbers and their associated neural graph is often called a *model*.

You've probably seen these graphs surfacing in technical articles, drawn as a collection of nodes from left to right like Figure 1-3.

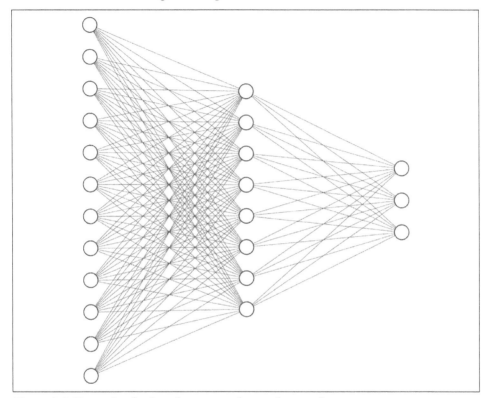

Figure 1-3. Example of a densely connected neural network

Our framework TensorFlow.js handles the API for specifying the structure or architecture of the model, loading data, passing data through our machine learning process, and ultimately tuning the machine to be better at predicting answers to the given input the next time. This is where the real benefits of TensorFlow.js come to bear. All we have to worry about is properly tuning the framework to solve the problem with sufficient data and then saving the resulting model.

What Is a Model?

When you create a neural network in TensorFlow.js, it's a code representation of the desired neural network. The framework generates a graph with intelligently selected randomized values for each neuron. The model's file size is generally fixed at this point, but the contents will evolve. When a prediction is made by shoving data through an untrained network of random values, we get an answer that is generally as far away from the right answer as pure random chance. Our model hasn't trained on any data, so it's terrible at its job. So as a developer, our code that we write is complete, but the untrained result is poor.

Once training iterations have occurred for some significant amount of time, the neural network weights are evaluated and then adjusted. The speed, often called the *learning rate*, affects the resulting solution. After taking thousands of these small steps at the learning rate, we start to see a machine that improves, and we are engineering a model with the probability of success far beyond the original machine. We have left randomness and converged on numbers that make the neural network work! Those numbers assigned to the neurons in a given structure are the trained model.

TensorFlow.js knows how to keep track of all these numbers and computational graphs so we don't have to, and it also knows how to store this information in a proper and consumable format.

Once you have those numbers, our neural network model can stop training and just be used to make predictions. In programming terms, this has become a simple function. Data goes in, and data comes out.

Feeding data through a neural network looks a lot like chance, as shown in Figure 1-4, but in the world of computing it's a delicate machine of balanced probability and sorting that has consistent and reproducible results. Data gets fed into the machine, and a probabilistic result comes out.

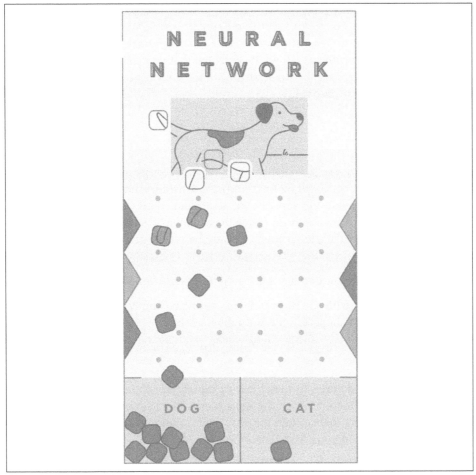

Figure 1-4. A balanced network metaphor

In the next chapter, we'll experiment with importing and predicting with an entirely trained model. We'll utilize the power of hours of training to get an intelligent analysis in microseconds.

In This Book

This book is constructed so that you could pack it away for a vacation and, once you've found your small slice of heaven, read along with the book, learn the concepts, and review the answers. The images and screenshots should suffice for explaining the deep underbelly of TensorFlow.js.

However, for you to really grasp the concepts, you'll need to go beyond simply reading the book. As each concept unfolds, you should be coding, experimenting, and testing the boundaries of TensorFlow.js on an actual computer. For any of you who are new to machine learning as a field, it's essential that you solidify the terminology and workflows you're seeing for the first time. Take your time to work through the concepts and code from this book.

Associated Code

Throughout the book, there is runnable source code to illustrate the lessons and functionality of TensorFlow.js. While in some cases the entire source is provided, in most cases the printed code will be limited to the salient portions. It's advisable that you immediately download the source code that aligns with this book. Even if you plan on writing code from scratch alongside the examples, it's likely that small configurations that you may struggle with will already be solved and referenceable in the associated code.

You can see the GitHub source page at *https://github.com/GantMan/learn-tfjs*.

If you are unfamiliar with GitHub and Git, you can simply download the latest project source code in a single ZIP file and reference that.

You can download the source ZIP file from *https://github.com/GantMan/learn-tfjs/archive/master.zip*.

The source code is structured to match each chapter. You should be able to find all chapter resources in the folder with the same name. In each chapter folder, you will find at most four folders that contain the lesson information. This will be reviewed in Chapter 2 when you run your first TensorFlow.js code. For now, familiarize yourself with the purpose of each folder so you can select the example code that works best for your learning needs.

The extra folder

This folder contains any extra materials referenced in a chapter, including documentation or additional reference material. The material in these sections are useful files for each chapter.

The node folder

This folder contains a Node.js-specific implementation of the chapter's code for a server-based solution. This folder will likely contain several specific projects within it. Node.js projects will come with some extra packages installed to simplify the experimentation process. The example projects for this book utilize the following:

nodemon

> Nodemon is a utility that will monitor for any changes in your source and auto-matically restart your server. This is used so you can save your files and immediately see their associated updates.

ts-node

> TypeScript has plenty of options, most notably strong typing. However, for approachability this book is focused on JavaScript and not TypeScript. The ts-node module is in place for ECMAScript support. You can write modern Java-Script syntax in these node samples, and via TypeScript, the code will work.

These dependencies are identified in the *package.json* file. The Node.js examples are to illustrate server solutions with TensorFlow.js and generally do not need to be opened in a browser.

To run these examples, install the dependencies with either Yarn or Node Package Manager (NPM), and then execute the start script:

```
# Install dependencies with NPM
$ npm i
# Run the start script to start the server
$ npm run start
# OR use yarn to install dependencies
$ yarn
# Run the start script to start the server
$ yarn start
```

After starting the server, you will see the results of any console logs in your terminal. When you're done reviewing the results, you can use Ctrl+C to exit the server.

The simple folder

This folder will contain solutions where NPM was not used. All resources are simply placed in solitary HTML files to be served. This is by far the simplest solution and the most often used. This folder will most likely contain the most results.

The web folder

If you're familiar with client-based NPM web applications, you will feel comfortable with the web folder. This folder will likely contain several specific projects within it. The web folder examples are bundled using Parcel.js (*https://parceljs.org*). It is a fast multicore bundler for web projects. Parcel provides Hot Module Replacement (HMR) so you can save your files and immediately see the page reflect your code changes, while also providing friendly error logging and access to ECMAScript.

To run these examples, install the dependencies with either Yarn or NPM, and then execute the start script:

```
# Install dependencies with NPM
$ npm i
# Run the start script to start the server
$ npm run start
# OR use yarn to install dependencies
$ yarn
# Run the start script to start the server
$ yarn start
```

After running the bundler, a web page with your default browser will open and access a local URL for that project.

 If a project uses a resource like a photo, a *credit.txt* file will exist in that project's root folder to properly credit the photographer and source.

Chapter Sections

Each chapter begins by identifying the goals of the chapter and then dives in immediately. At the end of each chapter, you're presented with a Chapter Challenge, which is a resource for you to immediately apply what you've just learned. The answers for each challenge can be found in Appendix B.

Finally, each chapter ends with a grouping of thought-provoking questions to verify you've internalized the information from the chapter. It's advised that you verify the answers for yourself by code when possible, but the answers are also provided for you in Appendix A.

Common AI/ML Terminology

You might be thinking to yourself, "Why isn't a model just called a function? Models already have a meaning in programming, and they don't need another!" The truth is this comes from the origin of problems that machine learning started with. Original data problems were rooted in statistics. Statistical models recognize patterns as statistical assumptions on sample data, and so our product from this mathematical operation on examples is a machine learning model. It's quite common for machine learning terminology to heavily reflect the field and culture of the scientists who invented it.

Data science comes with a good bit of mathematical terminology. We'll see this as a theme throughout the book, and we'll identify the reasons for each. Some terms make sense instantly, some collide with existing JavaScript and framework terms, and some new terminology collides with other new terminology! Naming things is hard. We'll do our best to explain some key terms in a memorable way and elaborate on etymology along the way. The TensorFlow and TensorFlow.js docs are replete with new vocabulary for developers. Read through the following machine learning terminology and see if you can grasp these fundamental terms. It's OK if you can't. You can come back to this chapter and reference these definitions at any time as we progress forward.

Training

Training is the process of attempting to improve a machine learning algorithm by having it review data and improve its mathematical structure to make better predictions in the future.

TensorFlow.js provides several methods to train and monitor training models, both on a machine and in a client browser.

> e.g., "Please don't touch my computer, it's been training for three days on my latest air-bending algorithm."

Training set

Sometimes called the *training data*, this is the data you're going to show your algorithm for it to learn from. You might think, "Isn't that all the data we have?" The answer is "no."

Generally, most ML models can learn from examples they've seen before, but teaching the test doesn't assure that our model can extrapolate to recognize data it has never seen before. It's important that the data that we use to train the AI be kept separate for accountability and verification.

> e.g., "My model keeps identifying hot dogs as sub sandwiches, so I'll need to add more photos to my training set."

Test set

To test that our model can perform against data it has never seen before, we have to keep some data aside to test and never let our model train or learn from it. This is generally called the *test set* or *test data*. This set helps us test if we've made something that will generalize to new problems in the real world. The test set is generally significantly smaller than the training set.

> e.g., "I made sure the test set was a good representation of the problem we're trying to train a model to solve."

Validation sets

This term is important to know even if you aren't at the level where you need it. As you'll hear often, training can sometimes take hours, days, or even weeks. It's a bit alarming to kick off a long-running process just to come back and find out you've structured something wrong and you have to start all over again! While we probably won't run into any of those mega-training needs in this book, those situations could use a group of data for quicker tests. When this is separate from your training data, it's a "holdout method" for validation. Essentially, it's a practice where a small set of training data is set aside to make validation tests before letting your model train on an expensive infrastructure or for an elongated time. This tuning and testing for validation is your validation set.

There's a lot of ways to select, slice, stratify, and even fold your validation sets. This goes into a science that is beyond the scope of this book, but it's good to know for when you discuss or read and advance your own mega-datasets.

TensorFlow.js has entire training parameters for identifying and graphing validation results during the training process.

> e.g., "I've carved out a small validation set to use while we construct our model architecture."

Tensors

We'll cover tensors in great detail in Chapter 3, but it's worth noting that tensors are the optimized data structure that allows for GPU and Web Assembly acceleration for immense AI/ML calculation sets. Tensors are the numerical holders of data.

> e.g., "I've converted your photo into a grayscale tensor to see what kind of speed boost we can get."

Normalization

Normalization is the action of scaling input values to a simpler domain. When everything becomes numbers, the difference in sparsity and magnitude of numbers can cause unforeseen issues.

For example, while the size of a house and the number of bathrooms in a house both affect the price, they are generally measured in different units with vastly different numbers. Not everything is measured in the same metric scale, and while AI can adapt to measure these fluctuations in patterns, one common trick is to simply scale data to the same small domain. This lets models train faster and find patterns more easily.

> e.g., "I've applied some normalization to the house price and the number of bathrooms so our model can find patterns between the two more quickly."

Data augmentation

In photo editing software, we can take images and manipulate them to look like the same thing in a completely different setting. This method effectively makes an entirely new photo. Perhaps you want your logo on the side of a building or embossed on a business card. If we were trying to detect your logo, the original photo and some edited versions would be helpful in our machine learning training data.

Oftentimes, we can create new data from our original data that fits the goal of our model. For example, if our model is going to be trained to detect faces, a photo of a person and a mirrored photo of a person are both valid and significantly different photos!

TensorFlow.js has libraries dedicated to data augmentation. We will see augmented data later in this book.

> e.g., "We've performed some data augmentation by mirroring all the pumpkins to double our training set."

Features and featurization

We mentioned featurizing earlier when we talked about the way eyes send what's most important to the brain. We do the same thing with ML. If we were trying to make an AI that guesses how much a house is worth, we then have to identify what inputs are useful and what inputs are noise.

There's no shortage of data on a house, from the number of bricks to the crown molding. If you watch a lot of home improvement TV, you know it's smart to identify a house's size, age, number of bathrooms, date the kitchen was last updated, and neighborhood. These are often key features in identifying a house's price, and you'll care more about feeding a model that information than something trivial. Featurization is the selection of these features from all the possible data that could be selected as inputs.

If we decided to throw in all the data we could, we give our model the chance to find new patterns at the cost of time and effort. There's no reason to choose features like the number of blades of grass, house smell, or natural lighting at noon, even if we have that information or we feel it's important to us.

Even once we've selected our features, there are often errors and outliers that will slow the training of a practical machine learning model. Some data just doesn't move the needle toward a more successful predictive model, and selecting smart features makes a quick-trained, smarter AI.

> e.g., "I'm pretty sure counting the number of exclamation marks is a key feature for detecting these marketing emails."

Chapter Review

In this chapter, we've ensnared the terms and concepts of the umbrella term AI. We've also touched on the key principles of what we'll cover in this book. Ideally, you are now more confident in the terms and structures that are essential in machine learning.

Review Questions

Let's take a moment and make sure you've fully grasped the concepts we mentioned. Take a moment to answer the following questions:

1. Can you give an adequate definition of machine learning?
2. If a person identifies an idea for a machine learning project, but they have no labeled data, what would you recommend?
3. What kind of ML would be useful for beating your favorite video game?
4. Is machine learning the only form of AI?
5. Does a model hold all the training example data that was used to make it work?
6. How is machine learning data broken up?

Solutions to these exercises are available in Appendix A.

Up Next...

In Chapter 2 you will get your machine ready to run TensorFlow.js and start getting your hands dirty with implementing actual TensorFlow.js libraries. You'll take all the concepts we covered in this chapter and start to see those terms in popular JavaScript libraries that are maintained by Google.

## CHAPTER 2

Introducing TensorFlow.js

"If your actions inspire others to dream more, learn more,
do more, and become more, you are a leader."

—John Quincy Adams

We've been talking about TensorFlow.js a bit and what it can do, but we haven't really dug into what a machine learning framework like TensorFlow.js actually is. In this chapter, we'll tackle the concept of a machine learning framework and then quickly dive into writing code. I know it's important to write code that has some kind of tangible outcome, so in this chapter, you'll finally get your computer running TensorFlow.js and producing results.

We will:

- Look at the concept of TensorFlow.js
- Set up TensorFlow.js
- Run a TensorFlow.js model package
- Take a deep look at what the AI did

Let's start with the framework we'll be using to make it all happen.

Hello, TensorFlow.js

Given how our previous chapter discussed the philosophies of ancient times and the birth of machine learning as a field, you'd expect AI frameworks to have a history that reaches as far back as the early 1960s. However, AI was stagnant for a long time, and this time is often called "AI winter." The concepts of AI were beleaguered by disbelief and extreme mathematical calculations for the small data that was available. Who could blame these researchers? Most software developers today depend on shipping apps without writing GPU-enabled linear algebra and calculus from scratch, and building your own AI shouldn't be the exception. Fortunately, due to some open source contributions from the Google Brain team, we have options.

There's a lot of buzzwords that get thrown around when you're starting machine learning. TensorFlow, TensorFlow Lite, and TensorFlow.js can all be mentioned, and it's not clear to most newcomers what these terms mean or why there are even three of them. For now, let's ignore the term *tensor*, as you've heard the word in Chapter 1 and you'll really get to understand it in subsequent chapters. Instead, let's focus on defining TensorFlow.js so we can use it.

TensorFlow, without any extra ".js" or "Lite," was Google's first public machine learning framework; the Google Brain team released it in late 2015.[1] This framework focused on effectively solving machine learning problems for Google in the cloud with Python. It wasn't long before Google realized there would be benefits to pushing this popular framework to IoT and mobile devices that have limited computing power, and that required an adaptation of TensorFlow, which is known as TensorFlow Lite. This successful adaptation paved the way to push TensorFlow ideals into other languages.

You can probably guess what happened next. In early 2018, Google announced a Google-backed JavaScript import of the machine learning framework TensorFlow for JavaScript, called TensorFlow.js. This new effort empowered the practicality of TensorFlow in a whole new way. Daniel Smilkov, Nikhil Thorat, and Shanqing Cai were part of a team that released TensorFlow.js. At the TensorFlow Developer Summit (*https://youtu.be/YB-kfeNIPCE*), Smilkov and Thorat train a model to control a *PAC-MAN* game using computer vision and a webcam in the browser.

It was this moment when the "Python-only" chains were removed from options of popular AI frameworks, and neural networks could effectively traverse the JavaScript domain. *If you can run JavaScript, you can run AI that is powered by TensorFlow.js ML.*

All three of these implementations are alive today and grow with their specific purpose. By expanding TensorFlow to a JavaScript implementation, we can now implement AI/ML with node servers and even the client browser. In the paper "TensorFlow.js: Machine Learning for the Web and Beyond" (Daniel Smilkov et al., 2019) (*https://oreil.ly/XkIjZ*), they state, "TensorFlow.js has empowered a new set of developers from the extensive JavaScript community to build and deploy machine learning models and enabled new classes of on-device computation." TensorFlow.js can leverage a vast platform of devices while still accessing the GPU and even Web

---

1 TensorFlow didn't reach 1.0.0 status until February 11, 2017.

Assembly. With JavaScript, our machine learning can venture to the horizon and back.

It's also worth noting that in several benchmarking tests, Node has outperformed Python 3 with lower CPU load,[2] so while Python has been the adopted language of most AI, JavaScript serves as a parimary language platform for products and services.

But there's no need to remove or promote any one language. TensorFlow models are based on directed acyclic graphs (DAGs), which are language-independent graphs that are the *output* of the training. These graphs can be trained by one language and then converted and consumed by a completely different programming language. It's the goal of this book to arm you with the tools you'll need to get the most out of using JavaScript and TensorFlow.js.

Leveraging TensorFlow.js

For a lot of people, "learning" can sometimes mean starting at the fundamentals, which means starting with the mathematics. For those people, a framework like TensorFlow and a pragmatic branch of a framework like TensorFlow.js is a poor start. In this book, we'll be building projects and touching on the fundamentals of the framework of TensorFlow.js, and we'll spend little time, if any, on the underlying mathematical magic.

Frameworks like TensorFlow and TensorFlow.js help us avoid the specifics of the linear algebra involved. You're freed from terms like *forward propagation* and *backpropagation*, as well as their computations and calculus. Instead, we'll be focused on industry terms like *inference* and *model training*.

While TensorFlow.js can access lower-layer APIs (such as `tfjs-core`) to do some fundamental optimization on classical problems, those moments are left to the academics and advanced users who have a strong foundation regardless of the framework at hand. This book is meant to show the power of TensorFlow.js, and utilizing the hard work and optimization of the framework is how we'll do that. We leave TensorFlow.js the job of configuring and optimizing our code to work with the wide variety of device constraints and WebGL APIs.

We might even take things a bit too far and apply machine learning to algorithms you could easily code by hand, but that's generally where most people really grasp concepts clearly. Solving simple problems you understand with machine learning helps you extrapolate the steps, logic, and trade-offs of solving advanced problems you could never code by hand.

---

2 2x boost with Node over Python case study: *https://oreil.ly/4Jrbu*

On the other side of the coin, some fundamentals of neurons, activation functions, and model initialization cannot be ignored and may require some explanation. It's the goal of this book to give you a healthy balance of theory and practicality.

As you might have surmised, the variety of platforms for TensorFlow.js means that there's no singular prescribed setup. We'll be able to run TensorFlow.js in a client or a server for this book. However, our most tacit interactive option is to take full advantage of the browser. For that reason, we'll perform the lion's share of examples in the browser. We will, of course, still cover the key aspects of hosting a node server solution where appropriate. Each of these two tools has their underlying drawbacks and benefits, which we'll mention as we venture into the power of TensorFlow.js.

Let's Get TensorFlow.js Ready

Like any popular tool, you might notice there are several flavors for the TensorFlow.js package, as well as several locations where you can access the code. The majority of this book will focus on the most available and "ready to run" versions of Tensor-Flow.js, which means the browser client. Optimized builds of the framework are made for the server side. These builds talk to the same underlying C++ core API that Python does, but via Node.js, which allows you to leverage all the performance of your server's graphics card or CPU. TensorFlow.js AI models run in a variety of locations and utilize a variety of optimizations for each environment (see Figure 2-1).

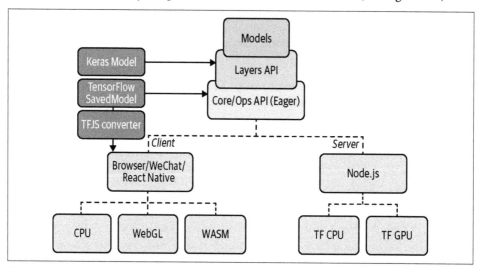

Figure 2-1. Options for TensorFlow.js

The knowledge you'll learn in this book can be applied to most platforms. For your convenience, we'll cover the setup process for the most common platforms. If you're uncomfortable setting up your environments from scratch, you can simply access the preconfigured projects built for you in the source code associated with this book, located at *https://github.com/GantMan/learn-tfjs*.

Getting Set Up with TensorFlow.js in the Browser

Let's jump into the fastest, most versatile, and simplest way of running TensorFlow.js. To get TensorFlow.js running in your browser, it's actually quite easy. I'm going to assume that you're familiar with the basics of JavaScript and that you've imported JavaScript libraries into existing code before. TensorFlow.js supports a wide variety of ways to be included, so developers of any experience can access it. If you're familiar with including JavaScript dependencies, you'll be familiar with these common practices. We can import TensorFlow.js into a page two ways:

- Using NPM
- Including a script tag

Using NPM

One of the most popular ways to manage your dependencies for your website is to use a package manager. If you're used to building projects with NPM or Yarn, you can access the code via the NPM registry at *https://oreil.ly/R2lB8*. Simply install the dependency at the command line:

```
# Import with npm
$ npm i @tensorflow/tfjs

# Or Yarn
$ yarn add @tensorflow/tfjs
```

Once you have imported the `tfjs` package, you can import this code in your Java-Script project with the following ES6 JavaScript import code:

```
import * as tf from '@tensorflow/tfjs';
```

Including a Script Tag

If a website does not use a package manager, you can simply add a script tag to the HTML document. This is the second way you can include TensorFlow.js in your project. You can download and host TensorFlow.js locally or utilize a content delivery network (CDN). We'll be pointing the script tag at a CDN-hosted script source:

```
<script src="https://cdn.jsdelivr.net/npm/@tensorflow/tfjs@2.7.0/dist/tf.min.js">
</script>
```

Besides caching across websites, CDNs are extremely quick because they utilize edge locations to ensure speedy delivery worldwide.

As you might have noticed, I've locked this code to a specific version (2.7.0), which I strongly recommend you always do in your projects regarding CDNs. You don't want to run into any issues with automatic breaking changes for your site.

Getting Set Up with TensorFlow.js Node

The TensorFlow.js package we use for the browser works just fine with Node.js, and this is a fine solution if you're planning on only temporarily experimenting with Node.js. A good rule is to use the simple /tfjs over the /tfjs-node import if you're not interested in hosting a live project for others or training on large amounts of data.

If your goal is to go beyond experimentation and into effective Node.js with TensorFlow.js, you should spend some time improving your Node.js setup with some of these alternative packages (*https://oreil.ly/zREQy*). There are two better distributions of TensorFlow.js that are built specifically for Node and speed. They are `tfjs-node` and `tfjs-node-gpu`. Keep in mind that each developer machine is unique and your installs and experiences may vary.

For Node.js you'll likely make a selection between `@tensorflow/tfjs-node` or `@tensorflow/tfjs-node-gpu`. You can utilize the latter GPU-powered package if your computer is configured with an NVIDIA GPU and properly set up with CUDA software. Compute Unified Device Architecture (CUDA) allows direct GPU-accelerated access through a parallel computing platform for NVIDIA hardware. While the GPU package is the absolute fastest of the TensorFlow.js options, it's also the least likely to be ready and configured for most machines, due to its hardware and software constraints. For now, our examples will work on installing `tfjs-node` and leave the optional CUDA configuration up to you.

```
# Import with npm
$ npm i @tensorflow/tfjs-node

# Or Yarn
$ yarn add @tensorflow/tfjs-node
```

Oftentimes, if your computer has not been set up to develop advanced C++ libraries, you might have to do a bit of installing to get your machine ready. This rabbit hole is only necessary if you're looking to actively work with `tfjs-node` or `tfjs-node-gpu`.

Install Tips

On Windows if you're having trouble with `node-gyp`, this can sometimes mean you will need to download Visual Studio and check the "Desktop development in C++" workload. See Figure 2-2 for a screenshot of the install process.

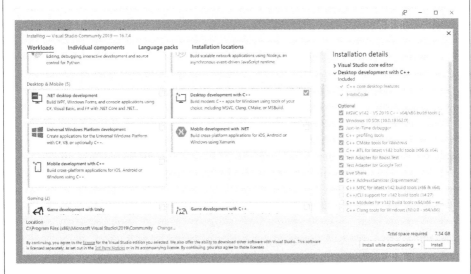

Figure 2-2. Installing C++ to get `node-gyp` to run `tfjs-node`

On a Mac, you might have to install Xcode and run `xcode-select --install`. Review the `node-gyp` GitHub for documentation (*https://github.com/nodejs/node-gyp*) specific to your machine.

Once you have the C++ workload and you're able to install the package, you may have to rebuild `tfjs-node` on your machine with the following command: **npm rebuild @tensorflow/tfjs-node --build-from-source**.

If you're looking to use `tfns-node-gpu`, you'll have to set up CUDA to work with your graphics card. That install can become quite time- and instruction- intensive. You should refer to the latest CUDA documentation for those instructions.

If your NPM install was successful, congratulations! You are ready to import from this package. If you have Node set up to handle ES6, you can import with the following:

```
import * as tf from '@tensorflow/tfjs-node';
```

If you haven't configured your Node.js package to handle ES6 imports, you can still access the code with a classic require:

```
const tf = require('@tensorflow/tfjs-node');
```

Verifying TensorFlow.js Is Working

All of the previous methods will make a variable `tf` available in your JavaScript code, which gives you access to TensorFlow.js. To make sure our import worked appropriately, let's log the version of the imported TensorFlow.js library.

Add this code to your JavaScript, and if you see a version printed in the console, your import is good to go!

```
console.log(tf.version.tfjs);
```

When the page is run, we can right-click the page and inspect to access the JavaScript console logs. There we'll find the output of our log command, "3.0.0" or whatever version of TensorFlow.js you imported. For the Node.js example, the value will simply print directly in the console.

 Before you access features of the `tf` variable (TensorFlow.js library), you would normally need to assure TensorFlow.js has properly loaded a backend and is ready. The aforementioned code bypasses this check, but it's always prudent to run your initial code awaiting the promise of `tf.ready()`.

Download and Run These Examples

As mentioned in Chapter 1, you have access to code from this book. To make sure you don't have to set up these projects from scratch on every example, ensure you have the source code for each project, including the simple code shown previously.

Download the project in your preferred way from the book's repo: *https://github.com/ GantMan/learn-tfjs*.

Navigate to the directory for Chapter 2, and make sure you can run the code on your machine.

Running the simple example

In *chapter2/simple/simplest-example* we are avoiding NPM and simply pulling our code from a CDN. With the way this code is currently structured, we don't even have to host the site! We can simply open *index.html* in any modern browser, and it will work!

At some point, we'll actually need to host these simple examples because we'll access additional assets that require full URIs. We can do this quite easily by using a small web server to host the files. The smallest web server I know is called Web Server for Chrome and has a funny hand-drawn "200 OK!" logo. Within five minutes, we can get our files properly served on a local server.

You can find Web Server for Chrome on the Chrome Web Store as an extension (*https://oreil.ly/ZOedW*). In this book we'll sometimes call this plug-in "200 OK!" When you point the web server at the *index.html* file, it will automatically serve the file for you, and all adjacent files will be accessible with their associated URLs, as we will require in later lessons. The app interface should look like Figure 2-3.

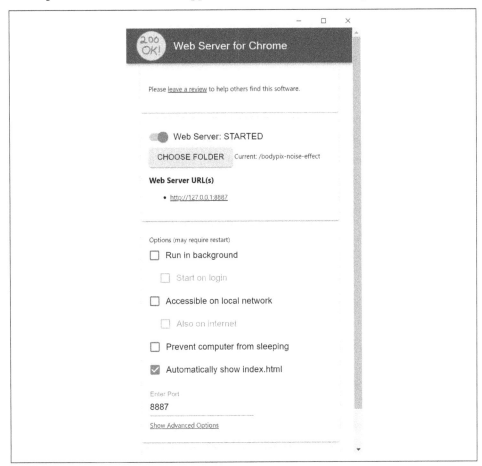

Figure 2-3. Web Server for Chrome 200 OK! dialog

If you'd like to peruse other options or want a link to the mentioned Chrome plug-in, take a look at *chapter2/extra/hosting-options.md* to find the one that works for you.

And of course, if you find a fantastic option that's not listed, please contribute a pull request.

Once you find a server that runs *simple-example* in a way you enjoy, you can use that service for all simple options going forward.

Running the NPM web example

If you're more familiar with NPM, the basic NPM example for this project uses Parcel. Parcel is the fastest application bundler with zero configuration. It also includes Hot Module Reloading to get real-time updates and excellent error logging.

To run the code, navigate to *chapter2/web/web-example* and do an NPM install (npm i). Once that's done, there's a script in the *package.json* that kicks everything off. You can simply run the start script:

```
$ npm run start
```

That's it! We'll be using this method to run all NPM-based code in the book.

Running the Node.js example

The Node.js example is just as easy to run as the Parcel NPM example. While Node.js is generally unopinionated, the Node.js examples in this book will include a few opinionated dev dependencies so we can make our Node.js example code align with the browser examples. The code throughout this book will take full advantage of ECMA-Script. We do this with some transpiling, file watching, and node magic.

To prep this example, navigate to *chapter2/node-example* and do an NPM install (npm i). If you have any issues, you may need to run npm i -g ts-node nodemon node-gyp to assure you have the needed libraries to make all our magic happen. Once your node packages are properly in place, you can start the project at any time by running the start script:

```
$ npm run start
```

The code is transpiled via TypeScript and reload-friendly nodemon. If everything ran properly, you'll see the installed TensorFlow.js version printed directly in the console/terminal where you ran the server.

Let's Use Some Real TensorFlow.js

Now that we have TensorFlow.js, let's use it to make something epic! OK, that's quite a simplification: if it were that easy, the book would be over. There's still a mountain of things to learn, but that doesn't stop us from taking a gondola to get a high-level view.

TensorFlow.js has plenty of prewritten code and models we can utilize. These pre-written libraries help us get the benefits of utilizing TensorFlow.js without fully grasping the underlying concepts.

While there are plenty of community-driven models that work quite well, the official maintained list of TensorFlow.js models is on the TensorFlow GitHub under a repo named `tfjs-models`. For stability, we'll use these as often as we can in this book. You can peruse the links here: *https://github.com/tensorflow/tfjs-models*.

For this foray into running actual TensorFlow.js models, let's pick something with a relatively simple input and output. We'll use the TensorFlow.js *Toxicity* classifier to check if text input is insulting or not.

The Toxicity Classifier

Google provides a few "ready-to-go" models of varying complexity. One beneficial model is called the Toxicity model, which is perhaps one of the most straightforward and useful models for beginners.

Like all programming, a model will require specific input and will provide specific output. To kick things off, let's take a look at what those are for in this model. Toxicity detects toxic content such as threats, insults, cussing, and generalized hate. Since those aren't necessarily mutually exclusive, it's important that each of these violations has their own probability.

The Toxicity model attempts to identify a probability that a given input is true or false for the following characteristics:

- Identity attack
- Insult
- Obscene
- Severe toxicity
- Sexually explicit
- Threat
- Toxicity

When you give the model a string, it returns an array of seven objects to identify the percentage-of-probability prediction for each specific violation. Percentages are represented as two `Float32` values between zero and one.

If a sentence is surely *not* a violation, the probabilities will give most of the value to the zero index in the `Float32` array.

For example, [0.7630404233932495, 0.2369595468044281] reads that the prediction for this particular violation is 76% not a violation and 24% likely a violation.

This can be quite a "Hold on, what!?" moment for most developers. It's a bit strange getting probabilities where we're used to true and false, isn't it? But in an intuitive way, we've always understood that language has a lot of gray area. The exact science of insults often depends on the person and even the day!

For this reason, the model has a bonus feature of allowing you to pass a threshold that will identify when a particular violation surpasses the allotted limit. When an insult is detected beyond the threshold, the match flag is set to true. This is a nice little bonus to help you quickly map the results for significant violations. Picking a valid threshold depends on your needs and the situation. You can shoot from the hip, but if you need some guidance, statistics has all kinds of tools you could review. Read up on Receiver Operating Characteristic (ROC) graphs for plotting and picking an optimal threshold for your needs.

 To activate the Toxicity model, we will have to write something insulting. The following example uses an insult based on looks. The insult avoids using profanity but is still offensive. This is not directed to anyone in particular and is meant to illustrate the capabilities of AI to understand and identify toxic comments.

It's important to choose an insult that is easy for humans to recognize, but difficult for a computer. Sarcasm detection is difficult in text form and has been a major problem in computer science. To seriously test this model, the insult should avoid common and blatant inflammatory wording. Running the Toxicity model on a particularly crafty insult with the threshold set to 0.5 yields the array shown in Example 2-1.

The insult input: "She looks like a cavewoman, only far less intelligent!"

Example 2-1. The full toxicity report on the input sentence

```
[{
    "label":"identity_attack",
    "results":[{
        "probabilities":{
            "0":0.9935033917427063,
            "1":0.006496586836874485
        }, "match":false
    }]
},{
    "label":"insult",
    "results":[{
        "probabilities":{
            "0":0.5021483898162842,
```

```
                    "1":0.4978516101837158
                }, "match":false
            }]
    },{
        "label":"obscene",
        "results":[{
                "probabilities":{
                    "0":0.9993441700935364,
                    "1":0.0006558519671671093
                }, "match":false
            }]
    },{
        "label":"severe_toxicity",
        "results":[{
                "probabilities":{
                    "0":0.9999980926513672,
                    "1":0.0000018614349528434104
                }, "match":false
            }]
    },{
        "label":"sexual_explicit",
        "results":[{
                "probabilities":{
                    "0":0.9997043013572693,
                    "1":0.00029564235592260957
                }, "match":false
            }]
    },{
        "label":"threat",
        "results":[{
                "probabilities":{
                    "0":0.9989342093467712,
                    "1":0.0010658185929059982
                }, "match":false
            }]
    },{
        "label":"toxicity",
        "results":[{
                "probabilities":{
                    "0":0.4567308723926544,
                    "1":0.543269157409668
                }, "match":true
            }]
    }]
}]
```

As you can see from Example 2-1, we snuck under the "insult" radar by a hair (50.2% false), but we got dinged by the toxicity indicator, which resulted in "match": true. This is quite impressive, because I don't have any explicitly offensive language in the sentence. As a programmer, it wouldn't be straightforward to write an algorithm to catch and identify this toxic insult, but AI was trained to identify the complex patterns of toxic language after studying heaps of labeled insults so we don't have to.

The previous example uses a single sentence in an array as input. If you include multiple sentences as input, your sentence index will correspond directly with your result index for each category.

But don't take my word for it; now it's your turn to run the code. You can add the model to your website with NPM via this:

```
$ npm install @tensorflow-models/toxicity
```

and then import the library:

```
import * as toxicity from "@tensorflow-models/toxicity";
```

Or you can add the script directly from a CDN.[3] Order matters with script tags, so make sure your tag is placed on the page before you try to use the model:

```
<script src="https://cdn.jsdelivr.net/npm/@tensorflow-models/toxicity@1.2.2">
</script>
```

Either of the previous examples will provide results in a ready-to-go `toxicity` variable. We'll use this variable's `load` method to load the ML model promise. And from that model, we can utilize the `classify` method on an array of sentences.

Here's an example of loading the model and running classification on three sentences. This exact example can be found in three different forms in the associated sections of the chapter code on GitHub (*https://oreil.ly/sTs5a*).

```
// minimum positive prediction confidence
// If this isn't passed, the default is 0.85
const threshold = 0.5;

// Load the model ❶
toxicity.load(threshold).then((model) => {
  const sentences = [
    "You are a poopy head!",
    "I like turtles",
    "Shut up!"
  ];

  // Ask the model to classify inputs ❷
  model.classify(sentences).then((predictions) => {
    // semi-pretty-print results
    console.log(JSON.stringify(predictions, null, 2)); ❸
  });
});
```

❶   The model is loaded into the browser with a threshold.

---

3 Notice this version is locked at 1.2.2.

❷ The loaded model is asked to classify inputs.

❸ The object is printed nicely using JavaScript Object Notation.

 If you run this code in a browser, you'll need to view the console to view the output. You can navigate to the console from inspecting the page, or generally, you can press Control+Shift+J on Windows or Command+Option+J on Mac. If you're running this from the command line with npm start, you should see the output immediately in the console.

The results for multiple sentences are grouped by toxicity category. So the previous code attempts to identify each sentence depending on each category. For instance, the "insult" output from the previous should read similar to Example 2-2.

Example 2-2. Insult section results

```
...
{
  "label": "insult",
  "results": [
    {
      "probabilities": {
        "0": 0.05905626341700554,
        "1": 0.9409437775611877
      },
      "match": true
    },
    {
      "probabilities": {
        "0": 0.9987999200820923,
        "1": 0.0012000907445326447
      },
      "match": false
    },
    {
      "probabilities": {
        "0": 0.029087694361805916,
        "1": 0.9709123373031616
      },
      "match": true
    }
  ]
},
...
```

Ta-daaaaa! The code works great. Each results index corresponds to the input sentence index, and it properly diagnoses the two insults among the three sentences.

Congratulations on running your first TensorFlow.js model. Now that you're a master of AI, let's talk through the steps and underlying concepts of this library.

Loading the Model

When we call `toxicity.load`, you might be thinking the model is being loaded into memory, but you'd only be half-right. Most of these libraries do not ship with the trained model in the JavaScript codebase. Read that sentence again. This might seem a bit alarming to our NPM developers, but it makes complete sense to our CDN users. The load method fires off a network call to download the model that the library uses. In some cases, the model that is loaded is optimized for the environment and device where the JavaScript is located. Review the network logs illustrated in Figure 2-4.

Name	Status	Type	Initiator	Size
group1-shard1of7	200	fetch	group1-shard1of7	4.2 MB
group1-shard2of7	200	fetch	group1-shard2of7	4.2 MB
group1-shard6of7	200	fetch	group1-shard6of7	4.2 MB
group1-shard5of7	200	fetch	group1-shard5of7	195 B
group1-shard4of7	200	fetch	group1-shard4of7	4.2 MB
group1-shard7of7	200	fetch	group1-shard7of7	123 B
group1-shard3of7	200	fetch	group1-shard3of7	143 B

Figure 2-4. Network download requests

 While the Toxicity NPM bundle can be minified and zipped to a mere 2.4 KB, there's an additional multimegabyte payload over the network for the actual model file when the library is used.

The load method for this Toxicity library takes a threshold that it will apply to all subsequent classifications and then fires off a network call to download the actual model file. When that model is fully downloaded, the library then loads the model into tensor-optimized memory for use.

It's important to evaluate each library appropriately. Let's review some common questions people ask when they learn a bit more about this.

TensorFlow.js Model Q&A

Q: Do all TensorFlow.js models do this download?

Answer: There's no rule that TensorFlow.js has to import the model file from a URL. In fact, it can pull the file from a multitude of places. In the world of lower-level TensorFlow.js, model files are placed wherever they're most useful. However, it is pretty common for Google-maintained libraries to pull their models from a singular hosted destination to be accessed when needed.

Q: Where is this hosted?

Answer: Because it's hard to assure updates and resolve the need for effective model hosting, Google has set up a model hosting service for popular community models called TensorFlow Hub (TFHub). You can review all the models at *https://tfhub.dev*. When our code calls `.load`, it is making a request to TensorFlow Hub for the model. If it helps, you can think of this as NPM for ML models.

Q: Why are the models in "shards"?

Answer: When a model is bigger than 4 MB, it is broken into shards of 4 MB to encourage the device to parallelize downloads and cache the model locally. Lots of mobile browser caches top out at 4 MB per file for a given session.

Q: Are all models this size?

Answer: No. Each model has a variety of sizes, pruning, and optimizations. I've made models that are 48 KB, and I've made models that are 20 MB. Toxicity at the time of this writing is 28.06 MB,[4] but large models can often be optimized down significantly. We'll get into how you can resize models in later chapters. It's important to know and evaluate the cost of each model and its effect on the user's internet plan.

Q: Can I host the model myself?

Answer: In many instances, you can. Most non-Google libraries will even encourage you to shoulder your own hosting of models and may depend on it entirely. However, others, like this one, leave you no option. This Toxicity model loads from TensorFlow Hub only. Fortunately, open source software means we can get around this by modifying a fork of the JavaScript library.

---

4 The Toxicity model info is available at *https://oreil.ly/Eejyi*.

Classifying

The next thing our Toxicity code did is run a `classify` method. This is the moment where our input sentences were passed through the model, and we got the results. While it seemed just as simple as any other JavaScript function, this library actually hid some fundamental processing that was necessary.

All data in and out of a model is converted to a tensor. We will cover tensors in greater detail in Chapter 3, but it's important to note that this conversion is essential for the AI. All the input strings are converted, and calculations are made, and the results that come out are tensors that are reconverted into normal JavaScript primitives.

It's nice that this library handled this for us. When you're finished with this book, you'll be able to wrap machine learning models with the same dexterity. You'll be able to keep your users in blissful ignorance of the intricacies of data conversions that are happening behind the scenes.

In the next chapter, we'll jump into that conversion. You'll fully grasp the transition of data into tensors and all the data manipulation superpowers that come with it.

Try It Yourself

Now that you've implemented one model, you can most likely implement the other models provided by Google (*https://oreil.ly/WFq62*). Most of the other Google models' GitHub pages have README documents explaining how to implement each library. Many of the implementations are similar to what we saw with Toxicity.

Take a moment to browse through the existing models to let your imagination run wild. You can begin working with these libraries immediately. Knowing these models exist will also be useful as you progress in this book. Not only are you going to better understand what these libraries are capable of, but you might want to combine and even improve on these existing libraries for your needs.

In the next chapter, we'll start digging into the details of what these well-wrapped libraries are hiding so we can unleash your TensorFlow.js skills without limit.

Chapter Review

We set up your computer for TensorFlow.js via a few common practice options. We assured our machine is ready to run TensorFlow.js, and we even pulled down and ran a packaged model for determining text toxicity.

Chapter Challenge: Truck Alert!

Take the time to try the MobileNet model (*https://oreil.ly/fUKoy*), which has the ability to look at images and attempt to classify the predominant artifact. This model can be passed any `<img>`, `<video>`, or `<canvas>` element, and it returns an array of most likely predictions for what it sees in that particular graphic.

The MobileNet model has been trained to classify 1,000 possible items (*https://oreil.ly/6PEAn*) from stone walls, to garbage trucks, to even an Egyptian cat. People have used this library to detect a wide variety of fun things. I once saw some code that connected a webcam to MobileNet to detect llamas (*https://oreil.ly/L0nBz*).

For this Chapter Challenge, you're tasked with creating a website that can detect trucks. Given an input image, you're looking to identify if it's a truck or not. When you detect a truck from a photo, do an `alert("TRUCK DETECTED!")`. By default, the MobileNet package returns the top three detections. If any of those three see a truck in the photo, your alert should notify the user just like in Figure 2-5.

Figure 2-5. Truck detector working

You can find the answer to this challenge in Appendix B.

Review Questions

Let's review the lessons we've learned from the code you've written in this chapter. Take a moment to answer the following questions:

1. Can regular TensorFlow run in the browser?
2. Does TensorFlow.js have access to the GPU?
3. Do you have to have CUDA installed to run TensorFlow.js?
4. If I don't specify a version on a CDN, what happens?
5. How does the Toxicity classifier identify violations?
6. When do we pass a threshold to Toxicity?
7. Does the Toxicity code contain all the needed files?
8. Do we have to do any tensor work to use this Toxicity library?

Solutions to these exercises are available in Appendix A.

Up Next...

In Chapter 3 you will finally dig into the most fundamental structure of machine learning, the tensor. You will convert data into tensors and back with a real-world example. You'll understand how tensors leave the world of iterative looping and become the concept of optimized batches of mathematical empowerment.

## CHAPTER 3

Introducing Tensors

"Whoa!"

—Keanu Reeves *(Bill & Ted's Excellent Adventure)*

We've mentioned the word *tensor* a few times, and it resides as the predominant word in TensorFlow.js, so it's time we get to know what these structures are. This critical chapter will give you hands-on experience with the fundamental concept of managing and accelerating data, which is at the heart of teaching machines with data.

We will:

- Explain the concept and terminology of tensors
- Create, read, and destroy tensors
- Practice concepts of structured data
- Take the leap into utilizing tensors to build something useful

Take your time with this chapter if you're new to tensors. Being comfortable with this aspect of data will help you be comfortable with machine learning altogether.

Why Tensors?

We live in a world full of data, and deep down, we all know it ends in 1s and 0s. To many of us, this happens quite magically. You take a photo with your phone, and some complex binary file gets created. Then, you swipe up and down, and our binary file changes from JPG to PNG within an instant. Thousands of unknown bytes are generated and destroyed in microseconds as files resize, reformat, and, for you hip kids, filter. You can't be mollycoddled anymore. As you venture into actually touching, feeling, and feeding data, you have to wave goodbye to ignorant bliss.

To quote the 1998 movie *Blade*:

> "You better wake up. The world you live in is nothing but a sugarcoated topping. There is another world beneath it."

OK, it's like that but not as intense. To train an AI, you'll need to make sure your data is uniform, and you'll need to understand and see it. You're not training your AI to do the task of decoding PNGs and JPGs uniformly; you're training it on the decoded and imitated versions of what's actually in a photo.

This means images, music, statistics, and whatever else you're using in your TensorFlow.js models all need a uniform and optimized data format. Ideally, our data would be converted into numeric containers that quickly scale and work directly with calculation optimizations in the GPU or Web Assembly. You need something clean and straightforward for our informational data in and out. These containers should be unopinionated so they can hold anything. Welcome to tensors!

 Understanding the use and properties of tensors is an ongoing exercise for even the most adept TensorFlow.js expert. While this chapter serves as an excellent introduction, you shouldn't feel laggardly for having difficulty with wielding tensors. This chapter can serve as a reference as you progress.

Hello, Tensors

Tensors are collections of data in a structured type. It's nothing new for a framework to convert everything to numbers, but it might be a new concept to realize that it's up to you to choose how the data is ultimately formed.

As mentioned in Chapter 1, all data needs to be distilled into numbers for the machines to understand it. Tensors are the preferred format of information, and they even have small abstractions for nonnumeric types. They are like electrical signals from the physical world to our AI's brain. While there's no specification of how your data should be structured, you do need to stay consistent to keep your signals organized so our brain can see the same pattern over and over. People generally organize their data in groups, like arrays and multidimensional arrays.

But what is a tensor? A *tensor*, as defined mathematically, is simply a structured set of values of any dimension. Ultimately, this resolves to an optimized grouping of data as numbers that are ready for calculation. That means, mathematically speaking, a traditional JavaScript array is a tensor, a 2D array is a tensor, and a 512D array is a tensor. TensorFlow.js tensors are the embodiment of these mathematical structures that hold the accelerated signals that feed data into and out of a machine learning model.

If you're familiar with multidimensional arrays in JavaScript, you should feel right at home with the syntax for tensors. As you add a new dimension to each array, it's often said you are increasing the *rank* of a tensor.

Array Dimensions Review

A one-dimensional (1D) array is your standard flat set of data. You probably work with these all the time in your JavaScript. These rank-one arrays are ideal for capturing sets of related data and sequences.

```
[1, 2, 3, 4]
```

A two-dimensional (2D) or rank-two array captures grids of related data. For instance, a 2D array can store the X and Y coordinates for a graph.

```
[
  [2, 3],
  [5, 6],
  [8, 9]
]
```

A three-dimensional (3D) array would be rank three. Rank three is the last commonly visual rank for us mere humans. It's hard to visualize beyond three dimensions.

```
[
  [
    [1, 2, 3],
    [4, 5, 6]
  ],
  [
    [6, 5, 4],
    [3, 2, 1]
  ]
]
```

To put it plainly, a 2D array is an array of arrays, and a 3D array is an array of arrays of arrays. You get the idea. Nesting arrays allows you to format data so that correlated information can map to one another, and patterns can emerge. After three dimensions, you can't easily graph the data, but you can utilize it.

Creating Tensors

Regardless of how you imported TensorFlow.js, the code in this book assumes you've consolidated the library to a variable named `tf`, which will be used to represent TensorFlow.js in all examples.

You can read along or write the code from scratch, or even run these fundamental examples in the browser-based /tfjs solution available with the book source code. For simplicity, we'll be avoiding the repetition of the <script> or import tags required to set up these examples and instead simply write the shared code.

To create your first tensor, we'll keep things simple, and you'll build it with a 1D Java-Script array (Example 3-1). The array syntax and structure are carried over to tensors.

Example 3-1. Creating your first tensors

```
// creating our first tensor
const dataArray = [8, 6, 7, 5, 3, 0, 9]
const first = tf.tensor(dataArray) ❶

// does the same thing
const first_again = tf.tensor1d(dataArray) ❷
```

❶ tf.tensor creates a 1D tensor if passed a 1D array. It would create a 2D tensor if passed a 2D array.

❷ tf.tensor1d creates a 1D tensor if passed a 1D array. It would error if passed a 2D array.

This code creates a 1D tensor data structure of seven numbers in memory. Now those seven numbers are ready for manipulation, accelerated operations, or simply input. However, I'm sure you noticed we supplied two ways to perform the same action.

The second method provides an extra level of runtime checking since you've defined the expected dimensionality. Determining the desired dimensionality is useful when you're looking to ensure the number of dimensions in the data you're working with. Methods exist for verifying up to six dimensions with tf.tensor6d.

In this book, we'll mostly be working with the generic tf.tensor, but if you find yourself deep into a complex project, don't forget you can save yourself the headache of receiving unexpected dimensions by explicitly identifying your desired dimensionality of a tensor.

As an extra note, while the tensors in Example 3-1 were an array of natural numbers, the default data type to store numbers is Float32. Floating-point numbers (that's numbers with decimal places, e.g., 2.71828) are quite dynamic and impressive. They can usually handle most numbers you'll need and be ready for values between. Unlike JavaScript arrays, a tensor's data type must be homogeneous (all the same type). These types can be only Float32, Int32, bool, complex64, or string, with no mixing between.

If you'd like to enforce that your tensor is created as a particular type, feel free to utilize the third parameter of the `tf.tensor` function, which explicitly defines the tensor's type structure.

```
// creating a 'float32' tensor (the default)
const first = tf.tensor([1.1, 2.2, 3.3], null, 'float32') ❶

// an 'int32' tensor
const first_again = tf.tensor([1, 2, 3], null, 'int32') ❷

// inferred type for boolean
const the_truth = tf.tensor([true, false, false]) ❸

// Guess what this does
const guess = tf.tensor([true, false, false], null, 'int32') ❹

// What about this?
const guess_again = tf.tensor([1, 3.141592654, false]) ❺
```

❶ This tensor is created as a `Float32` tensor. The third parameter was redundant in this case.

❷ The resulting tensor is Int32, and without the third parameter, it would have been a `Float32`.

❸ The resulting tensor is a Boolean tensor.

❹ The resulting tensor is an Int32 tensor, with the Boolean values cast to 0 for false, and 1 for true. So, the variable guess contains the data [1, 0, 0].

❺ You might think this wild array will error, but each of the input values gets converted to its corresponding `Float32` with the resulting tensor data [1, 3.1415927, 0].

How can you identify the tensor type that was created? Just like any JavaScript array, tensors are equipped with methods to explain their properties. Useful properties include length (`size`), dimensionality (`rank`), and data type (`dtype`).

Let's apply what we've learned:

```
const second = tf.tensor1d([8, 6, 7, 5, 3, 0, 9]) ❶

// Whoopsie!
try {
  const nope = tf.tensor1d([[1],[2]]) ❷
} catch (e) {
  console.log("That's a negative Ghost Rider")
}
```

```
console.log("Rank:", second.rank) ❸
console.log("Size:", second.size) ❹
console.log("Data Type:", second.dtype) ❺
```

❶ This creates a successful tensor. You should know the data type, dimension, and size.

❷ Since you're using `tensor1d` to create a rank-two tensor, this will throw and cause the `catch` to run and log a message.

❸ The simple array is rank one, so it will print 1.

❹ The size is the length of the array and will print 7.

❺ The tensor's data type from an array of numbers will print `float32`.

Congratulations on creating your first few tensors! It's safe to say that being a master of tensors is at the core of taming data for TensorFlow.js. These structured buckets of values are the foundation for getting data into and back out of machine learning.

Tensors for Data Exercises

Let's say you want to make an AI to play tic-tac-toe (noughts & crosses to my friends across the pond). As always with data, it's time to get a coffee or tea and think of the right way to convert real-world data to tensor data.

You could store images of games, strings of tutorials, or simply the Xs and Os of the game. Images and tutorials would be pretty impressive, but for now, let's just consider the idea of storing a game board's state. There are only nine possible boxes to play in, so a simple array of nine values should represent any given state of the board.

Should the values read left to right and top to bottom? It rarely matters as long as you're consistent. All encodings are made up. However, keep in mind a tensor resolves to numbers! This means that while you can store strings "X" and "O," they would have to turn into numbers anyway. Let's store our Xs and Os by mapping them to some kind of numeric value that makes sense. Does that mean you just assign one of them to 0 and the other to 42? I'm sure you can find a strategy that appropriately reflects the game state.

Let's evaluate the state of an active game for an exercise. Take a moment to review the grid of a match in progress, as shown in Figure 3-1. How could this be converted to tensors and numbers?

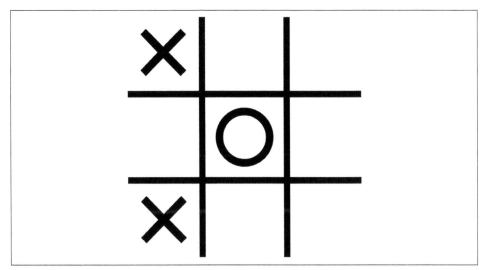

Figure 3-1. A game with data

Perhaps the board displayed here could be read and represented as a one-dimensional tensor. You could read the values left to right, top to bottom. As for numbers, let's choose -1, 0, and 1 to represent the three possible values for any square. Table 3-1 shows the lookup for each possible value.

Table 3-1. Value-to-number table

Board value	Tensor value
X	1
0	-1
Empty	0

This would create a tensor like so: [1, 0, 0, 0, -1, 0, 1, 0, 0]. Or, it would create a 2D tensor, like so: [[1, 0, 0],[0, -1, 0],[1, 0, 0]].

Now that you have a goal, let's write some code to convert the board into a tensor. We'll even explore the additional parameters of tensor creation.

```
// This code creates a 1D `Float32` tensor
const a = tf.tensor([1, 0, 0, 0, -1, 0, 1, 0, 0])

// This code creates a 2D `Float32` tensor
const b = tf.tensor([[1, 0, 0],[0, -1, 0],[1, 0, 0]])

// This does the same as the above but with a 1D input
// array that is converted into a 2D `Float32` tensor
const c = tf.tensor([1, 0, 0, 0, -1, 0, 1, 0, 0], [3, 3]) ❶
```

```
// This code turns the 1D input array into a 2D Int32 tensor
const d = tf.tensor([1, 0, 0, 0, -1, 0, 1, 0, 0], [3, 3], 'int32') ❷
```

❶ The second parameter of a tensor can identify the desired shape of the input data.
   Here, you convert the 1D array into a 2D tensor by specifying you would like the
   data to be rank-two structured as 3 x 3.

❷ The third parameter of the tensor identifies the data type you would like to use
   over the inferred data type. Since you are storing round numbers, you can specify
   the type int32. However, the range of the default float32 type is massive and
   can comfortably handle our numbers.

Tensors Are Forever...Kinda

We identified how to specify a tensor's size and data type when it's created, and of
course, you can edit the code, but once a tensor is created, you're stuck with it. Let's
pretend a library that we don't manage hands us a tensor of Float32s, and we really
needed the type to be Int32s; what can you do about it? The bittersweet news is that
tensors are immutable. While you cannot modify this tensor, you can easily create a
new tensor with the correct type and data. For this, you can use asType.

For example, convert a tensor like so:

```
const nope = tf.tensor([4], null, 'float32')
const yep = nope.asType('int32') ❶
```

❶ The variable yep is a *new* Int32 tensor with the value 4. The nope tensor still
   exists unaltered.

It's important to note these conversions are quick and dirty. If you have the value
3.9999 and you convert it to Int32, it becomes 3. There's no logic in bringing the
value to the nearest Int32. It merely removes the decimal portion like JavaScript's
Math.floor. Boolean tensors switch to 0 and 1, and string tensors will flat-out error.
If you're converting a tensor's data type, make sure you're ready for the results.

When you're creating tensors to represent data, it's up to you to decide how you're
formatting the input data and what the resulting tensor structure should be. As you
grasp the concepts of machine learning, you are always honing your intuition of what
kind of data works best.

We'll come back to this tic-tac-toe problem later in this book.

Tensors on Tour

We're going to get deeper into tensors as the book progresses, so it's essential to take a moment and discuss why they're so important. Without understanding the magnitude of the calculations we're leveraging, it's hard to understand the benefits of leaving the safety of the familiar JavaScript variables and engine for little old math.

Tensors Provide Speed

Now that you know you can make tensors and represent data as tensors, what's the benefit of performing this conversion? We've mentioned that calculations with tensors are optimized by the TensorFlow.js framework. When you convert JavaScript arrays of numbers to tensors, you can perform matrix operations at breakneck speeds, but what does that really mean?

Computers are excellent at doing a single calculation, and there are benefits to performing mass groupings of calculations. Tensors are engineered for an immense number of side-by-side calculations. If you've ever performed matrix and vector calculations by hand, you can start to appreciate the benefits of accelerated calculations.

Tensors Provide Direct Access

Without machine learning, you can still use tensors to make 3D graphics, content recommendation systems, and beautiful iterated function systems (IFSs) (*https://oreil.ly/jjnvk*) like the Sierpiński triangle illustrated in Figure 3-2.

Figure 3-2. IFS example: the Sierpiński triangle

There are plenty of libraries out there for images, sound, 3D models, video, and more. They all have one thing in common. Despite all the formats that exist, the libraries get you data in a universal format. Tensors are like that raw, unrolled data format, and with that access you can build, read, or predict anything you'd like.

You can even use these advanced structures to modify image data (you begin doing this in Chapter 4). You'll start having more fun with tensor functions after you've graduated from the basics.

Tensors Batch Data

In the data realm, you might find yourself looping through mountains of data and worrying about text editors crashing. Tensors are optimized for batch processing at high speeds. The small project at the end of this chapter has only four users to keep things simple, but any production environment needs to be ready to handle hundreds of thousands.

Most of the benefits of tensors will be recognized when you ask trained models to perform the calculations to predict human-like operations in milliseconds. You'll start to see examples of this as early as Chapter 5. We've identified that tensors are impressive structures that bring a lot of acceleration and mathematical power to JavaScript, so it makes sense that you'll commonly use this beneficial structure in batches.

Tensors in Memory

Tensor speed comes with an overhead cost. Usually, when we're done with a variable in JavaScript, the memory is cleanly removed when all references to that variable are completed. This is called *automatic garbage detection and collection* (AGDC), and it happens without most JavaScript developers understanding or caring how this works. However, your tensors don't get that same kind of automatic care. They persist long after the variable that uses them has been collected.

Deallocating Tensors

Because tensors survive garbage collection, they behave differently from standard JavaScript and have to be accounted for and deallocated manually. Even if a variable is garbage-collected in JavaScript, the associated tensor is then orphaned in memory. You can access the current count and size using `tf.memory()`. This function returns an object with a report of active tensors.

The code in Example 3-2 illustrates noncollected tensor memory.

Example 3-2. Tensors left in memory

```
/* Check the number of tensors in memory
 *  and the footprint size.
 *  Both of these logs should be zero.
 */
console.log(tf.memory().numTensors)
console.log(tf.memory().numBytes)
```

```
// Now allocate a tensor
let speedy = tf.tensor([1,2,3])
// remove reference for JS
speedy = null

/* No matter how long we wait
 *  this tensor is going to be there,
 *  until you refresh the page/server.
 */
console.log(tf.memory().numTensors)
console.log(tf.memory().numBytes)
```

The code from Example 3-2 will result in printing the following in the logs:

```
0
0
1
12
```

Since you already know tensors are for handling large accelerated data, the idea of leaving these sizable chunks in memory is a problem. With one small loop, you could leak an entire computer's available RAM and GPU.

Fortunately, all tensors and models have a `.dispose()` method that purges a tensor from memory. When you call `.dispose()` on a tensor, the `numTensors` will go down by the number of tensors you just released.

This does mean you will have to think of tensors as managed in two ways, yielding four possible states. Table 3-2 shows all the combinations of what happens when Java-Script variables and TensorFlow.js tensors are created and destroyed.

Table 3-2. Tensor states

	Tensor live	Tensor disposed
JavaScript variable is live	This variable is live; you can read the tensor.	An error will be raised if you attempt to use this tensor.
JavaScript variable has no reference	This is a memory leak.	This is a properly destroyed tensor.

To put it succinctly, keep your variables and your tensors alive to access them, and when you're done, dispose the tensor and do not attempt to access it.

Automatic Tensor Cleanup

Fortunately, tensors do have an auto-clean option called `tidy()`. You can use `tidy` to create a functional encapsulation that will clean all tensors that aren't returned or flagged for being kept with `keep()`. We'll do a demo in a moment to help you grasp `tidy`, and we'll be using it throughout the book.

You'll get used to cleaning up tensors in no time. Make sure to study the following code, which will demonstrate tidy() and keep() in action:

```
// Start at zero tensors
console.log('start', tf.memory().numTensors)

let keeper, chaser, seeker, beater
// Now we'll create tensors inside a tidy
tf.tidy(() => { ❶
  keeper = tf.tensor([1,2,3])
  chaser = tf.tensor([1,2,3])
  seeker = tf.tensor([1,2,3])
  beater = tf.tensor([1,2,3])
  // Now we're at four tensors in memory ❷
  console.log('inside tidy', tf.memory().numTensors)

  // protect a tensor
  tf.keep(keeper)
  // returned tensors survive
  return chaser
})

// Down to two ❸
console.log('after tidy', tf.memory().numTensors)

keeper.dispose() ❹
chaser.dispose() ❺

// Back to zero
console.log('end', tf.memory().numTensors)
```

❶ The tidy method takes a synchronous function and monitors the tensors created in this enclosure. You cannot use an async function or promise here. If you're going to need anything async, you will have to call .dispose explicitly.

❷ All four tensors are effectively loaded into memory.

❸ Even though you haven't called dispose explicitly, tidy has properly destroyed two of the created tensors (the two that weren't kept or returned). If you try to access them now, you will get an error.

❹ Explicitly destroy the tensor that you saved with tf.keep from inside tidy.

❺ Explicitly destroy the tensor that you returned from tidy.

If all of that makes sense, you've learned the practice of creating and removing tensors from their magical place in memory.

Functional Versus Object-Oriented Styling

If you're familiar with the differences between object-oriented programming (OOP) and functional programming, you might have noticed some mixing of styles in the previous code. That is, the tensors are created with `tf.tensor`, but destroyed with `<tensor variable here>.dispose()` rather than something like `tf.dispose(<ten sor variable here>)`. One follows a functional paradigm, and the other is quite object-oriented.

The answer is, both of these work. The awesome people who designed the API for TensorFlow.js support both syntaxes. Rather than strictly following one methodology over another, this book is going to use whichever syntax illustrates the point best. The code will use `<tensor>.method` or `tf.method(<tensor>)` interchangeably to create the most readable code for each example.

Feel free to choose and enforce your own standards as you follow along. When it comes to tensors, as with most frameworks, it's possible to handle transformations the same way, but with significantly different-looking code.

Tensors Come Home

It's worth noting that you can even mix tensors and JavaScript where applicable. The code in Example 3-3 creates a normal JavaScript array of tensors.

Example 3-3. Mixing JS and tensors

```
const tensorArray = []
for (let i = 0; i < 10; i++) {
  tensorArray.push(tf.tensor([i, i, i]))
}
```

The result of Example 3-3 is an array of 10 tensors, with values [0,0,0] up to [9,9,9]. Unlike creating a 2D tensor to hold these values, you access a particular tensor with ease by retrieving a normal JavaScript index in the array. So if you want [4,4,4], you can get it with `tensorArray[4]`. You can then destroy the whole collection from memory with a simple `tf.dispose(tensorArray)`.

After the dust settles, we've learned how to create and remove tensors, but we're missing the critical part where tensors return their data to JavaScript. Tensors are great for large calculations and speed, but JavaScript has its benefits too. With JavaScript you can iterate, grab a specific index, or perform a world of NPM library calculations that are far more cumbersome in tensor form.

It's safe to say that after you've reaped the benefits of calculating with a tensor, you'll always need the results of that data to end up back in JavaScript.

Retrieving Tensor Data

If you try to print a tensor to the console, you can see the object, but not the underlying data values. To print a tensor's data, you can call the tensor's `.print()` method, but that will send the values directly to `console.log` and not a variable. While viewing the values of a tensor is helpful to the developer, we'll need to ultimately get these values into JavaScript variables to use them.

There are two ways you retrieve tensors. Each of these methods has a synchronous method and an asynchronous method. First, if you'd like your data to be delivered in the same multidimensional array structure, you can use `.array()` for an asynchronous result or simply use `.arraySync()` for a sync value. Second, if you'd like to keep your values with extreme precision and flattened to a 1D typed array, you can use the synchronous `dataSync()` and an asynchronous method `data()`.

The following code explores converting, printing, and resolving tensors using the methods described earlier:

```
const snap = tf.tensor([1,2,3])
const crackle = tf.tensor([3.141592654])
const pop = tf.tensor([[1,2,3],[4,5,6]])

// this will show the structure but not the data
console.log(snap) ❶
// this will print the data but not the tensor structure
crackle.print() ❷

// Now let's go back to JavaScript
console.log('Welcome Back Array!', pop.arraySync()) ❸
console.log('Welcome Back Typed!', pop.dataSync()) ❹

// clean up our remaining tensors!
tf.dispose([snap, crackle, pop])
```

❶ This log shows the JavaScript structure that holds the tensor and its associated properties. You can see the shape, and `isDisposedInternal` is false because it hasn't been disposed, but this serves as a pointer to the data rather than containing the data. This log prints the following:

```
{
  "kept": false,
  "isDisposedInternal": false,
  "shape": [
    3
  ],
  "dtype": "float32",
  "size": 3,
  "strides": [],
  "dataId": {},
  "id": 4,
  "rankType": "1",
  "scopeId": 4
}
```

❷ Calling .print on the tensor gives us an actual printout of the internal value directly to the console. This prints the following:

```
Tensor
    [3.1415927]
```

❸ .arraySync gives us the values of the 2D tensor back as a 2D JavaScript array. This log prints the following:

```
Welcome Back Array!
[
  [
    1,
    2,
    3
  ],
  [
    4,
    5,
    6
  ]
]
```

❹ .dataSync gives us the values of the 2D tensor as a 1D Float32Array (*https:// oreil.ly/ozV2H*) object, effectively flattening the data. Logging a typed array looks like an object with indices as properties. This log prints:

```
Welcome Back Typed!
{
  "0": 1,
  "1": 2,
  "2": 3,
  "3": 4,
  "4": 5,
```

```
    "5": 6
}
```

Now you know how to manage tensors. You can take any JavaScript data and bring it into TensorFlow.js tensors for manipulation and then bring it back out cleanly when you're done.

Tensor Manipulation

It's time to cash in on the value of moving all this data around. You now know how to move large amounts of data to and from tensors, but let's get the perks of having done such a process. Machine learning models are driven by math. Any mathematical process that relies on linear algebra is going to benefit from tensors. You will also benefit because you don't have to write any complex mathematical operations.

Tensors and Mathematics

Let's say you had to multiply the contents of one array by another. In JavaScript, you'd have to write some iterative code. Additionally, if you're familiar with matrix multiplication, you know that code isn't as simple as you first thought. No developer at any level should resolve linear algebra for tensor manipulation.

Remember how to multiply matrices correctly? I forgot, too.

$$\begin{bmatrix} 91 & 82 & 13 \\ 15 & 23 & 62 \\ 25 & 66 & 63 \end{bmatrix} X \begin{bmatrix} 1 & 23 & 83 \\ 33 & 12 & 5 \\ 7 & 23 & 61 \end{bmatrix} = ?$$

It's not as simple as multiplying each number by the corresponding position; as some of you may recall, there's multiplication and addition involved. Calculating the top-left value would be 91 x 1 + 82 x 33 + 13 x 7 = 2888. Now do that eight more times for each index of the new matrix. The JavaScript to calculate that simple multiplication isn't completely trivial.

Tensors have mathematical benefits. I don't have to write any code to perform the previous calculation. While writing custom code would not be complicated, it would be unoptimized and redundant. Useful, scalable mathematical operations are builtin. TensorFlow.js makes linear algebra accessible and optimized for structures like tensors. I can get a speedy answer for the previous matrix with the following code:

```
const mat1 = [
  [91, 82, 13],
  [15, 23, 62],
  [25, 66, 63]
]
```

```
const mat2 = [
  [1, 23, 83],
  [33, 12, 5],
  [7, 23, 61]
]

tf.matMul(mat1, mat2).print()
```

In Chapter 2 the Toxicity detector downloaded megabytes and megabytes of numbers that are used in each classification calculation. The act of handling these large calculations in milliseconds is the power behind tensors. While we will continue to expand on the benefits of calculations in tensors, the whole reason for TensorFlow.js is that the complexity of such a large calculation is the domain of the framework and not the programmer.

Recommending Tensors

With the skills you've learned so far, you can construct a simple example of how TensorFlow.js can handle calculations for a real-world scenario. The following example has been chosen as an illustration of the power of tensors that welcomes the elite as well as the mathematical avoiders.

This section is probably the furthest you'll get into mathematics. If you'd like to dig further into the linear algebra and calculus that fuels machine learning, there's a fantastic free online course, offered by Stanford and taught by Andrew Ng, (*https://oreil.ly/OhvzW*) that I recommend.

Let's build something real with some tensor data. You'll do a simple group of calculations to identify some user preferences. These systems are often called *recommendation engines*. You might be familiar with recommendation engines as they suggest everything from what you should buy to what movie you should watch next. These algorithms are at the heart of digital product giants like YouTube, Amazon, and Netflix. Recommendation engines are quite popular with any business that sells anything and could probably fill a book by themselves. We'll be implementing a simple "content-based" recommendation system. Use your imagination because in a production system these tensors are significantly larger.

Here's what you'll do, at a high level:

1. Ask users to rank bands from 1 to 10.

2. Any unknown bands get a 0.

3. Bands and music styles will be our "features."

4. Use the matrix dot product to identify what styles each user likes!

Dot Product What?

The dot product might throw you for a loop. Don't worry too much about it. It's just a way to identify similarity between tensors represented as vectors. The more two tensors are similar, the higher their dot product will be.

The tensors your users created by rating bands will place them on a graph, and when two vectors on that graph are close together, their dot product (matMul in Tensor-Flow.js) is a larger number. When they are in opposite directions, the dot product is a negative number. This is how the recommender mathematically knows two things are similar. Figure 3-3 shows an example of two similar vectors, which create a positive value.

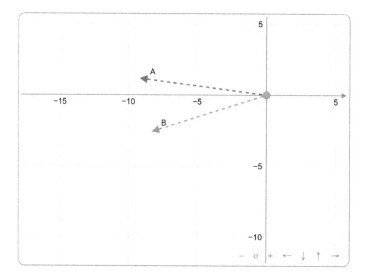

Dot Product = 69.01

Figure 3-3. Two negative vectors that are similar have a positive dot product

You can take my word for it, or you can open the extra code provided for this chapter and play with vectors A and B to verify (*https://oreil.ly/vv4rY*).

Regardless of the method for deciding similarity (yes, there are others), you can utilize tensors to handle the heavy lifting for calculations in a recommendation system.

Let's get started creating a recommender! This small dataset will serve as an example of what you need. As you'll notice, you mix JavaScript arrays with tensors in the code. It's quite common for labels to remain in JavaScript and calculations to be pushed into tensors. This not only keeps tensors focused on numbers; it also has the benefit

---

of internationalizing the tensor results. The labels are the only language-dependent part of this operation. You'll see this theme continue in several examples throughout the book and in the real world of practical machine learning.

Here's the data:

```
const users = ['Gant', 'Todd',  'Jed', 'Justin'] ❶
const bands = [ ❷
  'Nirvana',
  'Nine Inch Nails',
  'Backstreet Boys',
  'N Sync',
  'Night Club',
  'Apashe',
  'STP'
]
const features = [ ❸
  'Grunge',
  'Rock',
  'Industrial',
  'Boy Band',
  'Dance',
  'Techno'
]

// User votes ❹
const user_votes = tf.tensor([
  [10, 9, 1, 1, 8, 7, 8],
  [6, 8, 2, 2, 0, 10, 0],
  [0, 2, 10, 9, 3, 7, 0],
  [7, 4, 2, 3, 6, 5, 5]
])

// Music Styles ❺
const band_feats = tf.tensor([
  [1, 1, 0, 0, 0, 0],
  [1, 0, 1, 0, 0, 0],
  [0, 0, 0, 1, 1, 0],
  [0, 0, 0, 1, 0, 0],
  [0, 0, 1, 0, 0, 1],
  [0, 0, 1, 0, 0, 1],
  [1, 1, 0, 0, 0, 0]
])
```

❶ The four name labels are simply stored in a normal JavaScript array.

❷ You've asked our users to rate seven bands.

❸ Some simple music genres can be used to describe our seven bands, again in a JavaScript array.

❹ This is our first tensor, a rank-two description of each user's vote from 1 to 10, with "I don't know this band" as 0.

❺ This tensor is also a 2D tensor that identifies the genres that match each given band. Each line index represents an encoding of true/false for the genres it can be classified as.

Now you have all the data you need in tensors. As a quick review, you can see the way the information is organized. By reading the user_votes variable, you can see each user's votes. For example, you can see user 0, which maps to Gant, has rated Nirvana a 10 and Apashe 7, while Jed has given Backstreet Boys a 10.

The band_feats variable maps each band to the genres they fulfill. For example, the second band at index 1 is Nine Inch Nails and has a positive scoring for Grunge and Industrial styles of music. To keep this example simple, you're using a binary 1 and 0 per genre, but a normalized scale of numbers would work here, too. In other words, [1, 1, 0, 0, 0, 0] would represent Grunge and Rock for the 0th band, which is Nirvana.

Next, you'll calculate each user's favorite genres based on their votes:

```
// User's favorite styles
const user_feats = tf.matMul(user_votes, band_feats)
// Print the answers
user_feats.print()
```

Now user_feats contains a dot product of the user's votes across the features of each band. The result from our print will look like this:

```
Tensor
    [[27, 18, 24, 2 , 1 , 15],
     [14, 6 , 18, 4 , 2 , 10],
     [2 , 0 , 12, 20, 10, 10],
     [16, 12, 15, 5 , 2 , 11]]
```

This tensor shows the value of the features (in this case, genres) of each user. User 0, which aligns with Gant, has their highest value as 27 at index 0, which means their top preferred genre from the surveyed data is Grunge. This data looks pretty good. Using this tensor, you can identify each user's preferred tastes.

While the data is in tensor form, you can use a method called topk to help us identify the top values for each user with size k. To get the top k tensors or simply identify where the top values are via identifying their indices, you can call the function topk with the desired tensor and size. For this exercise, you'll set k to be the full feature set size.

Finally, let's take this data home to JavaScript. The code to do this can be written like so:

```
// Let's make them pretty
const top_user_features = tf.topk(user_feats, features.length)
// Back to JavaScript
const top_genres = top_user_features.indices.arraySync() ❶
// print the results
users.map((u, i) => {
  const rankedCategories = top_genres[i].map(v => features[v]) ❷
  console.log(u, rankedCategories)
})
```

❶ You are returning the index tensor to a rank-two JavaScript array for the results.

❷ You are mapping the indices back to musical genres.

The resulting log looks like this:

```
Gant
[
  "Grunge",
  "Industrial",
  "Rock",
  "Techno",
  "Boy Band",
  "Dance"
]
Todd
[
  "Industrial",
  "Grunge",
  "Techno",
  "Rock",
  "Boy Band",
  "Dance"
]
Jed
[
  "Boy Band",
  "Industrial",
  "Dance",
  "Techno",
  "Grunge",
  "Rock"
]
Justin
[
  "Grunge",
  "Industrial",
  "Rock",
  "Techno",
  "Boy Band",
  "Dance"
]
```

In the results, you can see Todd should check out more Industrial music, and Jed should brush up on his Boy Bands. Both will be happy with their recommendations.

What did you just do?

You successfully loaded data into tensors in a way that makes sense, and then you applied a mathematical calculation to the entire set, rather than an iterative approach across each person. Once you got your answers, you sorted the entire set and brought the data back to JavaScript for recommendations!

Can you do more?

You can do plenty more. From here, you can even use the 0s from each user's votes to identify what bands the user has never listened to and recommend them in order of most-liked genre! There's a really cool mathematical way to do this, but that's a bit outside the scope of our first tensor exercise. Regardless, congratulations on implementing one of the most demanded and trending features of online sales!

Chapter Review

In this chapter, you've done more than scratch the surface of tensors. You've dug your hands deep into the fundamental structure of TensorFlow.js and grasped the roots. You're on your way to wielding machine learning in JavaScript. Tensors are a concept that permeates all machine learning frameworks and fundamentals.

Chapter Challenge: What Makes You So Special?

Now that you're no longer a tensor-newb and you can manage tensors like a pro, let's attempt a small exercise to solidify your skills. As of the time of this writing, JavaScript has no built-in method for clearing duplicates in an array. While other languages like Ruby have had the `uniq` method for more than a decade, JavaScript developers have either hand-rolled their solutions or imported popular libraries like Lodash. For fun, let's use TensorFlow.js to solve the problem of unique values. As an exercise on lessons learned, muse over this problem:

> Given this array of US phone numbers, remove the duplicates.

```
// Clean up the duplicates
const callMeMaybe = tf.tensor([8367677, 4209111, 4209111, 8675309, 8367677])
```

Make sure your answer is a JavaScript array. If you get stuck with this exercise, you can review the TensorFlow.js online documentation (*https://oreil.ly/9thOd*). Searching the documentation for key terms will point you in the right direction.

You can find the answer to this challenge in Appendix B.

Review Questions

Let's review the lessons you've learned from the code you've written in this chapter. Take a moment to answer the following questions:

1. Why do we even use tensors?
2. Which one of these is not a tensor data type?
    a. `Int32`
    b. `Float32`
    c. Object
    d. Boolean
3. What is the rank of a six-dimensional tensor?
4. What is the dimensionality of the return array for the method `dataSync`?
5. What happens when you pass a 3D tensor to `tf.tensor1d`?
6. What is the difference between `rank` and `size` in relation to a tensor's shape?
7. What is the data type of the tensor `tf.tensor([1])`?
8. Is the input array dimension for a tensor always the resulting tensor dimension?
9. How can you identify the number of tensors in memory?
10. Can `tf.tidy` handle an async function?
11. How can I keep a tensor created inside of `tf.tidy`?
12. Can I see the values of a tensor with `console.log`?
13. What does the `tf.topk` method do?
14. Do tensors optimize for batch or iterative calculation?
15. What is a recommendation engine?

Solutions to these exercises are available in Appendix A.

Up Next...

In Chapter 4, you will get to see and feel the results of your tensor knowledge with tangible images. Machine learning commonly uses images, even for nonvisual applications. Becoming an expert in image tensors is a fun and rewarding way to manage data.

CHAPTER 4
Image Tensors

"But he who dares not grasp the thorn
Should never crave the rose."

—Anne Brontë

In the previous chapter, you created and destroyed simple tensors. However, our data was minuscule. As you might guess, printing tensors can take you only so far and in so many dimensions. You're going to need to learn how to deal with large tensors, which are more common. This is, of course, true in the world of images! This is an exciting chapter because you'll start working with real data, and we'll be able to see the effects of your tensor operations immediately.

We'll also get to utilize some existing best practices. As you recall, in the previous chapter, you converted a tic-tac-toe game to tensors. During this exercise with a simple 3 x 3 grid, you identified one method for converting a game's state, but another person might have come up with a completely different strategy. We'll need to identify some common practices and tricks of the trade, so you don't have to reinvent the wheel every time.

We will:

- Identify what makes a tensor an image tensor
- Build some images by hand
- Use fill methods to create large tensors
- Convert existing images to tensors and back
- Manipulate image tensors in useful ways

When you finish this chapter, you'll be confident in managing real-world image data, and a lot of this knowledge will apply to managing tensors in general.

Visual Tensors

You might assume that when an image is converted into a tensor, that resulting tensor will be rank two. If you've forgotten what a rank-two tensor looks like, review Chapter 3. It's easy to picture a 2D image as a 2D tensor, except that pixel color generally can't be stored as a single number. A rank-two tensor works only with grayscale images. The most common practice for a colored pixel is to represent it as three separate values. Those who were raised with paints were taught to use red, yellow, and blue, but us nerds prefer the red, green, blue (RGB) system.

 The RGB system is another instance of art imitating life. The human eye uses RGB, which is based on an "additive" color system —a system of emitting light, like computer screens do. Your art teacher probably used yellow over green to help lighten up paints that darken as you add more in a "subtractive" color system, like paint on paper.

A pixel is commonly colored by the ordered amounts of red, green, and blue within the confines of a singular byte. This 0-255 array of values looks like [255, 255, 255] for integers and like #FFFFFF for most websites seeking a hexadecimal version of the same three values. When our tensor is the data type int32, this is the interpretation method that is used. When our tensor is float32, the values are assumed to be in the range 0-1. So, an integer [255, 255, 255] represents pure white, but in float form the equivalent would be [1, 1, 1]. This also means [1, 1, 1] is pure white in a float32 tensor and interpreted as next to black in an int32 tensor.

Depending on the tensor data type, you get two color extremes from a pixel encoded as [1, 1, 1], as shown in Figure 4-1.

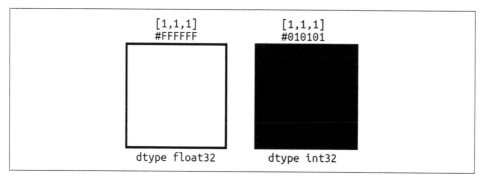

Figure 4-1. Significant color difference from the same data

This means to store images you'll need a 3D tensor. You'll need each three-value pixel stored at given width and height. Just as you saw in the tic-tac-toe problem, you'll have to identify what's the best format to do so. In TensorFlow and TensorFlow.js, it's common practice to store the RGB values in the final dimension of a tensor. It's also customary to store the values across height, then width, and then color dimension. This might seem odd for images, but referencing rows and then columns is the classic organizational reference order of matrices.

 Most of the world will mention an image size as width by height. A 1024 x 768 image is 1024px wide and 768px high, but as we just stated, TensorFlow image tensors store height first, which can be a little confusing. That same image would be a [768, 1024, 3] tensor. This often confuses developers who are new to visual tensors.

So if you wanted to make a 4 x 3 checkerboard of pixels, you could create that image by hand with a 3D array with the shape [3, 4, 3].

The code would be as simple as the following:

```
const checky = tf.tensor([
  [
    [1, 1, 1],
    [0, 0, 0],
    [1, 1, 1],
    [0, 0, 0]
  ],
  [
    [0, 0, 0],
    [1, 1, 1],
    [0, 0, 0],
    [1, 1, 1]
  ],
  [
    [1, 1, 1],
    [0, 0, 0],
    [1, 1, 1],
    [0, 0, 0]
  ],
])
```

A 4 x 3 pixel image would be pretty small, but if we zoomed in a few hundred times, we would be able to see the pixels we just created. The resulting image would look like Figure 4-2.

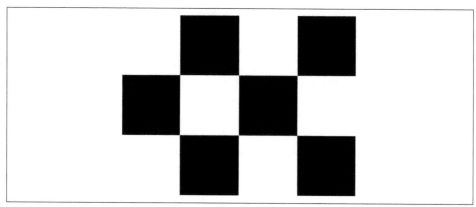

Figure 4-2. The checkered 4 x 3 TensorFlow.js image

You're not limited to RGB, as you might have expected; adding a fourth value to the RGB dimension of a tensor will add an alpha channel. Much like in web color, #FFFFFF00 would be white at zero opacity, and a tensor pixel with a red, green, blue, alpha (RGBA) value of [1, 1, 1, 0] would be similarly transparent. A 1024 x 768 image with transparency would be stored in a tensor with the shape [768, 1024, 4].

As a corollary to the two aforementioned systems, if the final channel has only one value instead of three or four, the resulting image would be grayscale.

Our black-and-white checkered pattern example from earlier could be significantly condensed using that last bit of knowledge. Now we can build the same image but with the tensor, with code like so:

```
const checkySmalls = tf.tensor([
  [[1],[0],[1],[0]],
  [[0],[1],[0],[1]],
  [[1],[0],[1],[0]]
])
```

And yes, if you simply remove those inner brackets and move this to a simple 2D tensor, that will work, too!

Quick Image Tensors

I know there's a line of people beating down your door to hand-draw images, pixel by pixel, so you might be surprised to learn some people find writing little 1s and 0s tedious. Of course, you could create arrays using Array.prototype.fill and then use that to fill arrays to create sizable 3D tensor constructors, but it's worth noting that TensorFlow.js comes with that functionality built in.

It's a common need to create large tensors with already populated values. In fact, if you were to continue working on our recommendation system from Chapter 3, you would need to utilize these exact features.

As it is now, you can use the methods `tf.ones`, `tf.zeros`, and `tf.fill` to create large tensors by hand. Both `tf.ones` and `tf.zeros` take a shape as a parameter, and then they construct that shape with every value equal to 1 or 0, respectively. So, the code `tf.zeros([768, 1024, 1])` would create a 1024 x 768 black image. The optional second parameter would be the data type for the generated tensor.

 Often, you can run an empty image made with `tf.zeros` through a model to preallocate memory. The result is immediately thrown away, and subsequent calls are much faster. This is often called *model warming*, and it's a speedup trick you might see when developers are looking for things to allocate while waiting for a webcam or network data.

As you might imagine, `tf.fill` takes a shape, and then the second parameter is the value to fill that shape with. You might be tempted to pass a tensor as the second parameter, essentially raising the rank of the resulting generated tensor, but it's important to note that this will not work. For a juxtaposition of what does and doesn't work, see Table 4-1.

Table 4-1. Fill params: scalar versus vector

This works	This fails
`tf.fill([2, 2], 1)`	`tf.fill([2, 2], [1, 1, 1])`

Your second parameter must be a single value to fill the tensor of the shape you gave. This nontensor value is often called a *scalar*. To recap, the code `tf.fill([200, 200, 4], 0.5)` would create a 200 x 200 gray semitransparent square, as illustrated in Figure 4-3.

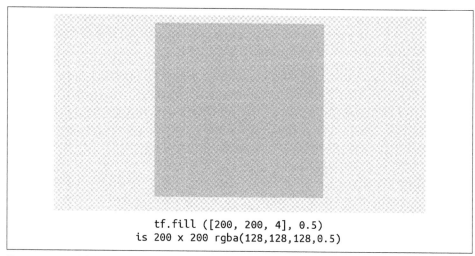

```
tf.fill ([200, 200, 4], 0.5)
is 200 x 200 rgba(128,128,128,0.5)
```

Figure 4-3. Alpha channel image tensor with background

If you're disappointed that you can't fill a tensor with some elegant color other than grayscale, have I got a treat for you! Our next way to create large tensors not only lets you fill with tensors, but it also enables you to fill with patterns.

Let's return to the 4 x 3 checkered image you made earlier. You hand-coded 12 pixel values. If you wanted to make a 200 x 200 checkered image, that would be 40,000 pixel values for simple grayscale. Instead, we'll use the `.tile` method to expand a simple 2 x 2 tensor.

```
// 2 x 2 checker pattern
const lil = tf.tensor([   ❶
  [[1], [0]],
  [[0], [1]]
]);
// tile it
const big = lil.tile([100, 100, 1])  ❷
```

❶ The checker pattern is a 2D black-and-white tensor. This could be any elegant pattern or color.

❷ The tile size is 100 x 100 because the repeated pattern is 2 x 2, which results in a 200 x 200 image tensor.

Checkered pixels are hard for a human eye to see. The checkered pattern can look gray without zooming in. Much like how printed dots make up multiple colors for magazines, you can see the checkered pattern clearly once you zoom in, like in Figure 4-4.

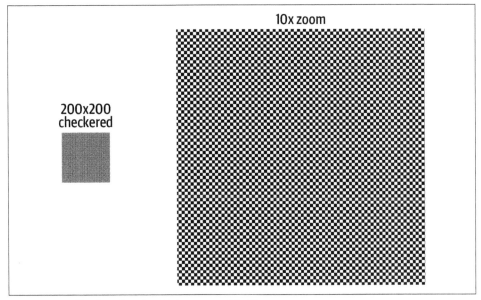

Figure 4-4. Checkered 200 x 200 tensor with 10x zoom

Lastly, if all these methods are far too structured for your taste, you can unleash the chaos! While JavaScript has no built-in method to generate arrays of random values, TensorFlow.js has a wide variety of methods (*https://oreil.ly/tg46b*) to do precisely this.

For simplicity, my favorite is called `.randomUniform`. This tensor method takes a shape and also optionally a min, max, and data type.

If you want to build a 200 x 200 random static of grayscale colors, you can use `tf.ran domUniform([200, 200, 1])` or even `tf.randomUniform([200, 200, 1], 0, 255, 'int32')`. Both of these will make the same (as same as random can be) result.

Figure 4-5 shows some example output.

Figure 4-5. 200 x 200 random value-filled tensor

JPGs and PNGs and GIFs, Oh My!

OK, Gant! You've been talking about images for a bit now, but we can't see them; all we see are tensors. How does a tensor turn into an actual visible image? And probably more important for machine learning, how does an existing image turn into a tensor?

As you might have intuited, this will vary significantly according to where the Java-Script is running, specifically the client and server. To decode an image to a tensor and back on a browser, you'll be limited and empowered by the magic of the browser's built-in functionality for a sandbox. Conversely, images on a server running Node.js will not be sandboxed but lack easy visual feedback.

Fear not! You will cover both of these options in this section so you can confidently apply TensorFlow.js to images, regardless of the medium.

We'll review the following common scenarios in detail:

- Browser: tensor to image
- Browser: image to tensor
- Node.js: tensor to image
- Node.js: image to tensor

Browser: Tensor to Image

For visualizing, modifying, and saving images, you will utilize HTML elements and a canvas. Let's start by giving us a way to visualize all the graphical lessons we've learned. We'll render a tensor to a canvas in a browser.

First, create a 400 x 400 tensor of random noise, and then convert the tensor to an image in the browser. To accomplish this, you will use `tf.browser.toPixels`. This method takes a tensor as the first parameter, and optionally a canvas to draw to for the second parameter. It returns a promise that resolves when the render is complete.

 At first glance, having the canvas be an optional parameter is quite confusing. It's worth noting that the promise resolves with a `Uint8ClampedArray` of the tensor as a parameter, so it's a good way to have a "canvas ready" value created, even if you don't have an active canvas in mind. It will likely decrease in utility as the concept of an OffscreenCanvas (*https://oreil.ly/gaiVn*) moves from experimental mode to an actual supported web API.

To set up our first ever canvas render, you'll need to have a canvas in our HTML with an ID that you can reference. For those of us who are familiar with the complexity of HTML load order, you'll need the canvas to exist *before* you attempt to access it from our JavaScript (or follow any best practice for your site, like checking for a document-ready state):

```
<canvas id="randomness"></canvas>
```

And now you can access this canvas by ID and pass it to our `browser.toPixels` method.

```
const bigMess = tf.randomUniform([400, 400, 3]); ❶
const myCanvas = document.getElementById("randomness"); ❷
tf.browser.toPixels(bigMess, myCanvas).then(() => { ❸
  // It's not bad practice to clean up and make sure we got everything
  bigMess.dispose();
  console.log("Make sure we cleaned up", tf.memory().numTensors);
});
```

❶ Creating an RGB 400 x 400 image tensor

❷ Grabbing a reference to our canvas in the Document Object Model (DOM)

❸ Calling `browser.toPixels` with our tensor and canvas

If this code were run in an async function, you could have simply awaited the `browser.toPixels` call and then cleaned up. Without utilizing the promise or async functionality, the `dispose` would most assuredly win the possible race condition and cause an error.

Browser: Image to Tensor

As you may have guessed, `browser.toPixels` has a counterpart named `browser.from Pixels`. This method takes an image and converts it to a tensor. Fortunately for us, the input for `browser.fromPixels` is quite dynamic. You can pass in a wide variety of elements, from JavaScript ImageData to Image objects, to HTML elements like <img>, <canvas>, and even <video>. This makes it pretty simple to encode any image into a tensor.

As a second parameter, you can even identify the number of channels you'd like for an image (1, 3, 4), so you can optimize for the data you care about. For example, if you were identifying handwriting, there's no real need for RBG. You can get a grayscale tensor immediately from our tensor conversion!

To set up our image to tensor conversion, you'll explore the two most common inputs. You'll convert a DOM element, and you'll convert an in-memory element, too. The in-memory element will load an image via URL.

If you've been opening *.html* files locally up to this point, this is where that will stop working. You'll need to actually use a web server like 200 OK! or one of the other mentioned hosting solutions to access images loaded by URL. See Chapter 2 if you get stuck.

To load an image from the DOM, you simply need a reference to that item on the DOM. In the source code associated with this book, I've set up an example to access two images. The simplest way to follow along is to read Chapter 4 on GitHub (*https://oreil.ly/ZzWPP*).

Let's set our DOM image up with a simple img tag and id:

```
<img id="gant" src="/gant.jpg" />
```

Yes, that's a strange image of me I decided to use. I have adorable dogs, but they are shy and have refused to sign a release to be models for my book. Being a dog lover can be "ruff." Now that you have an image, let's write the simple JavaScript to reference the desired image element.

 Be sure the document is finished loading before trying to access the image element. Otherwise, you might get a cryptic message like "The source width is 0." This happens most frequently on implementations with no JavaScript frontend framework. In situations where there's nothing awaiting the DOM load event, I suggest subscribing to the window's load event before trying to access the DOM.

With the img in place and the DOM loaded, you can call browser.fromPixels for results:

```
// Simply read from the DOM
const gantImage = document.getElementById('gant')  ❶
const gantTensor = tf.browser.fromPixels(gantImage)  ❷
console.log(  ❸
  `Successful conversion from DOM to a ${gantTensor.shape} tensor`
)
```

❶ Grabbing a reference to the img tag.

❷ Creating a tensor from the image.

❸ Logging proof that we now have a tensor! This prints the following:

```
Successful conversion from DOM to a 372,500,3 tensor
```

If you are getting an error similar to `Failed to execute 'getIma geData' on 'CanvasRenderingContext2D': The canvas has been tainted by cross-origin data.`, this means you're trying to load an image from another server rather than local. For security reasons browsers protect against this. See the next example for loading external images.

Perfect! But what if our image is not in an element on our page? So long as the server allows cross-origin loading (`Access-Control-Allow-Origin "*"`), you'll be able to dynamically load and process external images. This is where the JavaScript Image object example (*https://oreil.ly/dSjiI*) comes in. We can convert an image into a tensor like so:

```
// Now load an image object in JavaScript
const cake = new Image() ❶
cake.crossOrigin = 'anonymous' ❷
cake.src = '/cake.jpg' ❸
cake.onload = () => { ❹
  const cakeTensor = tf.browser.fromPixels(cake) ❺
  console.log( ❻
    `Successful conversion from Image() to a ${cakeTensor.shape} tensor`
  )
}
```

❶ Create a new Image web API object.

❷ This is not necessary here because the file is on the server, but you commonly need to set this to access external URLs.

❸ Give the path to the image.

❹ Wait for the image to fully load into the object before you try to turn it into a tensor.

❺ Convert the image to a tensor.

❻ Print our tensor shape to make sure everything went as planned. This prints the following: `Successful conversion from Image() to a 578,500,3 tensor`.

By combining the two previous methods, you can have a single page that shows one image element and prints the values of two tensors to the console (see Figure 4-6).

Figure 4-6. The console log of two images becoming tensors

By the logs of the images, you can see both of them are 500-pixel-wide RGB. If you modify the second parameter, you can easily convert either of these images to grayscale or RGBA. You'll get into modifying our image tensors later in this chapter.

Node: Tensor to Image

In Node.js, there's no canvas for rendering, just the quiet efficiency of writing files. You'll be saving a random 400 x 400 RGB with `tfjs-node`. While image tensors are pixel-by-pixel values, typical image formats are much smaller. JPG and PNGs have various compression techniques, headers, features, and more. The resulting file internals will look nothing like our pretty 3D image tensors.

Once tensors are converted to their encoded file formats, you'll use the Node.js filesystem library (`fs`) to write the file out. Now that you have a plan, let's explore the features and settings to save a tensor to JPG and PNG.

Writing JPGs

To encode a tensor into a JPG, you will use a method called node.encodeJpeg. This method takes an Int32 representation of the image and some options and returns a promise with the resulting data.

The first hiccup you might notice is that the input tensor *must* be that Int32 encoding with values of 0-255, where the browser could handle float and integer values. Perhaps this is an excellent opportunity for an open source contributor!?

 Any Float32 tensor with values 0-1 can be transformed into a new tensor by multiplying by 255 and then converting to int32 with code like so: myTensor.mul(255).asType('int32').

Writing a JPG from a tensor, as found in *chapter4/node/node-encode*, in Chapter 4 on GitHub (*https://oreil.ly/Nn9nX*), can be as simple as this:

```
const bigMess = tf.randomUniform([400, 400, 3], 0, 255); ❶
tf.node.encodeJpeg(bigMess).then((f) => { ❷
  fs.writeFileSync("simple.jpg", f); ❸
  console.log("Basic JPG 'simple.jpg' written");
});
```

❶ You create random RGB pixels for a 400 x 400 image tensor.

❷ node.encodeJpeg is called with the tensor input.

❸ The resulting data is written with the filesystem library.

Because the file you're writing is a JPG, there's a wide variety of configuration options you can enable. Let's write another image and modify the defaults along the way:

```
const bigMess = tf.randomUniform([400, 400, 3], 0, 255);
tf.node
  .encodeJpeg(
    bigMess,
    "rgb", ❶
    90,    ❷
    true,  ❸
    true,  ❹
    true,  ❺
    "cm",  ❻
    250,   ❼
    250,   ❽
    "Generated by TFJS Node!" ❾
  )
  .then((f) => {
```

```
    fs.writeFileSync("advanced.jpg", f);
    console.log("Full featured JPG 'advanced.jpg' written");
  });
```

❶ format: you can override the default color channels with grayscale or rgb instead of matching the input tensor.

❷ quality: adjust the quality of the JPG. Lower numbers degrade quality, usually for size.

❸ progressive: JPGs have the ability to load from the top down, or slowly become clear as a progressive load. Setting this to true enables progressive load format.

❹ optimizeSize: spend a few extra cycles to optimize an image size without modifying the quality.

❺ chromaDownsampling: this is a trick where lighting is more important in the encoding than colors. It modifies the raw distribution of the data so it's clearer to the human eye.

❻ densityUnit: choose either pixels per inch or centimeter; a strange few fight the metric system.

❼ xDensity: set the pixels-per-density unit on the x-axis.

❽ yDensity: set the pixels-per-density unit on the y-axis.

❾ xmpMetadata: this is a nonvisible message to store in the image metadata. Generally, this is reserved for licensing and scavenger hunts.

Depending on why you're writing the JPG, you can adequately configure or ignore these options from Node.js! Figure 4-7 shows the file size difference of the two JPGs you just created.

Figure 4-7. File sizes of our two examples

Writing PNGs

The features for writing a PNG are significantly more limited than a JPG. As you might have guessed, we'll have a friendly method that helps us along the way, and it's called `node.encodePng`. Just like our friend the JPG, this method expects an integer representation of our tensor with values ranging `0-255`.

We can easily write a PNG with the following:

```
const bigMess = tf.randomUniform([400, 400, 3], 0, 255);
tf.node.encodePng(bigMess).then((f) => {
  fs.writeFileSync("simple.png", f);
  console.log("Basic PNG 'simple.png' written");
});
```

The PNG parameters aren't nearly as advanced. You have only one new parameter, and it's a cryptic one! The second parameter to `node.encodePng` is a compression setting. This value can be anywhere between `-1` and `9`. The default value is 1, which means a little compression, and 9 means max compression.

You might think -1 means no compression, but from experimenting, 0 means no compression. Actually, -1 activates max compression. So, -1 and 9 are effectively the same.

Since PNGs are terrible at compressing randomness, you can set this second parameter to 9 and get a file around the same size as the default setting:

```
tf.node.encodePng(bigMess, 9).then((f) => {
  fs.writeFileSync("advanced.png", f);
  console.log("Full featured PNG 'advanced.png' written");
});
```

If you'd like to see an actual file size difference, try printing something easy to compress, like `tf.zeros`. Regardless, you can now generate PNG files from tensors with ease.

If your tensor utilizes an alpha channel, you cannot use formats like JPG; you'll have to save a PNG to preserve that data.

Node: Image to Tensor

Node.js is a fantastic tool for training a machine learning model because of the direct file access and speed of decoding images. Decoding into a tensor on Node.js is quite similar to the encoding process.

Node provides functions for decoding BMP, JPG, PNG, and even GIF file formats (*https://oreil.ly/pRjb5*). However, as you might expect, there is also a generic `node.decodeImage` method, which is capable of doing the simple identification lookup and conversion of any of these files automatically. You'll use `decodeImage` for now and leave `decodeBMP`, etc., for you to review as needed.

The simplest decode for an image is to pass the file directly into the command. To do this, you can use the standard Node.js libraries `fs` and `path`.

This example code depends on a single *cake.jpg* file for loading and decoding into a tensor. The code and image resources used in this demo are available at *chapter4/node/node-decode* in Chapter 4 on GitHub (*https://oreil.ly/k8jjE*).

```
import * as tf from '@tensorflow/tfjs-node'
import * as fs from 'fs'
import * as path from 'path'

const FILE_PATH = 'files'
const cakeImagePath = path.join(FILE_PATH, 'cake.jpg')
const cakeImage = fs.readFileSync(cakeImagePath) ❶

tf.tidy(() => {
  const cakeTensor = tf.node.decodeImage(cakeImage) ❷
  console.log(`Success: local file to a ${cakeTensor.shape} tensor`)

  const cakeBWTensor = tf.node.decodeImage(cakeImage, 1) ❸
  console.log(`Success: local file to a ${cakeBWTensor.shape} tensor`)
})
```

❶ You load the designated file into memory using the filesystem library.

❷ You decode the image into a tensor that matches the imported image's number of color channels.

❸ You decode this image into a grayscale tensor.

As we mentioned earlier, the decoding process also allows the decoding of GIF files. One obvious question is, "Which frame of the GIF?" For this, you can choose either all frames or the first frame for animated GIFs. The `node.decodeImage` method has a flag that allows you to identify what you prefer.

 Physicists often argue about the fourth dimension being or not being time. Regardless of the debates on 4D Minkowski spacetime being a reality, it is a proven reality for animated GIFs! To represent animated GIFs in a tensor, you use a rank-four tensor.

This example code decodes an animated GIF. The example GIF you're going to use is a 500 x 372 animated GIF with 20 frames:

```
const gantCakeTensor = tf.node.decodeImage(gantCake, 3, 'int32', true)
console.log(`Success: local file to a ${gantCakeTensor.shape} tensor`)
```

For the `node.decodeImage` parameters, you're providing the image data, followed by three channels for color, as an `int32` result tensor, and the final parameter is `true`.

Passing `true` lets the method know to unroll animated GIFs and return a 4D tensor, where `false` would clip this down to 3D.

Our resulting tensor shape, as you might have expected, is `[20, 372, 500, 3]`.

Common Image Modifications

Importing images into tensors for training is powerful but rarely direct. When images are used for machine learning, they generally have some common modifications.

Common modifications include:

- Being mirrored for data augmentation
- Resizing to the expected input size
- Cropping out faces or other desired portions

You'll perform many of these operations in machine learning, and you'll see these skills being utilized in the next two chapters. The capstone project in Chapter 12 will depend on this skill extensively. Let's take a moment to implement a few of these everyday operations to round out your comfort with image tensors.

Mirroring Image Tensors

If you're trying to train a model on identifying cats, you can double your dataset by mirroring your existing cat photos. Slightly adjusting training images to augment datasets is a common practice.

To flip tensor data for an image, you have two options. One is to modify the image tensor's data in a way that flips the image along the width axis. The other way is to use `tf.image.flipLeftRight`, which is commonly used for batches of images. Let's do both.

To flip a single image, you can use `tf.reverse` and specify you want to flip only the axis that holds the pixels for the width of an image. As you already know, this is the second axis of the image, and thus the index you will pass is 1.

In the corresponding source code for this chapter, you display an image and then mirror that image in a canvas right next to it. You can access this example at *simple/*

simple-image-manipulation/mirror.html on GitHub (*https://oreil.ly/83b9B*). The full code for this operation looks like this:

```
// Simple Tensor Flip
const lemonadeImage = document.getElementById("lemonade");
const lemonadeCanvas = document.getElementById("lemonadeCanvas");
const lemonadeTensor = tf.browser.fromPixels(lemonadeImage);
const flippedLemonadeTensor = tf.reverse(lemonadeTensor, 1) ❶
tf.browser.toPixels(flippedLemonadeTensor, lemonadeCanvas).then(() => {
  lemonadeTensor.dispose();
  flippedLemonadeTensor.dispose();
})
```

❶ The reverse function flips the axis index 1 to reverse the image.

Because you understand the underlying data, it was trivial to apply this transformation to your image. You can experiment with flipping along the height or even RGB axis. Any data can be reversed.

Figure 4-8 shows the result of `tf.reverse` on axis 1.

Figure 4-8. tf.reverse for lemonadeTensor with axis set to 1

> Reverse and other data manipulation methods are not unique to images. You could use this to augment nonvisual datasets like tic-tac-toe and similar games.

We should also review the other method of mirroring an image, because this method can handle mirroring a group of images, and this exposes some pretty important concepts when it comes to image data. After all, our goal is to rely on the optimization of tensors as much as possible and to stay away from JavaScript iterative looping.

The second way you can mirror an image is to use `tf.image.flipLeftRight`. This method is geared toward handling batches of images, and batches of 3D tensors are basically 4D tensors. For our demo, you'll take one image and make it a batch of one.

To expand the dimensionality of a single 3D image, you can use tf.expandDims, and then when you're looking to reverse that (throw away the unnecessary bracket), you can use tf.squeeze. This way, you can move a 3D image to 4D for batch processing and back. This seems a bit silly with a single image, but it's an excellent exercise in the concept of understanding batches and changing dimensions of tensors.

So, a 200 x 200 RGB image starts as [200, 200, 3], and then you expand it, essentially making it a stack of one. The resulting shape becomes [1, 200, 200, 3].

You can perform tf.image.flipLeftRight on a single image with the following code:

```
// Batch Tensor Flip
const cakeImage = document.getElementById("cake");
const cakeCanvas = document.getElementById("cakeCanvas");
const flipCake = tf.tidy(() => {
  const cakeTensor = tf.expandDims(  ❶
    tf
      .browser.fromPixels(cakeImage)  ❷
      .asType("float32")  ❸
  );
  return tf
    .squeeze(tf.image.flipLeftRight(cakeTensor))  ❹
    .asType("int32");  ❺
})
tf.browser.toPixels(flipCake, cakeCanvas).then(() => {
  flipCake.dispose();
});
```

❶ The dimensions of the tensor are expanded.

❷ Import the 3D image as a tensor.

③ As of the writing of this section, `image.flipLeftRight` expects images to be a `float32` tensor. This may change in the future.

④ Flip the image batch and then squeeze it down into a 3D tensor again when you're done.

⑤ The `image.flipLeftRight` returned 0-255 values, so you'll need to make sure our tensor you send to `browser.toPixels` is an `int32`, so it renders correctly.

That was a bit more complicated than our use of `tf.reverse`, but each strategy has its own benefits and drawbacks. It's essential to take full advantage of the speed and massive calculation capabilities of tensors whenever possible.

Resizing Image Tensors

Lots of AI models expect a specific input image size. That means that while your users upload 700 x 900 images, the model is looking for a tensor that is 256 x 256. Resizing images is at the core of dealing with image input.

 Resizing image tensors for input is a common practice for most models. This means any image that is wildly out of proportion to the desired input, like a panoramic photo, will likely perform terribly when it is resized for input.

TensorFlow.js has two excellent methods for resizing images, and both support batches of images: `image.resizeNearestNeighbor` and `image.resizeBilinear`. I recommend that you use `image.resizeBilinear` for any visual resizing and save `image.resizeNearestNeighbor` for when the specific pixel values of an image cannot be compromised or interpolated. There is a small speed difference, `image.resizeNearestNeighbor` being around 10x faster than `image.resizeBilinear`, but the difference is still measured in milliseconds per resize.

To put it bluntly, `resizeBilinear` blurs and `resizeNearestNeighbor` pixelates when they have to extrapolate for new data. Let's upscale an image with both methods and compare. You can access this example at *simple/simple-image-manipulation/resize.html* (*https://oreil.ly/ieQLD*).

```
// Simple Tensor Flip
const newSize = [768, 560] // 4x larger ❶
const littleGantImage = document.getElementById("littleGant");
const nnCanvas = document.getElementById("nnCanvas");
const blCanvas = document.getElementById("blCanvas");
const gantTensor = tf.browser.fromPixels(littleGantImage);

const nnResizeTensor = tf.image.resizeNearestNeighbor( ❷
```

```
    gantTensor,
    newSize,
    true ❸
  )
  tf.browser.toPixels(nnResizeTensor, nnCanvas).then(() => {
    nnResizeTensor.dispose();
  })

  const blResizeTensor = tf.image.resizeBilinear( ❹
    gantTensor,
    newSize,
    true ❺
  )
  const blResizeTensorInt = blResizeTensor.asType('int32') ❻
  tf.browser.toPixels(blResizeTensorInt, blCanvas).then(() => {
    blResizeTensor.dispose();
    blResizeTensorInt.dispose();
  })

  // All done with ya
  gantTensor.dispose();
```

❶ Increase an image size 4x so you can see the difference between these two.

❷ Resize using the nearest neighbor algorithm.

❸ The third parameter is `alignCorners`; just always set this to true.[1]

❹ Resize with the bilinear algorithm.

❺ Always set this to `true` (see 3).

❻ As of this writing, `resizeBilinear` returns a `float32`, which you have to convert.

If you look closely at the result in Figure 4-9, you can see sharp pixelation for the nearest neighbor and a softening blur for bilinear.

---

1 TensorFlow has a mistaken implementation of `alignCorners` that can be problematic (*https://oreil.ly/Ir9Gy*).

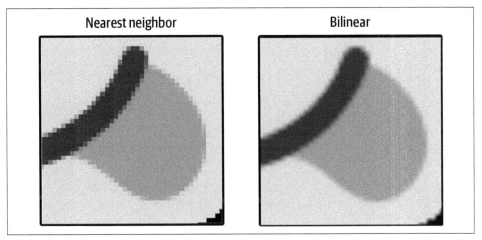

| Nearest neighbor | Bilinear |

Figure 4-9. Emoji with resize methods (for image license see Appendix C)

Resizing with the nearest neighbor algorithm can be maliciously manipulated. If someone knew your final image size, they could construct a wicked image that looks different only at that resize. It's called *adversarial preprocessing*. For more information see *https:// scaling-attacks.net.*

If you want to see a stark contrast, you should try resizing the 4 x 3 image you created at the beginning of this chapter with both methods. Can you guess which method would create a checkerboard at the new size and which would not?

Cropping Image Tensors

For our final round of essential image tensor tasks, we'll crop an image. I'd like to note, just like our mirror exercise earlier, there is a batch-friendly version of cropping large groups of images called `image.cropAndResize`. Know that this method exists and that you can utilize it for gathering and normalizing sections of images for training, e.g., grabbing all the faces detected in a photo and resizing them to the same input size for a model.

For now, you'll just do a simple example of carving out some tensor data from a 3D tensor. If you were to imagine this in space, it would be like carving a small rectangle slice from a larger rectangle cake.

You can carve out whatever portion you want in any axis by giving a starting position and size of our slice. You can access this example at *simple/simple-image-manipulation/crop.html* on GitHub (*https://oreil.ly/QDmBD*). To crop a single image, use the following code:

```
// Simple Tensor Crop
const startingPoint = [0, 40, 0]; ❶
const newSize = [265, 245, 3]; ❷
const lemonadeImage = document.getElementById("lemonade");
const lemonadeCanvas = document.getElementById("lemonadeCanvas");
const lemonadeTensor = tf.browser.fromPixels(lemonadeImage);

const cropped = tf.slice(lemonadeTensor, startingPoint, newSize) ❸
tf.browser.toPixels(cropped, lemonadeCanvas).then(() => {
  cropped.dispose();
})
lemonadeTensor.dispose();
```

❶ Start 0 pixels down, 40 pixels over, and at the red channel.

❷ Grab the next 265 pixels height, 245 pixels width, and all three RGB values.

❸ Pass everything into the tf.slice method.

The result is an exact crop of the original image, as you can see in Figure 4-10.

Figure 4-10. Using tf.slice *to crop a single image tensor*

New Image Tools

You just learned three of the most important image manipulation methods, but this is no limitation to what you can do. New AI models will require new image tensor functionality, and for that reason, TensorFlow.js and assistive libraries are continuously adding methods for handling and processing images. Now you can feel more comfortable utilizing and leaning on these tools in singular and batch forms.

Chapter Review

Encoding and decoding images from an editable tensor gives you the ability to do pixel-by-pixel manipulation on a level few people could ever do. Of course, you've learned visual tensors for our goals in AI/ML, but there's a significant bonus in the fact that if you wanted, you could experiment with wild image manipulation ideas. If you so desired, you could do any of the following:

- Tile a pixel pattern of your making
- Subtract an image from another for an artistic design
- Hide a message inside an image by manipulating pixel values
- Code fractals or other mathematical visualizations
- Remove a background image color like a green screen

In this chapter, you harnessed the ability to create, load, render, modify, and save large tensors of structured data. Dealing with image tensors is not only easy; it's quite rewarding. You're ready for whatever comes your way.

Chapter Challenge: Sorting Chaos

Using the methods you learned in this chapter and previous chapters, you can do some pretty exciting and interesting things with tensors. While this challenge doesn't have any specific utility that I can think of, it's a fun exploration of what you've covered. As an exercise on lessons learned, muse over this problem:

> How can you generate a random 400 x 400 grayscale tensor and then sort the random pixels along an axis?

If you complete this challenge, the resulting tensor image will look like Figure 4-11.

Figure 4-11. 400 x 400 randomness sorted across the width axis

You can solve this problem using methods learned so far in this book. If you get stuck, review the TensorFlow.js online documentation (*https://js.tensorflow.org/api/ latest*). Searching the documentation for key terms will point you in the right direction.

You can find the answer to this challenge in Appendix B.

Review Questions

Let's review the lessons you've learned from the code you've written in this chapter. Take a moment to answer the following questions:

1. If an image tensor contains values 0-255, what kind of data type is needed for it to render correctly?

2. What would a 2 x 2 red Float32 look like in tensor form?

3. What would tf.fill([100, 50, 1], 0.2) create as an image tensor?

4. True or false: to hold an RGBA image, you must use a rank-four image tensor.

5. True or false: randomUniform, if given the same input, will create the same output.

6. What is the method you should use to convert an image to a tensor in the browser?

7. When encoding a PNG in Node.js, what number should you use in the second parameter to get max compression?

8. If you want to flip an image tensor upside down, how could you do that?

9. Which is faster?

    a. Looping over a collection of images and resizing them

    b. Batching a group of images as a rank-four tensor and resizing the entire tensor

10. What is the rank and size of the result for:

    ```
    [.keep-together]#`tf.slice(myTensor, [0,0,0], [20, 20, 3])`?#
    ```

Solutions to these exercises are available in Appendix A.

Up Next...

In Chapter 5 you will finally get access to a model without the training wheels. Your tensor skills will guide your data through conversion, a model, and back to JavaScript.

## CHAPTER 5

Introducing Models

"Where does he get those wonderful toys?"

—Jack Nicholson (*Batman*)

Now you're in the big leagues. Way back in Chapter 2 you accessed a fully trained model, but you didn't need to understand tensors at all. Here in Chapter 5, you will get to utilize your tensor skills to work directly with your models, with no training wheels.

Finally, you're going to dive into utilizing the brain of most machine learning. Models can seem like a black box. Generally, they expect a specific tensor shape in, and a specific tensor shape comes out. For instance, let's say you've trained a dog or cat classifier. The input might be a 32 x 32 3D RGB tensor, and the output might be a single tensor value of zero to one to indicate the prediction. Even if you don't know the inner workings of such a device, at the least, consuming and utilizing models with a defined structure should be simple.

We will:

- Utilize trained models to predict a variety of answers
- Identify the benefits of our existing tensor manipulation skills
- Learn about Google's TFHub.dev hosting
- Learn about object localization
- Learn how to overlay a bounding box to identify some aspect of an image

This chapter will teach you direct access to models. You won't be dependent on cute wrapper libraries for coddling. If you want, you'll even be able to write your own wrapper library around existing TensorFlow.js models. Armed with the skills in this chapter, you can start applying breakthrough machine learning models to any website.

Loading Models

We know we need to get our models into memory and preferably into GPU-accelerated memory like tensors, but from where? As a blessing and a curse, the answer is "anywhere!" Loading files is common in software, so it corresponds to a variety of answers in TensorFlow.js.

To compound this problem, TensorFlow.js supports two different model formats. Fortunately, this assortment of options isn't complicated. You just need to know what kind of model you need and from where you'll be accessing it.

Currently, there are two model types in TensorFlow.js, each with their own benefits and costs. The simplest and most extensible model is called a *Layers model*. This model format lets you inspect, modify, and even take a model apart for adjustment. The format is perfect for retuning and adjusting later. The other model format is a *Graph model*. Graph models are generally more optimized as well as computationally efficient. The cost of using a Graph model is that the model is even more "black box," and due to its optimizations, it's more difficult to inspect or modify.

Model types are simple. If you're loading a Layers model, you'll need to use the method loadLayersModel, and if you're loading a GraphDef model, you'll need to use the method loadGraphModel. There are benefits and drawbacks to these two model types, but that's beyond the scope of this chapter. The key takeaway is that there's little complexity in loading the desired model type; it's just a question of which type and then using the corresponding method. The most important facet is the first parameter, which is the location of the model data.

 By the end of this book, you'll have a pretty solid understanding of the critical differences between a Layers and a Graph model type. Each time a model is introduced, take note of which one was used.

This section explains the diversity of options for model locations and the simple unifying URI syntax that binds them.

Loading Models Via Public URL

Loading models with a public URL is the most common method of accessing a model in TensorFlow.js. As you remember in Chapter 2, when you loaded the Toxicity detection model, you downloaded several shards of the file in small 4 MB cacheable chunks from a public network. The model knew the location of the file to download.

This is done with a single URL to a single file. The model file that was originally requested was a simple JavaScript Object Notation (JSON) file, and the subsequent files were weights for the neural network that were identified from that JSON file.

Loading TensorFlow.js models from a URL requires actively hosted adjacent model files (the same relative folder). This means that once you give a path for a model's JSON file, it usually references the weights in successive files at the same directory level. The desired structure looks like this:

```
Site
├── Example Folder
├── index.html
├── Model Folder
|   ├── model.json
|   └── group1-shard1of3
|   └── group1-shard2of3
|   └── group1-shard3of3
...
```

Moving or denying access to these extra files will cause your model to be unusable and error. Depending on the security and configuration of your server environment, this can be a bit of a sticking point. Therefore, you should always verify that each file has proper URL access.

 We've covered three major ways to run TensorFlow.js so far. They are simple hosted with 200 OK!, NPM packed with Parcel, and server hosted with Node.js. Before we tell you how to properly load models for these situations, can you identify which of these will have complications?

200 OK! Web Server for Chrome examples will have no issues because everything in the folder is hosted with no optimization or security. Parcel gives us some bells and whistles with transforms, error logging, HMR, and bundling. With those features, our JSON and weight files are not passed into the distribution, aka dist folder, without some coaching.

In Parcel.js 2.0 (which is not officially out at the time of this writing), you'll have more options for static files, but for now, there is a simple solution that works for Parcel 1.x that we'll be using. You can install a plug-in called parcel-plugin-static-files-copy to green-light model files for local static hosting. The code used in the associated repo for this book utilizes this plug-in.

The plug-in works by effectively making any files placed in the static directory publicly accessible from the root URL. For example, a *model.json* file placed in *static/model* would be accessible as *localhost:1234/model/model.json*.

Whatever web solution you use, you'll need to verify that the security and bundling of the model files work for you. For unprotected public folders, this is as simple as uploading all the files to services like Amazon Web Services (AWS) and Simple Storage Service (S3). You'll need to make the entire bucket public, or each adjacent file will have to explicitly be made public. It's important to verify you can access the JSON *and* the BIN files. The error messages for missing or restricted shards of a model are perplexing. You'll see a `404`, but errors continue on to a secondary and more cryptic error like that shown in Figure 5-1.

```
● Failed to load resource: the server responded with a status of 404 (Not Found)
● Uncaught (in promise) Error: Based on the provided shape, [144,64], the tensor should have 9216 values but has 10
    at lv (util_base.js:154)
    at cy (tensor_ops_util.js:48)
    at py (tensor.js:56)
    at my (io_utils.js:225)
    at mF (models.js:334)
    at models.js:316
    at u (runtime.js:45)
    at Generator._invoke (runtime.js:274)
    at Generator.forEach.e.<computed> [as next] (runtime.js:97)
    at Um (runtime.js:728)
```

Figure 5-1. Error: JSON available but no bin files

Create React App is a popular tool for simple React websites. If you use Create React App, files in the `public` folder will be accessible from the root URL out of the box. Think of `public` like our Parcel solution's `static` folder. Both work great and have been tested for model hosting.

Loading Models from Other Locations

Models don't have to be in public URLs. TensorFlow has methods to allow you to load from local browser storage (*https://oreil.ly/BHYc1*), IndexedDB storage (*https://oreil.ly/MHYA4*), and, in the case of Node.js, local filesystem access to model files.

One significant benefit of this is that you can locally cache a model you loaded from a public URL so your app can be offline-ready. Other reasons include speed, security, or simply because you can.

Browser files

Local browser storage and IndexedDB storage are two web APIs for saving files specified to a particular page. Unlike cookies, which store a small piece of data like a single variable, `Window.localStorage` and the IndexedDB API are client-side storage capable of handling files among other significant structured data across browser sessions.

Public URLs have the `http` and `https` schemes; however, these methods utilize different schemes in the URI. To load a model from local storage, you would use a `local storage://model-name` URI, and to load a model from IndexedDB, you would use a `indexeddb://model-name` URI.

Besides the supplied methods, there's no limit to the various locations you can store and retrieve a TensorFlow.js model. At the end of the day, it's just data that you need, so you can load a model with any custom `IOHandler`. For instance, there has even been proof-of-concept work on converting models completely to JSON files (*https://github.com/infinitered/tfjs-runway*) with the weights encoded so you can call `require` as needed from any location, even via a bundler.

Filesystem files

To access files on a filesystem, you'll need to use a Node.js server that has permission to get at the desired files. Browsers are sandboxed and cannot currently use this feature.

Fortunately, it's similar to the previous API. Use the *file:* scheme to identify a path to a given file like so: *file://path/to/model.json*. Just like in the browser examples, the ancillary files must be in the same folder and accessible.

Our First Consumed Model

Now that you're familiar with the mechanics of loading a model into memory, you can utilize models in your projects. This was automated for you when you used the Toxicity model in Chapter 2, but now, with your familiarity with tensors and model access, you can handle a model without all the protective package code.

You need a simple model to use for the first example. As you recall, you encoded a board of tic-tac-toe as an exercise in Chapter 3. Let's build from the foundation of your existing knowledge and not only encode a tic-tac-toe match but also pass that information into a trained model for analysis. The trained model will then predict and return an answer for the best next move.

Your goal for this section will be to ask the AI model what moves it recommends for the three board states illustrated in Figure 5-2.

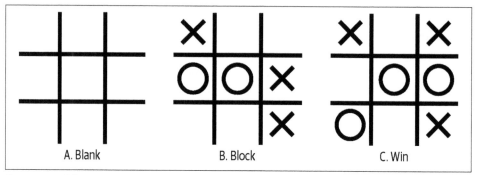

Figure 5-2. Three game states

Each of these games is in a different situation:

Scenario A
   This is blank and allows the AI to make the first move.

Scenario B
   This is O's turn, and we expect the AI to block the potential loss by playing in the top-right square.

Scenario C
   This is X's move, and we expect the AI to move in the top-middle and claim victory!

Let's see what the AI recommends, by encoding these three states and printing the output of the model.

Loading, Encoding, and Asking a Model

You'll be using the simple URL for loading the model. This model will be a Layers model. That means you will use `tf.loadLayersModel` and the path to the locally hosted model files to load. For this example, the model file will be hosted at *model/ttt_model.json*.

The trained tic-tac-toe model for this example can be accessed in the associated GitHub (*https://github.com/GantMan/learn-tfjs*) for this book. The JSON file is 2 KB, and the weights file (*ttt_model.weights.bin*) is 22 KB in size. This 24 KB load for a tic-tac-toe solver isn't bad at all!

To transcribe the game board state, there will be a slight difference in encoding. You'll need to tell the AI which team it's playing for. You'll also need an AI that can be X and O agnostic. Because scenario B is asking the AI for advice on O and not X, we need a flexible system for encoding. Instead of X always meaning 1, assign the AI to 1 and the adversary to -1. This way we can put the AI in a situation where it's playing X or O. Table 5-1 shows each possible value for the lookup.

Table 5-1. Grid-to-number conversion

Board value	Tensor value
AI	1
Opponent	-1
Empty	0

All three games need to be encoded and then stacked into a single tensor to pass to the AI model. The model then supplies three answers, one for each situation.

This is the full process:

1. Load the model.
2. Encode the three separate game states.
3. Stack the states into a single tensor.
4. Ask the model to print the results.

Stacking input to a model is a common practice and allows your model to handle any number of predictions in accelerated memory.

Stacking increases the dimensionality of the result. Performing this action on 1D tensors creates a 2D tensor, and so on. In this instance, you have three board states represented in 1D tensors, so stacking them will create a [3, 9] rank-two tensor. Most models support stacking or batching for their input, and the output will be similarly stacked with matching answers to the input indices.

The code, which can be found at *chapter5/simple/simple-ttt-model* in the GitHub repo (*https://oreil.ly/38zZx*), looks like this:

```
tf.ready().then(() => {  ❶
  const modelPath = "model/ttt_model.json"  ❷
  tf.tidy(() => {
    tf.loadLayersModel(modelPath).then(model => {  ❸
      // Three board states
      const emptyBoard = tf.zeros([9])  ❹
      const betterBlockMe = tf.tensor([-1, 0, 0, 1, 1, -1, 0, 0, -1])  ❺
      const goForTheKill = tf.tensor([1, 0, 1, 0, -1, -1, -1, 0, 1])  ❻

      // Stack states into a shape [3, 9]
      const matches = tf.stack([emptyBoard, betterBlockMe, goForTheKill])  ❼
      const result = model.predict(matches)  ❽
      // Log the results
      result.reshape([3, 3, 3]).print()  ❾
    })
  })
})
```

❶ Use `tf.ready`, which resolves when TensorFlow.js is ready. No DOM access is needed.

❷ Though the model is two files, only the JSON file needs to be identified. It knows about and loads any additional model files.

❸ The `loadLayersModel` model resolves with the fully loaded model.

❹ An empty board is nine zeros, which represents scenario A.

❺ Encoded as X equal to `-1` for scenario B.

❻ Encoded as X equal to `1` for scenario C.

❼ Use `tf.stack` to combine three 1D tensors into a single 2D tensor.

❽ Use `.predict` to ask the model to identify the best next moves.

❾ The original output was going to be shaped as [3, 9], but it's a good situation where reshaping the output makes it more readable. Print the result in three 3 x 3 grids so we can read them like game boards.

When using `loadLayersModel` and even `loadGraphModel`, the TensorFlow.js library is depending on the presence of the `fetch` web API. If you're using this method in Node.js, you'll need to polyfill `fetch` with a package like node-fetch (*https://oreil.ly/rwPMW*).

The aforementioned code successfully converts the three matches to tensors in a format that the AI model expects, and then runs these values through the model's `predict()` method for analysis. The results are printed to the console and look like what we see in Figure 5-3.

```
         Elements   Console   Sources   Network

      top                    ▼    ◉    Tensor

  Tensor
     [[[0.2287459, 0.0000143, 0.2659601],
       [0.0000982, 0.0041204, 0.0001773],
       [0.2301052, 0.0000206, 0.270758 ]],

      [[0.0011957, 0.0032045, 0.9908957],
       [0.000263 , 0.0006491, 0.0000799],
       [0.0010194, 0.0002893, 0.0024035]],

      [[0.0000056, 0.9867876, 0.0000028],
       [0.0003809, 0.0001524, 0.0011258],
       [0.0000328, 0.0114983, 0.0000139]]]
  >|
```

Figure 5-3. The resulting [3, 3, 3] shaped tensor from our code

The method that does all the magic is the model's `predict()` function. The function lets the model know to generate output predictions for the given input.

Interpreting the Results

For some people this resulting tensor makes complete sense, and for others, you might need a moment of context. The resulting answers are again in probabilities of the next best moves. The highest number wins.

For this to be a proper probability, the answers need to sum up to 100%, and they do. Let's take a look at the empty tic-tac-toe board result shown here in scenario 1:

```
[
  [0.2287459, 0.0000143, 0.2659601],
  [0.0000982, 0.0041204, 0.0001773],
  [0.2301052, 0.0000206, 0.270758 ]
],
```

If you were to be silly like me and enter these nine values into your calculator (TI-84 Plus CE for life!), they would sum up to the number 1. That means each corresponding value is a percentage vote for that spot. We can see the four corners all have a significant (nearly 25%) portion of the result. This makes sense, because strategically starting in a corner is the best move possible in tic-tac-toe, followed by the middle, which has the next highest value.

Because the bottom right has 27% of the vote, this would be the AI's most likely move. Let's see how the AI performs in another scenario. If you recall, in scenario B from Figure 5-2, the AI would need to move in the top right to block. The resulting tensor from the AI is shown here in scenario 2:

```
[
  [0.0011957, 0.0032045, 0.9908957],
  [0.000263 , 0.0006491, 0.0000799],
  [0.0010194, 0.0002893, 0.0024035],
],
```

The top-right value is 99%, so the model has correctly blocked the given threat. One funny aspect of a machine learning model is that the other moves still have values, including spaces that are already taken.

The last scenario was an encoded tensor to see if the model would strike and win tic-tac-toe. The results are shown here in scenario 3 of the predicted batch:

```
[
  [0.0000056, 0.9867876, 0.0000028],
  [0.0003809, 0.0001524, 0.0011258],
  [0.0000328, 0.0114983, 0.0000139]
],
```

The result is 99% (rounded) certain that top middle is the best move, which is correct. No other move even comes close. All three predicted results seem to be not only functioning moves, but also the correct move for a given state.

You have successfully loaded and interacted with a model to have it provide results. With the skills you just attained, you could write your own tic-tac-toe game app. I imagine there's not much demand for tic-tac-toe games on the internet, but if provided a trained model of the same structure, you could use the AI to make all kinds of games!

 Most models will have some associated documentation to help you identify the proper inputs and outputs, but Layers models have properties that you can access if you need help. The expected input shape can be seen at `model.input.shape`, and the output can be seen at `model.outputShape`. These properties do not exist on Graph models.

Cleaning the Board After

The TensorFlow.js model in this example is wrapped in a `tidy` and will automatically free memory after the code has completed. In most situations, you will not be done with your model so quickly. It's important to note that you must call `.dispose()` on models, just like you do tensors. Models are accelerated the same way, and therefore they have the same cleanup cost.

Reloading web pages tends to clear tensors, but long-running Node.js servers will have to monitor and verify that tensors and models are disposed of.

Our First TensorFlow Hub Model

Now that you've properly encoded, loaded, and processed a small amount of data through a custom model, you should take a moment to push the envelope. In this section, you'll load a significantly larger model from TensorFlow Hub, and you'll process an image. Tic-tac-toe was an input of nine values, whereas most images are tensors with thousands of values.

The model you'll be loading will be one of the biggest and most impressive models out there, Inception v3. The Inception model is an impressive network first created in 2015. This third version has been, impressively, trained on hundreds of thousands of images. Weighing in at a whopping 91.02 MB, this model can classify 1,001 different objects. The MobileNet-wrapped NPM package from the Chapter Challenge in Chapter 2 is awesome, but not nearly as powerful as what you're about to use.

Exploring TFHub

Google has begun hosting models like Inception v3 for free on its own CDN. In situations for this large model size, it's quite useful to have a reliable and impressive versioned CDN for models like we often do for JavaScript. You can access hundreds of trained and ready-to-go models for TensorFlow and TensorFlow.js in one location at *https://tfhub.dev*. TensorFlow.js has a special way to identify when your model is hosted on TFHub; we just add `{ fromTFHub: true }` to our configuration after we've identified our model URL.

As you peruse TFHub, you can see a variety of publishers and explanations for each model. These explanations are critical, because as we've already identified, models are quite specific on what they expect for input and what they will supply for output. We can learn more about Inception v3 on its associated TFHub page (*https://oreil.ly/Utstp*). This model was built by Google, and the version it provides has been extensively trained. If you're hungry for more information, it's not a bad idea to scan through the published paper on the model (*https://arxiv.org/abs/1512.00567*).

On the TFHub page, you get both of those critical insights for using a model. First, the expected input image sizes should be 299 x 299, have values 0-1, and be batched just like we did in the previous tic-tac-toe example. Second, the result that the model returns is a single-dimensional tensor with 1,001 values, with the largest being the most likely (similar to the nine values returned by tic-tac-toe). It might sound confusing, but the page uses some statistics-based terminology to express this:

> The output is a batch of logits vectors. The indices into the logits are the num_classes = 1001 classes of the classification from the original training.

Returning a numeric result is useful, but as always, we have to map this back to a useful label. In tic-tac-toe we mapped the index to a location on the board, and in this case, we map the index of a value to the corresponding label that follows the same index. The TFHub page shares a TXT file (*https://oreil.ly/bzUeD*) of all the necessary labels in their correct order, which you will use to create an array to interpret the predicted results.

Wiring Up Inception v3

Now you know the Inception v3 model classifies photos, and you have the input and output specification. It's like a larger version of the tic-tac-toe problem. However, there will be new hurdles. For instance, printing 1,001 numbers won't be helpful information. You'll need to use `topk` to parse the giant tensor back into a useful context.

The following code is available in the *chapter5/simple/simple-tfhub* in the GitHub repo (*https://oreil.ly/X7TpN*) folder. The code depends on a mysterious image that has the id `mystery`. Ideally, the AI can solve the mystery for us:

```
tf.ready().then(() => {
  const modelPath =
    "https://tfhub.dev/google/tfjs-model/imagenet/inception_v3/classification/3
    /default/1"; ❶
  tf.tidy(() => {
    tf.loadGraphModel(modelPath, { fromTFHub: true }).then((model) => { ❷
      const mysteryImage = document.getElementById("mystery");
      const myTensor = tf.browser.fromPixels(mysteryImage);
      // Inception v3 expects an image resized to 299x299
      const readyfied = tf.image
        .resizeBilinear(myTensor, [299, 299], true) ❸
        .div(255) ❹
        .reshape([1, 299, 299, 3]); ❺

      const result = model.predict(readyfied); ❻
      result.print(); ❼

      const { values, indices } = tf.topk(result, 3); ❽
      indices.print(); ❾
```

```
        // Let's hear those winners
        const winners = indices.dataSync();
        console.log(` ❿
          ↑ First place ${INCEPTION_CLASSES[winners[0]]},
          ↑ Second place ${INCEPTION_CLASSES[winners[1]]},
          ↑ Third place ${INCEPTION_CLASSES[winners[2]]}
        `);
      });
    });
  });
```

❶ This is the URL to the TFHub for the Inception model.

❷ Load the graph model and set fromTFHub to true.

❸ The image is resized to 299 x 299.

❹ Convert the fromPixels results to values between 0 and 1 (normalizing the data).

❺ Convert the 3D tensor to a single batch 4D tensor like the model expects.

❻ Predict on the image.

❼ The print is so big it gets trimmed.

❽ Recover the top three values as our guesses.

❾ Print the top three prediction indices.

❿ Map the indices to their labels and print them. INCEPTION_CLASSES is an array of labels that maps to the model output.

In the associated code for this chapter, you'll find three images that you can set as the mystery image in this section. Inception v3 impressively identifies all three correctly. Take a look at the captured results in Figure 5-4.

Console Log for Result

Figure 5-4. Resulting classification of an image from Inception v3

As you can see from the photo, Inception's first choice was a "tape player," which I would say is very accurate. Second, it saw a "cassette player," and to be honest I don't know how that's different from a "tape player," but I'm no mega-model. Lastly, the third highest value was a "radio," which is what I would have said.

It's not often you need a large model like this, but as new models get added to TFHub, you know you have options. Peruse the existing models every so often. You'll see quite a few on image classification. Classifying images is one of the more impressive tasks of beginning AI, but why stop there?

Our First Overlayed Model

So far, the models you've been working with have simple output. Tic-tac-toe identified your next move, Inception classified a photo, and just to round things out, you'll implement a classic visual effect in movies that feature AI, the bounding box that identifies an object in a photo. Rather than classifying an entire photo, the AI highlights a specific bounding box within a photo, like in Figure 5-5.

Figure 5-5. Bounding box overlay

Normally, the bounding box output of a model is fairly complex because it handles a variety of classes and overlapping boxes. Usually, the model leaves you to use some math to properly clean up the results. Rather than dealing with that, let's just focus on drawing a single rectangle on predicted output in TensorFlow.js. This is sometimes called *object localization*.

The model for this final exercise will be a pet face detector. The model will do its best to give us a bounding set of coordinates for where it thinks the pet's face is located. It's not generally hard to talk people into looking at cute dogs and cats, but this model could have all kinds of applications. Once you have the location of a pet's face, you could use that data to train additional models, like recognizing pets or checking if their cute noses need a boop. You know...science!

The Localization Model

This model was trained on a public dataset called the Oxford-IIIT Pet Dataset (*https://oreil.ly/Pz0D9*). The small, 2-ish MB model expects a 256 x 256 Float32 input RGB image of a pet and outputs four numbers to identify a bounding box around the pet's face. The four numbers in the 1D tensor are the top-left point and the bottom-right point.

Screen Coordinates

Just like in a normal Cartesian coordinate system, points are identified as X and Y. X is the horizontal indicator, and Y is the vertical indicator. So, the given four values from the model will identify two points.

Unlike a normal Cartesian coordinate system, the origin is the top left, and points only exist in the positive domain. Positive Y values move right along the image, and positive X values move down along the image, from the origin. Make sure you're familiar with the Screen coordinate system before continuing.

The points are represented as values between 0 and 1, as a percentage of the image. You can define a rectangle with the model result information, as shown in Figure 5-6.

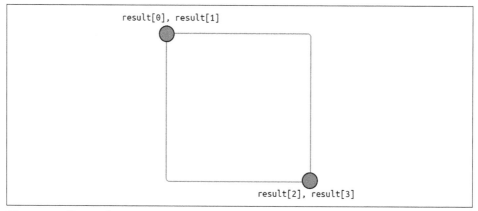

Figure 5-6. Four values into two points

The beginning of the code will be similar to the previous code. You'll start off by converting the image to a tensor and running it through the model. The following code can be found in *chapter5/simple/simple-object-localization* in the GitHub repo (*https://oreil.ly/zkSfM*).

```
const petImage = document.getElementById("pet");
const myTensor = tf.browser.fromPixels(petImage);
// Model expects 256x256 0-1 value 3D tensor
const readyfied = tf.image
  .resizeNearestNeighbor(myTensor, [256, 256], true)
  .div(255)
  .reshape([1, 256, 256, 3]);

const result = model.predict(readyfied);
// Model returns top left and bottom right
result.print();
```

Labeling the Detection

Now you can draw the result coordinates as a rectangle over the image. Drawing detections is a common task in TensorFlow.js. The basics of drawing a tensor result over an image require you to place the image in a container and then position an absolute canvas over that image. Now when you draw to the canvas, you'll be drawing over the image.[1] From a side view, the layout will resemble Figure 5-7.

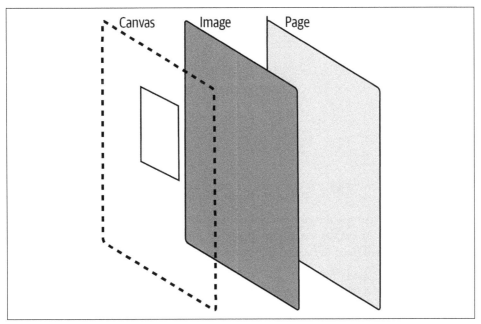

Canvas   Image   Page

Figure 5-7. Stacking view of the canvas

For this lesson, the CSS has been embedded directly in the HTML for ease. The image and canvas layout looks like this:

```
<div style="position: relative; height: 80vh"> ❶
  <img id="pet" src="/dog1.jpg" height="100%" />
  <canvas
    id="detection"
    style="position: absolute; left: 0;"
  ><canvas/> ❷
</div>
```

❶ The containing div is relative positioned and locked at 80% the page height.

---

1 You don't have to use the canvas; you can move a DOM object if you'd like, but the canvas provides simple and complex animations with significant speed.

❷ The canvas is placed over the image with an absolute position.

For a simple rectangle, you can use the canvas context's strokeRect method. The strokeRect method doesn't take two points like the model returns. It takes a starting point and then a width and height. To convert the model points to width and height, you can just subtract each vertex to get a distance. Figure 5-8 shows a visual representation of this calculation.

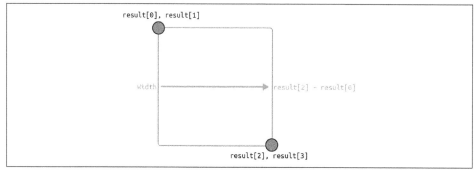

Figure 5-8. Width and height are calculated as the difference between Xs and Ys

Armed with the starting point, the width and height of the overlaid rectangle, you can draw it to scale on the canvas with a few lines of code. Remember, the tensor output is a percentage and will need to be scaled in each dimension.

```
// Draw box on canvas
const detection = document.getElementById("detection");
const imgWidth = petImage.width;
const imgHeight = petImage.height;
detection.width = imgWidth; ❶
detection.height = imgHeight;
const box = result.dataSync(); ❷
const startX = box[0] * imgWidth; ❸
const startY = box[1] * imgHeight;
const width = (box[2] - box[0]) * imgWidth; ❹
const height = (box[3] - box[1]) * imgHeight;
const ctx = detection.getContext("2d");
ctx.strokeStyle = "#0F0";
ctx.lineWidth = 4;
ctx.strokeRect(startX, startY, width, height); ❺
```

❶ Make the detection canvas the same size as the image it's over.

❷ Grab the bounding box result.

❸ Scale the starting point X and Y back to the image.

❹ Find the width of the box by subtracting X_1 from X_2 and then scaling it by the image width. The same goes for Y_1 and Y_2.

❺ Now use the canvas 2D context to draw the desired rectangle.

The result is a perfectly placed bounding box at the given points. See for yourself in Figure 5-9.

Figure 5-9. Pet face localization

A misconception when running this project might be that the detection and drawing you've experienced are slow. This is false. It's noticeable that when the page loads, there's a delay before the bounding box appears; however, the delay you're experiencing includes loading a model and loading it into accelerated memory of some type (sometimes called *model warmup*). Though doing so is a bit outside the goals of this chapter, if you were to call `model.predict` and draw again, you would see results in microseconds. The canvas + TensorFlow.js structure you created in this final section can easily support 60+ frames per second on a desktop computer.

Models that have plenty of bounding boxes and labels use similar `strokeRect` calls to outline the location of identified objects. There's a wide variety of models, and each of them identify various aspects of images. The practice of modifying the canvas to draw information over an image comes in handy in the TensorFlow.js world.

Chapter Review

Knowing the input and output of models is key. In this chapter, you finally saw data all the way through. You converted input, passed it into a trained model, and interpreted the results. Models can take a wide array of inputs and provide equally wide outputs. Now, regardless of what a model requires, you have some impressive experience to draw from.

Chapter Challenge: Cute Faces

Imagine our pet face localization was the first step in a larger process. Let's pretend you were identifying pet faces to then pass the pet's face to another model that would look for a tongue to see if the pet was hot and panting. It's common to organize multiple models in a pipeline like this, with each tuned to their own specific purpose.

Given a pet's face location from the previous code, write the additional code to extract the pet's face and prep it for a model that requires a 96 x 96 image input. Your answer will be a single batched crop like Figure 5-10.

Figure 5-10. The goal [1, 96, 96, 3] tensor of just the face

Though this exercise is to crop the pet's face for a secondary model, it could just as easily have been a "pet anonymizer" that required you to blur the pet's face. The applications of AI in the browser are limitless.

You can find the answer to this challenge in Appendix B.

Review Questions

Let's review the lessons you've learned from the code you've written in this chapter. Take a moment to answer the following questions:

1. What are the types of models you can load in TensorFlow.js?
2. Do you need to know the number of shards a model is broken into?
3. Other than public URLs, name another place you can load models from.
4. What does `loadLayersModel` return?
5. How do you clean the memory of a loaded model?
6. What is the expected input shape of the Inception v3 model?
7. What canvas context method should you use to draw an empty rectangle?
8. When loading a model from TFHub, what parameter must you pass to your load method?

Solutions to these questions are available in Appendix A.

Up Next...

In Chapter 6 you'll continue advancing your knowledge of consuming and utilizing TensorFlow.js models. Combining AI with the web is where TensorFlow.js shines, and this next chapter is constructed to give you a tour of some of the most important tools you'll need.

## CHAPTER 6

Advanced Models and UI

"It always seems impossible until it's done."

—Nelson Mandela

You have a baseline for understanding models. You've consumed and utilized models and even displayed the results in overlays. It might seem like the sky is the limit. However, you've already seen that models tend to return information in various and complex ways. For the Tic-Tac-Toe model, you wanted only one move, but it still returns all nine possible boxes, leaving some cleanup work for you before you could utilize the model's output. As models get more complicated, this problem can compound. In this chapter, we will select a widespread and complex model type for object detection and work through the UI and concepts to give you a full sense of what kind of tasks might befall you.

Let's review what your current workflow looks like. First, you select a model. Identify if it is a Layers or Graph model. Even if you didn't have this information, you'd be able to figure it out by trying to load it one way or another.

Next, you'll need to identify the inputs and outputs for the model—not just the shape, but what the data actually represents. You batch your data, call `predict` on the model, and the output is good to go, right?

Unfortunately, there's just a little more you should know. Some of the latest and greatest models have significant differences from what you've come to expect. In many ways, they are far superior, and in other ways, they are more cumbersome. Don't fret, because you've built a strong foundation in tensors and canvas overlays from the previous chapter. With a little coaching, you can handle this new world of advanced models.

We will:

- Dive into how theory can challenge your tensor skills
- Learn about advanced model characteristics
- Learn lots of new image and machine learning terminology
- Identify the best way to draw multiple boxes for object detection
- Learn how to draw labels for detections on a canvas

When you finish this chapter, you'll have a strong understanding of the theoretical demands of implementing advanced TensorFlow.js models. This chapter serves as a cognitive walk-through of one of the most powerful models you can use today, and with that comes a lot of learning. It won't be hard, but get your learning cap on, and don't shy away from the complexities. If you follow the logic explained in this chapter, you'll have a deep understanding and command of theories and practices core to machine learning.

MobileNet Again

As you cruise around TFHub.dev (*https://tfhub.dev*), you might have seen our old friend MobileNet mentioned in quite a few flavors and versions. One version has a simple name, `ssd_mobilenet_v2`, for image object detection (see the highlighted selection in Figure 6-1).

How exciting! It seems you can take your code from your previous TensorFlow Hub example and change the model to view a collection of bounding boxes and their associated classes, correct?

Figure 6-1. MobileNet for object detection

Upon doing so, you immediately get a failure that asks for you to use `model.executeA sync` instead of `model.predict` (see Figure 6-2).

```
⊗  ▶Uncaught (in promise) Error: This execution    graph_executor.js:162
   contains the node 'Preprocessor/map/while/Exit_1', which has the
   dynamic op 'Exit'. Please use model.executeAsync() instead.
   Alternatively, to avoid the dynamic ops, specify the inputs
   [Preprocessor/map/TensorArrayStack/TensorArrayGatherV3]
       at e.t.compile (graph_executor.js:162)
       at e.t.execute (graph_executor.js:212)
       at e.t.execute (graph_model.js:323)
       at e.t.predict (graph_model.js:276)
       at (index):25
```

Figure 6-2. Predict won't work

So what went wrong? By now, you might have a flurry of questions.

- What is this `executeAsync` that the model wants?
- Why is this MobileNet model for object detection?
- Why does this model spec not care about input size?

- What is the "SSD" part of the name in regard to machine learning?

 In Parcel, you might have gotten errors about a `regeneratorRuntime` not being defined. This is due to deprecation in a Babel polyfill. If you get this error, you can add the packages `core-js` and `regenerator-runtime` and import them in your main file. See the associated GitHub code for this chapter (*https://oreil.ly/LKc8v*) if you have this issue.

This is a perfect example of an advanced model that needs a little more information, theory, and history to comprehend. It's also a great time to learn some concepts we've kept buried for convenience. By the end of this chapter, you'll be ready to handle some new terminology, best practices, and features of complex models.

SSD MobileNet

The book has mentioned two models by name up to this point, but there's been no elaboration. MobileNet and Inception are published model architectures created by the Google AI team. You'll be architecting your own models in the next chapter, but it's fair to say they won't be as advanced as these two well-known models. Each model has a specific set of benefits and pitfalls. Accuracy isn't always the only metric for a model.

MobileNet is a specific architecture for low-latency, low-power models. That makes it excellent for devices and the web. While an Inception-based model will be more accurate, MobileNet's speed and size make it a standard tool for classification and object detection on edge devices.

Check out the performance and latency charts published by Google that compare model versions on devices (*https://oreil.ly/dHEKZ*). You can see that while Inception v2 is several times larger and requires significantly more calculations to make a single prediction, MobileNetV2 is much faster, and while it's not as accurate, it's still close. MobileNetV3 is even promising to be more accurate with only a small bump in size. The core research and advancements of these models make them excellent battle-tested resources with known trade-offs. It's for these reasons you'll see the same model architectures used over and over for novel problems.

Both of the aforementioned architectures have been trained by Google with millions of images. The classic 1,001 classes MobileNet and Inception can identify come from a well-known dataset called ImageNet (*https://image-net.org/about.php*). So after being trained for a long time on many computers in the cloud, the models are tuned for immediate use. While these models are classification models, they can be repurposed to detect objects as well.

Just like a building, models can be modified slightly to handle different objectives. For example, a theater can be modified from its original purpose of hosting live performances to facilitate 3D feature films. Yes, some small changes will need to be made, but the overall architecture is significantly reusable. The same goes for models that are repurposed from classification to object detection.

There are several different ways to perform object detection. One way is called a *region-based convolutional neural network* (R-CNN). Don't confuse R-CNNs with RNNs, which are wholly different and a real thing in machine learning. Region-based convolutional neural networks might sound like a spell from *Harry Potter*, but they're just a popular way of detecting objects by looking at patches of an image with a sliding window (i.e., sampling a smaller part of the image repeatedly until you have covered the whole image). R-CNNs are often slow but extremely accurate. The slow aspect doesn't work well with websites and mobile devices.

The second popular way of detecting objects is to use another buzzword, a "fully convolutional" approach (more about convolutions in Chapter 10). These approaches do not have a deep neural network, and that's why they avoid requiring a specific input size. That's right, you don't need to resize images for a fully convolutional approach, and they're fast, too.

This is where the "SSD" in SSD MobileNet matters. It stands for *single-shot detector*. Yes, you and I were probably thinking of solid-state drives, but naming things can be hard, so we'll give data science a pass. SSD model types are architected as fully convolutional models that get one shot to identify features of an image as a whole. This "single-shot" makes SSDs significantly faster than R-CNNs. Without getting too far into details, an SSD model has two major components, a *backbone model* that understands how to recognize objects, and an *SSD head* to localize the objects. The backbone, in this case, is the fast and friendly MobileNet.

Combining MobileNet and SSD requires a little magic called *control flow* that allows you to conditionally run operations in your model. That is what makes the `predict` method move from being straightforward to requiring the async call `executeAsync`. When a model implements control flow, the synchronous `predict` method will not work.

Conditional logic is normally handled in the native language, but that slows things down significantly. While most of TensorFlow.js can be optimized by utilizing GPU or web assembly (WASM) backends, a conditional statement in JavaScript would require unloading optimized tensors and reloading them. The SSD MobileNet model hides that headache for you at the low, low cost of utilizing control flow operations. While implementing control flow is outside the scope of this book, consuming models that utilize these advanced features is not.

Because of the modern nature of this model, it's not set up to handle batches of images. That means the only limitation of the input is not the image size but the batch size. It does, however, expect a batch of one, so a 1,024 × 768 RGB image would go into this model in the shape [1, 768, 1024, 3], with 1 being the stack size for the batch, 768 being the image height, 1024 being the image width, and 3 being the RGB values for each pixel.

It's always important to dig into what kind of input and output you'll be dealing with. It's worth noting that the model's output bounding boxes follow the classic height and then width architecture of the input, unlike the pet faces detector. That means the bounding boxes will be [y1, x1, y2, x2] instead of [x1, y1, x2, y2]. Small hiccups like these can be quite frustrating if they aren't caught. Your bounding boxes would look completely broken. Whenever you implement a new model, it's important that you verify the specification from all available documentation.

There's one last caveat before digging into code. In my experience, object detection in production is rarely used to identify thousands of different classes, as you've seen in MobileNet and Inception. There are many good reasons for this, so object detection is usually tested and trained on a few classes. One common group of labeled data that people use for object detection training is the Microsoft Common Objects in Context (COCO) (*https://cocodataset.org/#home*) dataset. This SSD MobileNet used that dataset to teach the model to see 80 different classes. While 80 is a significant drop from 1,001 possible classes, it's still an impressive set.

Now you understand more about SSD MobileNet than most people who use it. You know it's an object detection model that uses control flow to link the MobileNet speed to SSD results for 80 classes. This knowledge will help you later in interpreting the model's results.

Bounding Outputs

Now that you understand the model, you can get the results. The value returned by executeAsync in this model is a normal JavaScript array of two tensor stacks. The first tensor stack is what was detected, and the second tensor stack is the bounding box stack for each detection—in other words, scores and their boxes.

Reading Model Outputs

You can review the results of an image with a few lines of code. The following does just that and is also available in the chapter's source code (*https://oreil.ly/JLo5C*):

```
tf.ready().then(() => {
  const modelPath =
    "https://tfhub.dev/tensorflow/tfjs-model/ssd_mobilenet_v2/1/default/1"; ❶
  tf.tidy(() => {
    tf.loadGraphModel(modelPath, { fromTFHub: true }).then((model) => {
```

```
        const mysteryImage = document.getElementById("mystery");
        const myTensor = tf.browser.fromPixels(mysteryImage);
        // SSD Mobilenet batch of 1
        const singleBatch = tf.expandDims(myTensor, 0); ❷

        model.executeAsync(singleBatch).then((result) => {
          console.log("First", result[0].shape); ❸
          result[0].print();
          console.log("Second", result[1].shape); ❹
          result[1].print();
        });
      });
    });
  });
```

❶ This is the TFHub URL for the JavaScript model.

❷ The input is expanded in rank to be a batch of one with the shape [1, height, width, 3].

❸ The resulting tensor is [1, 1917, 90], which has returned 1,917 detections with the 90 probability values in each row adding up to 1.

❹ The tensor is shaped as [1, 1917, 4], providing the bounding boxes for each of the 1,917 detections.

Figure 6-3 displays the output of the model.

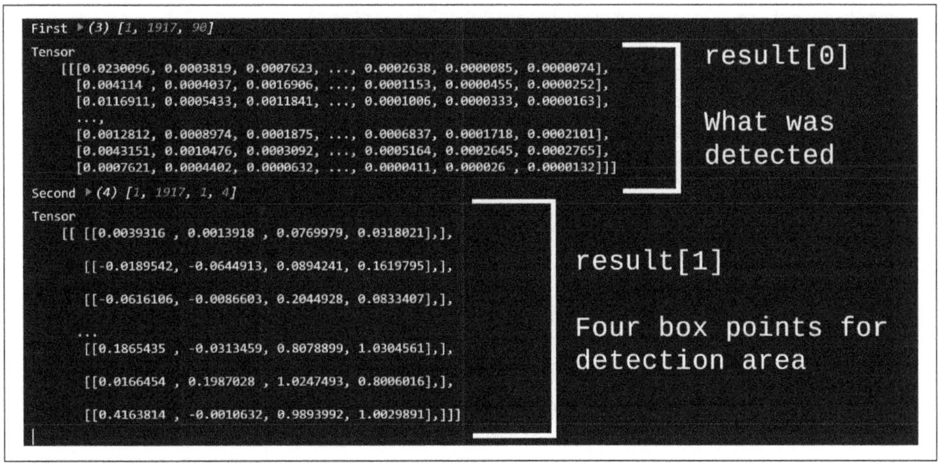

Figure 6-3. The output from the previous code

You're likely surprised to see 90 values instead of 80 for the possible classes. It's still only 80 possible classes. Ten of the result indices in that model aren't used.

While it looks like you're done, there are a few red flags. As you might assume, drawing 1,917 boxes isn't going to be useful or effective, but try it and see.

Displaying All Outputs

It's time to write the code to draw multiple bounding boxes. The gut reaction is that 1,917 detections is excessive. It's time to write some code to verify this. Since the code is getting a bit promise-heavy, it's a good time to switch over to async/await. This will stop the code from indenting further and will increase readability. If you're unfamiliar with switching between promises and async/await, please review that aspect of JavaScript.

The full code to draw the model detections can be found in the book source code file *too_many.html* (*https://oreil.ly/bMPVa*). This code is using the same techniques as described in the object localization section in the previous chapter, but with the parameter order adjusted to fit the expected output of the model.

```
const results = await model.executeAsync(readyfied);
const boxes = await results[1].squeeze().array();

// Prep Canvas
const detection = document.getElementById("detection");
const ctx = detection.getContext("2d");
const imgWidth = mysteryImage.width;
const imgHeight = mysteryImage.height;
detection.width = imgWidth;
detection.height = imgHeight;

boxes.forEach((box, idx) => {
  ctx.strokeStyle = "#0F0";
  ctx.lineWidth = 1;
  const startY = box[0] * imgHeight;
  const startX = box[1] * imgWidth;
  const height = (box[2] - box[0]) * imgHeight;
  const width = (box[3] - box[1]) * imgWidth;
  ctx.strokeRect(startX, startY, width, height);
});
```

Drawing every single detection regardless of the model's confidence wasn't hard, but the resulting output is completely unusable, as shown in Figure 6-4.

Figure 6-4. 1,917 bounding boxes, rendering the image useless

The mess you're seeing in Figure 6-4 indicates that there are plenty of detections, but there's no clarity. Can you guess what's causing this noise? There are two factors in the noise you're seeing.

Detection Cleanup

The first criticism of the resulting boxes is that there's no quality or quantity check. The code isn't checking the probability of the detection values or filtering for the most confident. For all you know, the model might be 0.001% sure of a detection, and that infinitesimal detection is not worth drawing a box. The first step to cleaning this up is to set a minimum threshold for a detection score and a maximum number of boxes.

Second, after close inspection, the boxes that are being drawn seem to be detecting the same objects over and over with slight variations. This will be verified in a bit. It would be best that their overlap was limited when they have identified the same class. If two overlapping boxes detect a person, just take the one with the highest detection score.

The model did (or did not do) a great job at finding things in the photo, so now it's your job to apply the cleanup.

Quality Checking

You'll want the highest-ranked predictions. You can do this by suppressing any bounding box below a given score. Identify the highest scores of the entire detection series with a single call to topk like so:

```
const prominentDetection = tf.topk(results[0]);
// Print it to be sure
prominentDetection.indices.print()
prominentDetection.values.print()
```

Calling topk on all the detection results returns an array with only the best of the best, as k defaults to 1. The index of each detection corresponds with the class, and the value is the confidence of the detection. The output would look like Figure 6-5.

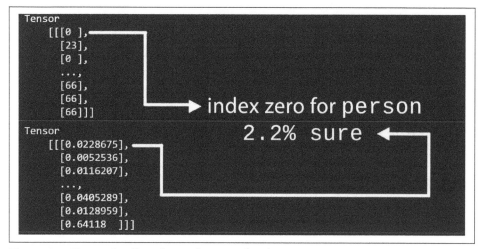

Figure 6-5. The topk call works on the entire batch

If the prominent detection is lower than a given threshold, you can deny drawing the box. You could then limit the boxes you're drawing to draw only the top N predictions. We'll leave the code for this exercise to the Chapter Challenge, because it does nothing to solve the second issue. Quality checking alone causes clusters of boxes around your strongest predictions, rather than singular predictions. The resulting boxes look like your detection system drank too much coffee (see Figure 6-6).

Figure 6-6. Drawing the 20 top predictions creates fuzzy boxing

Fortunately, there's a built-in way to solve these fuzzy boxes, and it provides you with some new terminology for your dinner parties.

IoUs and NMS

Until now, you might have thought IoUs were just an approved fiat currency backed by Lloyd Christmas, but in the world of object detection and training, they stand for *intersection over union*. Intersection over union is an evaluation metric for identifying accuracy and overlap of object detectors. The accuracy part is great for training, and the overlap is great for cleaning up overlapping output.

IoU is the formula for identifying how much area two boxes share in their overlap. If the boxes overlap perfectly, the IoU is one, and the less they fit, the closer the number is to zero. The title "IoU" comes from the formula for this calculation. The intersection area of the boxes is divided by the union area of the boxes, as illustrated in Figure 6-7.

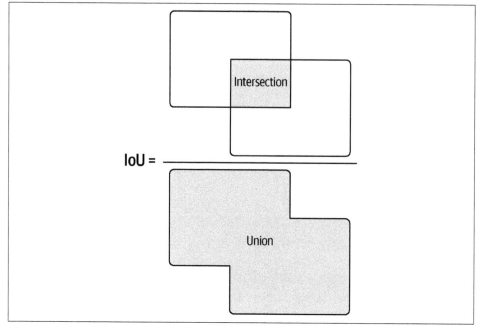

$$\text{IoU} = \frac{\boxed{\text{Intersection}}}{\boxed{\text{Union}}}$$

Figure 6-7. Intersection over union

Now you have a quick formula to check the similarity of bounding boxes. Using the IoU formula, you can enact an algorithm called *nonmaximum suppression* (NMS) to remove duplicates. NMS automatically grabs the highest-scoring boxes and dismisses any similar boxes with IoU over a designated level. Figure 6-8 shows a simple example with three scored boxes.

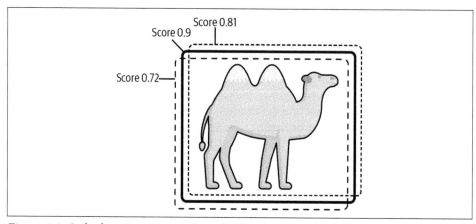

Figure 6-8. Only the max survives; the other lower-scoring boxes are removed

If you set the IoU for NMS to 0.5, then any box that shares 50% of its area with a higher-scoring box will get deleted. This works expertly for eliminating boxes that overlap the same object. However, it can be a problem for two objects that overlap each other and should have two bounding boxes. This is an issue for real objects that have an unfortunate angle that places them on top of one another because their bounding boxes will cancel each other out, and you'll get only one detection for two actual objects. For this situation, you can enable an advanced version of NMS called Soft-NMS (*https://arxiv.org/pdf/1704.04503.pdf*), which will decay scores of overlapping boxes rather than removing them. If their scores are still high enough after being decayed, the detections will survive and get their own bounding box, even if the IoU was extremely high. Figure 6-9 properly identifies two objects with extreme intersection with Soft-NMS.

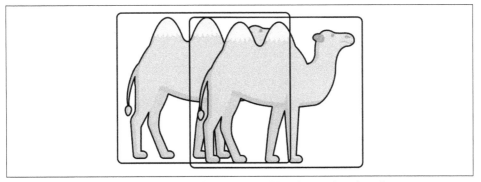

Figure 6-9. Real-world overlapping objects can still be detected with Soft-NMS

The best part about Soft-NMS is that it's built into TensorFlow.js. I recommend that you utilize this TensorFlow.js function for all your object detection needs. For this exercise, you will use that incorporated method, named `tf.image.nonMaxSuppres sionWithScoreAsync`. TensorFlow.js has quite a few NMS algorithms built in, but `tf.image.nonMaxSuppressionWithScoreAsync` has two qualities that make it excellent for use:

- `WithScore` provides Soft-NMS support.
- `Async` stops the GPU from locking up the UI thread.

Be careful when using nonasync advanced methods because they can lock the entire UI. If you would like to remove the Soft-NMS aspect for any reason, you can set the last parameter (the Soft-NMS Sigma) to zero, and then you've got a traditional NMS.

```
const nmsDetections = await tf.image.nonMaxSuppressionWithScoreAsync(
  justBoxes, // shape [numBoxes, 4]
  justValues, // shape [numBoxes]
  maxBoxes, // Stop making boxes when this number is hit
  iouThreshold, // Allowed overlap value 0 to 1
```

```
    detectionThreshold, // Minimum detection score allowed
    1 // 0 is normal NMS, 1 is max Soft-NMS
);
```

In just a few lines of code, you've clarified the SSD results to a few unclouded detections.

The result will be an object with two properties. The `selectedIndices` property will be a tensor of the indices of the boxes that made the cut, and the `selectedScores` would be their corresponding scores. You could loop over the chosen results and draw your bounding boxes.

```
const chosen = await nmsDetections.selectedIndices.data(); ❶
chosen.forEach((detection) => {
  ctx.strokeStyle = "#0F0";
  ctx.lineWidth = 4;
  const detectedIndex = maxIndices[detection]; ❷
  const detectedClass = CLASSES[detectedIndex]; ❸
  const detectedScore = scores[detection];
  const dBox = boxes[detection];
  console.log(detectedClass, detectedScore); ❹

  // No negative values for start positions
  const startY = dBox[0] > 0 ? dBox[0] * imgHeight : 0; ❺
  const startX = dBox[1] > 0 ? dBox[1] * imgWidth : 0;
  const height = (dBox[2] - dBox[0]) * imgHeight;
  const width = (dBox[3] - dBox[1]) * imgWidth;
  ctx.strokeRect(startX, startY, width, height);
});
```

❶ Create a normal JavaScript array from the indices of the resulting high-scoring boxes.

❷ Get the highest-scoring index from a previous `topk` call.

❸ The classes are imported as an array to match the given result indices. This structure is just like the code from the Inception example in the previous chapter.

❹ Log what is being boxed in the canvas so you can verify the results.

❺ Disallow negative numbers, so boxes at least start in frame. Otherwise, some boxes would be cut off from the top left.

The number of detections returned varies but is limited to the specifications set in the NMS. The example code resulted in five correct detections, as illustrated in Figure 6-10.

Figure 6-10. The clean Soft-NMS detected results

The console logs from the loop print out that the five detections were three "person" detections, one "wine glass," and one "dining table." Compare the five logs in Figure 6-11 with the five bound boxes in Figure 6-10.

person 0.8153703808784485	non_max.html:83
person 0.7834617495536804	non_max.html:83
person 0.7107626795768738	non_max.html:83
dining table 0.7050056457519531	non_max.html:83
wine glass 0.570665180683136	non_max.html:83

Figure 6-11. The result log classes and confidence levels

The UI has come so far. It only makes sense that the overlays should identify the detections and their percentage confidence. Average users don't know to look at the console for logs.

Adding Text Overlays

There are all kinds of fancy ways you can add text to a canvas and have it identify the bounding box associated. For this demo, we'll review the simplest method and leave the more aesthetic layouts as a task for the reader.

Drawing text to a canvas can be done with the canvas 2D context's `fillText` method. You can position the text at the top left of every box by reusing the `X, Y` coordinates you used to draw the boxes.

There are two issues to note with drawing text:

- Text can easily have low contrast with the background.
- Text that is drawn at the same time as a box might be covered by boxes drawn afterward.

Fortunately, both of these are easy to solve.

Solving Low Contrast

The typical method for creating readable labels is to draw a background box and then place your text. As you know, `strokeRect` creates a box with no fill color, so it should be no surprise that `fillRect` draws a box with a fill color.

How big should the rectangle be? A simple answer would be to draw the rectangle to the width of the detection box, but there's no guarantee that the box will be wide enough, and when the box is very wide, this creates large blocking bars in your results. The only effective solution is to measure the text and draw the box accordingly. Text height can be set by utilizing the context `font` property, and the width can be determined with `measureText`.

Finally, you might consider that you have to subtract the font height from your drawing position so that it draws the text inside the box rather than on top of the box, but context already has a property you can set to keep life simple. The `context.textBaseline` property has all kinds of options. Figure 6-12 shows starting points for each of the possible property options.

Figure 6-12. Setting the `textBaseline` to `top` keeps the text inside the X and Y coordinates

Now you know how to draw a filled rectangle to the appropriate size and place your labels inside. You can combine these methods inside your `forEach` loop where you're drawing detections and draw your results. The labels are drawn in the upper-left side of each detection, as shown in Figure 6-13.

Figure 6-13. The labels are drawn with each box

It's important that the text is drawn *after* the background box; otherwise, the box will be painted on top of the text. For our purposes, the labels will be drawn with a slightly different color green than the bounding boxes.

```
// Draw the label background.
ctx.fillStyle = "#0B0";
ctx.font = "16px sans-serif"; ❶
ctx.textBaseline = "top"; ❷
const textHeight = 16;
const textPad = 4; ❸
const label = `${detectedClass} ${Math.round(detectedScore * 100)}%`;
const textWidth = ctx.measureText(label).width;
ctx.fillRect( ❹
  startX,
  startY,
  textWidth + textPad,
  textHeight + textPad
);
// Draw the text last to ensure it's on top.
ctx.fillStyle = "#000000"; ❺
ctx.fillText(label, startX, startY); ❻
```

❶ Set the font and size to use on the labels.

❷   Set `textBaseline` as mentioned.

❸   Add a little horizontal padding to be used in the `fillRect` render.

❹   Draw the rectangle using the same `startX` and `startY` that were used to draw the bounding boxes.

❺   Change the `fillStyle` to be black for the text render.

❻   Finally, draw the text. This probably should have been padded a little, too.

Now each detection has a nearly readable label. However, depending on your image, you might have noticed a few issues that we will now solve.

Solving Draw Order

Even though the labels are drawn on top of the boxes, the boxes are drawn at separate times and can easily overlap with some existing label text, rendering them difficult or even impossible to read. As you can see in Figure 6-14, the dining table percentage is tough to read due to an overlapping detection.

Figure 6-14. Context draw order overlap issue

One way to solve this problem is to iterate over the detections and draw boxes, and then do a second pass and draw the text. This would ensure the text was drawn last at the cost of iterating over the detections in two subsequent loops.

As an alternative, you could handle this with code. You can set the context `globalCom positeOperation` to do all kinds of amazing things. One simple operation is to tell the context to render above or below existing content, effectively setting a z-order.

The strokeRect calls can be set with globalCompositeOperation to destination-over. This means any pixels that exist in the destination will win and be placed over the added content. This effectively draws under any existing content.

Then, when you're drawing your labels, return globalCompositionOperation to its default behavior, which is source-over. This draws the new source pixels over any existing drawings. If you flip back and forth between these two operations, you can ensure your labels are top priority and handle everything inside the master loop.

Altogether, the singular loop to draw bounding boxes, label boxes, and labels looks like this:

```
chosen.forEach((detection) => {
  ctx.strokeStyle = "#0F0";
  ctx.lineWidth = 4;
  ctx.globalCompositeOperation='destination-over'; ❶
  const detectedIndex = maxIndices[detection];
  const detectedClass = CLASSES[detectedIndex];
  const detectedScore = scores[detection];
  const dBox = boxes[detection];

  // No negative values for start positions
  const startY = dBox[0] > 0 ? dBox[0] * imgHeight : 0;
  const startX = dBox[1] > 0 ? dBox[1] * imgWidth : 0;
  const height = (dBox[2] - dBox[0]) * imgHeight;
  const width = (dBox[3] - dBox[1]) * imgWidth;
  ctx.strokeRect(startX, startY, width, height);
  // Draw the label background.
  ctx.globalCompositeOperation='source-over'; ❷
  ctx.fillStyle = "#0B0";
  const textHeight = 16;
  const textPad = 4;
  const label = `${detectedClass} ${Math.round(detectedScore * 100)}%`;
  const textWidth = ctx.measureText(label).width;
  ctx.fillRect(
    startX,
    startY,
    textWidth + textPad,
    textHeight + textPad
  );
  // Draw the text last to ensure it's on top.
  ctx.fillStyle = "#000000";
  ctx.fillText(label, startX, startY);
});
```

❶ Draw under any existing content.

❷ Draw over any existing content.

The result is a dynamic human-readable result that you can share with your friends (see Figure 6-15).

Figure 6-15. Using `destination-over` *fixes overlap issues*

Connecting to a Webcam

What's the benefit of all this speed? As mentioned earlier, there was a choice of SSD over R-CNN, MobileNet over Inception, and drawing the canvas in one pass instead of two. When you load the page, it looks pretty slow. It seems to take at least four seconds just to load and render.

Yes, getting everything in place takes a moment, but after the memory has been allocated and the model is downloaded, you can see some pretty significant speed. Yes, it's enough to run live detection on your webcam.

The key to speeding up the process is to run your setup code once and then move on to running a loop of detections. This does mean you need to break up the monolithic codebase from this lesson; otherwise, you'll get an unusable interface. For simplicity you can break up the project as shown in Example 6-1.

Example 6-1. Breaking up a codebase

```
async function doStuff() {
  try {
```

```
    const model = await loadModel()  ❶
    const mysteryVideo = document.getElementById('mystery')  ❷
    const camDetails = await setupWebcam(mysteryVideo)  ❸
    performDetections(model, mysteryVideo, camDetails)  ❹
  } catch (e) {
    console.error(e)  ❺
  }
}
```

❶ The longest delay is when loading the model; this should happen first and only once.

❷ For efficiency, you can capture the video element once and pass that reference into the places it's needed.

❸ Setting up the webcam should happen only once.

❹ The performDetections method can loop forever when detecting the content in the webcam and drawing the boxes.

❺ Don't let the errors get swallowed up with all these awaits.

Moving from Image to Video

It's actually not complicated to move from a still image to video because the hard part of turning what you see into a tensor is handled by tf.fromPixels. The tf.fromPix els method can read a canvas, an image, and even a video element. So the complexity lies in changing out the img tag for a video tag.

You start by switching out the tags. The original img tag:

```
<img id="mystery" src="/dinner.jpg" height="100%" />
```

becomes the following:

```
<video id="mystery" height="100%" autoplay></video>
```

It's worth noting that the video element is a bit more complicated with width/height properties because there's the input video width/height and the actual client width/ height. For this reason, all the calculations that were using width will need to use cli entWidth, and similarly, height will need to be clientHeight. If you use the wrong property, the boxes will not align or might not even show up at all.

Activating a Webcam

For our purposes, we'll only set up the default webcam. This corresponds to point four in Example 6-1. If you're unfamiliar with `getUserMedia`, take a moment to analyze how the video element is connected to the webcam. This is also the time when you can move your canvas context setup to fit the video element.

```
async function setupWebcam(videoRef) {
  if (navigator.mediaDevices && navigator.mediaDevices.getUserMedia) {
    const webcamStream = await navigator.mediaDevices.getUserMedia({ ❶
      audio: false,
      video: {
        facingMode: 'user',
      },
    })

    if ('srcObject' in videoRef) { ❷
      videoRef.srcObject = webcamStream
    } else {
      videoRef.src = window.URL.createObjectURL(webcamStream)
    }

    return new Promise((resolve, _) => { ❸
      videoRef.onloadedmetadata = () => { ❹
        // Prep Canvas
        const detection = document.getElementById('detection')
        const ctx = detection.getContext('2d')
        const imgWidth = videoRef.clientWidth ❺
        const imgHeight = videoRef.clientHeight
        detection.width = imgWidth
        detection.height = imgHeight
        ctx.font = '16px sans-serif'
        ctx.textBaseline = 'top'
        resolve([ctx, imgHeight, imgWidth]) ❻
      }
    })
  } else {
    alert('No webcam - sorry!')
  }
}
```

❶ These are the webcam user media configuration constraints. There are several options (*https://oreil.ly/MkWml*) you can apply here, but for simplicity, it's kept quite simple.

❷ This conditional check is to support older browsers that do not support the new `srcObject` configuration. This can likely be deprecated depending on your support needs.

❸ You can't access the video until it is loaded, so the event is wrapped in a promise so it can be awaited.

❹ This is the event you'll need to wait for before you can pass the video element to `tf.fromPixels`.

❺ While taking this opportunity to set up the canvas, notice the use of `clientWidth` instead of `width`.

❻ The promise resolves with information you'll need to pass along to the detect and draw loop.

Drawing Detections

Lastly, you perform your detections and drawing just like you did for an image. At the beginning of each call you will need to remove all the detections from the previous call; otherwise, your canvas will slowly fill up with old detections. Clearing the canvas is simple; you can use `clearRect` to remove anything from the designated coordinates. Passing the entire canvas width and height will wipe the slate clean.

```
ctx.clearRect(0, 0, ctx.canvas.width, ctx.canvas.height)
```

At the end of each drawn detection, *do not* dispose the model in your cleanup, as you'll need it in each detection. Everything else, however, can and should get disposed.

The `performDetections` function that was identified in Example 6-1 should call itself recursively in an infinite loop. The function can loop faster than a canvas can draw. To assure it's not wasting cycles, use the browser's `requestAnimationFrame` to throttle this:

```
// Loop forever
requestAnimationFrame(() => {
  performDetections(model, videoRef, camDetails)
})
```

And that's it. You've moved from a still image to video input at real-time speeds with a few logical adjustments. On my computer I was seeing around 16 frames per second. In the world of AI, that is more than fast enough to handle most use cases. I used it to facilitate proof I'm at least 97% a person, as shown in Figure 6-16.

Figure 6-16. Fully functioning webcam with SSD MobileNet

Chapter Review

Congratulations on tackling one of the most useful yet complex models to exist on TensorFlow Hub. While it's simple to hide the complexity of this model with Java-Script, you're now familiar with some of the most impressive concepts in object detection and clarification. Machine learning is burdened with the concept of solving a problem quickly and then solving the follow-up code to attach the majestic properties of AI to a given domain. You can expect a good bit of research to accompany any significantly advanced model and field.

Chapter Challenge: Top Detective

NMS simplifies both sorting and eliminating detections. Let's pretend you wanted to solve the problem of identifying the top predictions and then sorting them from highest to lowest, so you could create a graphic like Figure 6-6. Rather than relying on NMS to find your most viable and highest values, you'll need to solve the highest-value problem yourself. Take this small but similar grouping as the entire dataset of detection. Imagine this [1, 6, 5] tensor collection of detections is your result[0], and you want only the top three detections with the highest confidence values for any class. How could you solve this?

```
const t = tf.tensor([[
  [1, 2, 3, 4, 5],
  [1.1, 2.1, 3.1, 4.1, 5.1],
  [1.2, 2.2, 3.2, 4.2, 5.2],
  [1.2, 12.2, 3.2, 4.2, 5.2],
  [1.3, 2.3, 3.3, 4.3, 5.3],
  [1, 1, 1, 1, 1]
]])
```

```
// Get the top-three most confident predictions.
```

Your resulting solution should print [3, 4, 2] because the tensor at index 3 has the largest value (12.2) in its set of all the values, followed by index 4 (which contains 5.3) and then index 2 (5.2).

You can find the answer to this challenge in Appendix B.

Review Questions

Let's review the lessons you've learned from the code you've written in this chapter. Take a moment to answer the following questions:

1. What does SSD stand for in the world of object detection machine learning?
2. What method do you need to use to predict on a model that uses dynamic control flow operations?
3. How many classes and how many values does SSD MobileNet predict?
4. What is the method for deduplicating detections of the same object?
5. What is a drawback of using large synchronous TensorFlow.js calls?
6. What method should you use to identify the width of a label?
7. What globalCompositeOperation overwrites existing content on the canvas?

Solutions to these questions are available in Appendix A.

Up Next...

In Chapter 7 you'll start learning some of the key aspects and terminology of training your own model. The chapter will give you a world of resources for converting, training, and managing data.

## CHAPTER 7

Model-Making Resources

"By seeking and blundering we learn."
—Johann Wolfgang von Goethe

You're not limited to the models from TensorFlow Hub. Every day there are new and exciting models being tweeted, published, and highlighted in the community spotlight. These models and ideas are shared outside the Google-approved hubs, and sometimes they are even outside the realm of TensorFlow.js.

You're starting to advance beyond the garden walls and work with models and data in the wild. This chapter is specifically geared toward arming you with new ways to make models from existing models, as well as charge you with the challenges of gathering and understanding data.

We will:

- Introduce model conversion
- Introduce Teachable Machine
- Train a computer vision model
- Review where training data comes from
- Cover some key concepts of training

When you finish this chapter, you'll be armed with a few ways of making a model and a better understanding of the process of using data to make a machine learning solution.

Out-of-Network Model Shopping

TensorFlow.js hasn't been around for long. Consequently, the number of models available is limited, or at least there are fewer than other frameworks. That doesn't mean you're out of luck. You can often convert models that were trained on other frameworks to TensorFlow.js. Converting existing models to make new models that work in a new environment is a great way to find recently developed resources and create exciting and contemporary models.

Model Zoos

One somewhat endearing term that has emerged from the machine learning world is that a collection of models is sometimes called a *zoo*. These model zoos are a treasure trove of models that do a wide variety of tasks for a given framework, much like TensorFlow Hub.

The model zoos are a fantastic place to find unique models that could inspire or fit your needs. Zoos often link you to published works that explain the choices that were made for both the model architecture and the data that was used to create them.

The real benefit comes from the principle that once you've learned how to convert one of these models to TensorFlow.js, you could likely convert a lot of them.

It's worth taking a moment to review converting models so you can comprehend how accessible each model zoo or published model might be to TensorFlow.js.

Converting Models

Lots of Python-programmed TensorFlow models are saved in a format called Keras HDF5. HDF5 stands for Hierarchical Data Format v5, but is most commonly referred to as Keras or merely an h5 file. This file format is portable as one file with an h5 extension. The Keras file format has lots of data inside:

- An architecture that specifies the layers of the model
- A set of weight values, analogous to the bin files
- An optimizer and the loss metric for the model

This is one of the more popular model formats, and more importantly, they are easy to convert to TensorFlow.js even though they were trained in Python.

 With the knowledge of being able to convert TensorFlow Keras models, it means that any TensorFlow tutorial that you find can be read as a tutorial where the final product can likely be used in TensorFlow.js.

Running conversion commands

To convert from h5 to TensorFlow.js *model.json* and bin files, you'll need `tfjs-converter` (*https://oreil.ly/g46CE*). The `tfjs-converter` can also convert TensorFlow model types other than just HDF5, so it's a great tool for handling any TensorFlow to TensorFlow.js format.

The converter requires that your computer is set up with Python. Install the converter with `pip`. The `pip` command is the package installer for Python, similar to `npm` in JavaScript. There are multitudes of tutorials on installing Python and `pip` if your computer is not ready. You can run `tfjs-converter` once you have `pip` and Python installed.

This is the install command for the converter:

```
$ pip install tensorflowjs[wizard]
```

This installs two things: a no-nonsense converter that you can use in automation (`tensorflowjs_converter`) and a walk-through converter that you can run by typing **tensorflowjs_wizard**. For our purposes, I suggest using the wizard interface for conversion so you can take advantage of new capabilities as they become available.

You run the wizard by calling your newly installed `tensorflowjs_wizard` command from the command line, and you'll be prompted with questions like you see in Figure 7-1.

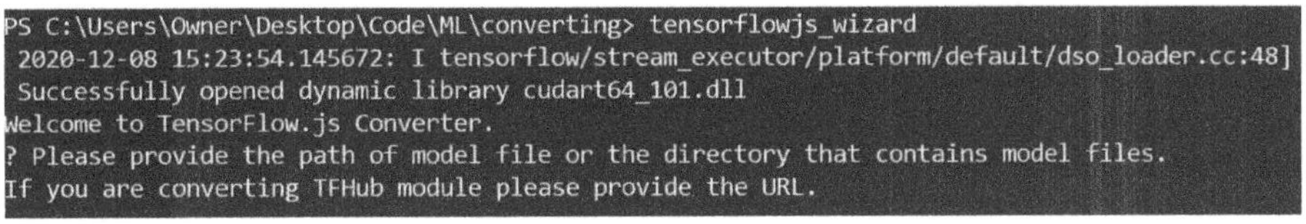

```
PS C:\Users\Owner\Desktop\Code\ML\converting> tensorflowjs_wizard
2020-12-08 15:23:54.145672: I tensorflow/stream_executor/platform/default/dso_loader.cc:48]
Successfully opened dynamic library cudart64_101.dll
Welcome to TensorFlow.js Converter.
? Please provide the path of model file or the directory that contains model files.
If you are converting TFHub module please provide the URL.
```

Figure 7-1. The wizard starts asking questions

This wizard will ask you for your input model format and your desired output model format. It will also ask quite a few questions depending on your answers. While the wizard will continue to be updated, here are some concepts you should keep in mind while selecting your desired settings:

When choosing between Graph/Layers models
Remember, Graph models are faster but lack some of the introspective and customization properties that Layers models provide.

Compression (via quantization)
This moves your model from storing 32-bit accuracy weights down to 16- or even 8-bit accuracy weight values. Using fewer bits means your model is substantially smaller in a possible sacrifice for accuracy. You should retest your model

after quantization. Most of the time, this compression is worth it for client-side models.

Shard size

The suggested shard size is to optimize your model for client-side browser caching. This should stay the recommended size unless you're not using the model in the client browser.

The quantization affects the model size on disk only. This provides significant network transfer benefits for websites, but when the model is loaded into RAM, the values are returned to 32-bit variables in the current TensorFlow.js.

Features continue to show up in the wizard interface. If a new feature shows up that confuses you, keep in mind documentation for converting models will be available in the tfjs-converter README source code (*https://oreil.ly/ldAPf*). Your experience will be similar to Figure 7-2.

```
Welcome to TensorFlow.js Converter.
? Please provide the path of model file or the directory that contains model files.
If you are converting TFHub module please provide the URL.  ./mnist.h5
? What is your input model format? (auto-detected format is marked with *)  Keras (HDF5) *
? What is your output format?  TensorFlow.js Layers Model
? Do you want to compress the model? (this will decrease the model precision.)  float16 quantization (2x smaller, Mi
? Please enter the layers to apply float16 quantization (2x smaller, minimal accuracy tradeoff).
Supports wildcard expansion with *, e.g., conv/*/weights  *
? Please enter shard size (in bytes) of the weight files?  4194304
```

Figure 7-2. An example wizard walk-through on Windows

The resulting folder contains a converted TensorFlow.js model, ready for use. The h5 file is now a *model.json* and the cachable bin files in chunks. You can see the resulting conversion in Figure 7-3.

```
PS C:\Users\Owner\Desktop\Code\ML\converting> ls tfjs-yay

    Directory: C:\Users\Owner\Desktop\Code\ML\converting\tfjs-yay

Mode                LastWriteTime         Length Name
----                -------------         ------ ----
-a----        12/8/2020     9:34 AM            640 group1-shard1of1.bin
-a----        12/8/2020     9:34 AM          36992 group2-shard1of1.bin
-a----        12/8/2020     9:34 AM        2359552 group3-shard1of1.bin
-a----        12/8/2020     9:34 AM           2580 group4-shard1of1.bin
-a----        12/8/2020     9:34 AM           4695 model.json
```

Figure 7-3. The TensorFlow.js model result

Intermediate models

If you find a model you'd like to convert to TensorFlow.js, you can now check if there's a converter to move that model to the format Keras HDF5, and then you know you can convert it to TensorFlow.js. It's worth noting that there's a significant effort to standardize models converting to and from a format called Open Neural Network Exchange (ONNX) (*https://onnx.ai*). Currently, Microsoft and many other partners are working on the proper conversion of models in and out of ONNX format, which will allow for a framework-independent model format.

If you find a published model that you'd like to utilize in TensorFlow.js, but it wasn't trained in TensorFlow, don't give up hope. You should check if there's ONNX support for that model type.

Some models do not have a direct conversion to TensorFlow, and because of that, you might need a more circuitous route through other conversion services. Outside of TensorFlow, the other popular framework library most machine learning enthusiasts use is called PyTorch. While ONNX is getting closer every day, currently the best way to convert from PyTorch to TensorFlow.js is to convert through a chain of tools, as shown in Figure 7-4.

Figure 7-4. Converting models

While it might seem like a good bit of work to do a model conversion, converting models from existing formats to TensorFlow.js can save you days or even weeks of re-creating and retraining a model on the published data.

Your First Customized Model

If downloading existing models was all you needed to do, you'd be done. But we can't all wait for Google to release models that classify what we need. You might have an idea that requires an AI to have an intimate knowledge of pastries. Even Google's Inception v3 might not be strong enough if you need to know the difference between a variety of items in a single domain.

Fortunately for you, there's a trick that allows us to ride the coattails of existing models. Some models can be slightly adjusted so they classify new things! Rather than retraining the entire model, we train the last few layers to look for different features. This allows us to take an advanced model like Inception or MobileNet and turn it into a model that identifies things we want. As a bonus, this method allows us to retrain a model with a minuscule amount of data. This is called *transfer learning*, and it's one of the most common methods for (re)training models on new classes.

We'll cover the code for transfer learning in Chapter 11, but there's no reason you can't experience it right now. Google has an entire transfer learning UI built for people to try training models.

Meet Teachable Machine

To start things off, you'll use a tool provided by Google called Teachable Machine. This tool is a simple website that is powered by TensorFlow.js, and it lets you upload images, upload audio, or even use your webcam for training, capturing data, and creating TensorFlow.js models. The models are trained directly in your browser and then hosted for you to try your code immediately. Your resulting model is a transfer learning version of MobileNet, PoseNet, or some other practical model that fits your needs. Because it uses transfer learning, you don't need much data at all.

Models created with a small amount of data will appear to work wonders but have a significant bias. That means they will work well with the conditions they were trained in, but they will error with background, lighting, or positional changes.

The website for training a model is located at *teachablemachine.withgoogle.com* (*https://oreil.ly/CAy4H*). When you access the site, you can get started with various projects, like audio, image, and even body poses. While you can and should experiment with each of these, this book will cover the Image Project option. This is the first option shown in Figure 7-5.

Image Project

Teach based on images, from files or your webcam.

Audio Project

Teach based on one-second-long sounds, from files or your microphone.

Pose Project

Teach based on images, from files or your webcam.

Figure 7-5. Awesome Teachable Machine options

On the resulting page, you're given the option to either upload or use your webcam to collect sample images for each class.

Here are a few ideas you can use to create your first classifier:

- Thumbs up or thumbs down?
- Am I drinking water?
- Which cat is this?
- Secret hand signal to unlock something?
- Book or banana!?

Use your creativity! Whatever model you create could be something easy to show off to friends and social media or something that could be turned into a web page to help you. For instance, the "Am I drinking water?" classifier could be hooked up to a timer for your self-hydration project. You can come up with all kinds of fun projects as long as you train the model with a few samples.

Personally, I'll be training a "Is Daddy working?" classifier. Many of you might have experienced difficulty with family in a remote work environment. If I'm sitting at my desk and the door is closed, you'd think that would tell people I'm working, right? But if the door is open, "come on in!" I'll ask Teachable Machine to use my webcam to classify what I look like when I'm working and what I look like when I'm not working.

The cool part is that since the detector will be tied to a website, "Is Daddy working?" could be expanded to do all kinds of awesome things. It could send text messages, turn on an "unavailable" light, or even tell my Amazon Echo devices to answer "yes" when asked if I am working. There's a whole world of opportunity as long as I can make a quick AI image classifier that is dependable.

Training from scratch is a scalable solution, but the task at hand is to train my presence in my office, and for that, we'll use Teachable Machine.

Use Teachable Machine

Let's take a quick tour through the UI for creating a model with Teachable Machine. The UI is set up like a network graph where information is filled in top-down from left to right. Utilizing the site is easy. Follow along as we review Figure 7-6.

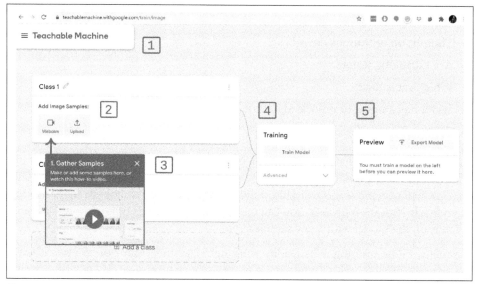

Figure 7-6. Image project UI tour

1. This upper header is meant to be small and stay out of the way on larger monitors. From the header, you can use Google Drive to manage your data and your results, so you can pick up where you left off or share the training of your model with others.

2. The top item is called "Class 1" and indicates one of the classes for your classification. Of course, you can rename it! I've renamed mine to "Working." Inside this workflow card, you can provide access to your webcam or upload image files that would fit this classification.

3. This second workflow card is any second class. This could be "Free" or "Not Working" in the case of my example I'm trying to build. Here you provide the data that fits your secondary classification.

4. All classes feed into the training workflow. When you have examples of what you want to build, you can click the Train Model button and actively train the model. We'll dig deeper into what this is doing with the Advanced tab when we get to it.

5. The Preview section immediately displays the model's real-time classifications in action.

Gathering Data and Training

You can hold down the webcam's "Hold to Record" button and instantly provide hundreds of images for example data. It's crucial that you evaluate and include variation as much as possible in your dataset. For example, if you're doing "Thumbs up or thumbs down," it's important that you move your hands around the screen, catch different angles, and put your hands in front of your face, shirt, and any other complex background.

For me, I adjusted my lighting, as sometimes I have a camera keylight, and sometimes I have backlights. Within a few seconds, I had hundreds of various conditions with my office door open and closed. I even did some photos where my door is closed but I'm not sitting at my desk.

One of the great things about Teachable Machine is that it gives you the results quickly in your browser, so if the model needs more data, you can always come back and add more right away.

Once you have a few hundred photos, you can click the Train Model button, and you'll see a "Training…" progress graph (see Figure 7-7).

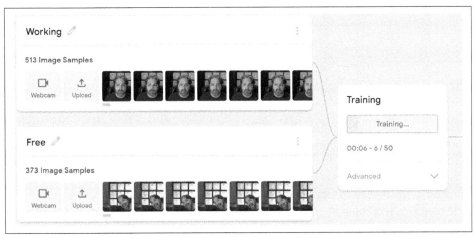

Figure 7-7. Teachable Machine active training

So what's happening now? Succinctly put, Teachable Machine is using your images to perform transfer learning to retrain the MobileNet model. A random 85% of your data has been used to train the model, and the other 15% is reserved for testing the model's performance.

Click the Advanced tab to view the details of this particular configuration. This will expose some of what are often called the *hyperparameters* for machine learning training (see Figure 7-8). These hyperparameters are parameters tunable to the model training.

Figure 7-8. Teachable Machine hyperparameters

In here, you'll see some new terminology. While it's not critical for you to learn these terms now, you'll need to learn them eventually, so we'll go over them quickly. Each of these concepts will show up when you get into coding your own models in Chapter 8.

Epochs

If you're coming from coding, especially JavaScript coding, the epoch was January 1, 1970. That is *not* what epoch means in this domain. An epoch in machine learning training is one full pass through the training data. At the end of an epoch, the AI has seen all the training data at least once. Fifty epochs means the model will have to see the data 50 times. A good analogy is flashcards. This number is how many times you're going through the entire deck of flashcards with the model for it to learn.

Batch size

The model is trained in batches that are loaded into memory. With a few hundred photos, you can easily handle all of the images in memory at the same time, but it's nicer to batch in reasonable increments.

Learning rate

The learning rate affects how much the machine learning model should adapt with each prediction. You might assume higher learning rates are always better, but you'd be wrong. Sometimes, especially when fine-tuning a transfer learning model, it's about the details (as covered in Chapter 11).

There's also a button at the bottom of the card with the text "Under the hood," which will give you lots of detailed information on the progress of the trained model. Feel free to look at the reports. You'll implement metrics like these later.

Verifying the Model

Once Teachable Machine is done, it immediately hooks the model up to your webcam and shows you what the model predicts. This is a great opportunity for you to test the results of the model.

For me, when I'm at my desk and my door is closed, the model predicted I was working. Hurray! I have a usable model ready to go. Both classes were performing impressively well, as illustrated in Figure 7-9.

Figure 7-9. The model works

Ideally, your training went just as well. Now it's essential to retrieve the trained model so it can be implemented in your more extensive project. If you'd like to share your model with your friends, you can click the Export Model button in the preview, where you're given a variety of options. The new modal window provides paths for applying your model in TensorFlow, TensorFlow Lite, and TensorFlow.js. There's even an option for hosting your trained model for free, rather than downloading and hosting your model yourself. We get all these friendly options and some nifty copy-and-paste code for you to quickly implement these models. The export code screen should be similar to Figure 7-10.

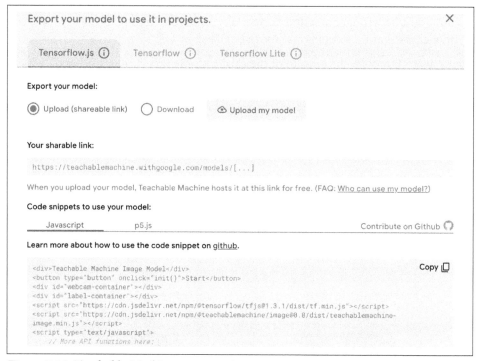

Figure 7-10. Teachable Machine export options

When your model is downloaded or published, your data is not published with it. To save the dataset, you'll have to save your project in Google Drive. Keep this in mind if you plan on advancing your model or growing your dataset over time. Identifying and handling edge cases is part of the data science process.

The code provided for free in the copy-and-paste section of Teachable Machine hides the nitty-gritty of webcams and tensors with an NPM package called @teachablemachine/image (*https://oreil.ly/kY7YJ*). While this is great for people who don't understand webcams and tensors, it's pretty useless for a finalized product. Your advanced UI skills from Chapter 6 make your creative potential far superior to the copy-and-paste code option.

 Each Teachable Machine model will be different; the visual model you just trained is built on top of our old friend MobileNet classifier. So when you implement the model, resize the input to 224 x 224.

You've just trained your first model. However, we cut as many corners as we could. Training models with a UI is going to be a large part of machine learning, and it helps everyone new to machine learning to get a fantastic start. But a tensor wizard like yourself can train a much more dynamic model. You're obviously looking to command your machines with explicit instructions like code. So let's get started on training a model by writing some JavaScript.

Machine Learning Gotchas

When coding, there are a wide variety of issues any developer might have to face. Even as programming languages vary, there's a core set of potholes that carries over to every infrastructure. Machine learning is no different. While there are issues that might be specific to any chosen genre and problem, it's important to identify these early so you can spot some of the most common complications with data-driven algorithms.

We'll quickly elaborate on a few concepts now, but each of these will be revisited when they apply to the work in the rest of this book:

- Small amounts of data
- Poor data
- Data bias
- Overfitting
- Underfitting

Let's review these so we can look out for them in upcoming chapters.

Small Amounts of Data

I've had people come to me with an excellent idea for a machine learning solution, and they have three labeled samples. Few things in this world could benefit from such a small training set. When data is how you train an algorithm, you'll need a fair amount of data. How much? There's never an answer that fits every problem, but you should lean toward more data over less.

Poor Data

Some people have clean, situated, and organized lives, but in the real world, data doesn't end up that way by accident. If your data has missing, mislabeled, or downright outrageous data, it can cause problems in your training. Lots of times, data needs to be scrubbed, and outliers need to be removed. Just getting the data ready is a big and critical step.

Data Bias

Your data can be clearly labeled, with every detail in the correct place, but it might be missing information that would make it work in a real-world case. In some cases, this can cause severe ethical issues, and in other cases, this can cause your model to perform poorly in various conditions. For instance, my "Is Daddy working?" model that I trained earlier (Figure 7-9) probably won't work for other people's office configurations because the data was only for my office.

Overfitting

Sometimes a model is trained to the point where it only works well on the training set data. In some cases, a more straightforward but lower-scoring accuracy would generalize better to fit new data points.

See how this separation graph in Figure 7-11 is overfitting the data? While it solves the given problem perfectly, it's likely to be slower and fail as new points it's never seen get added.

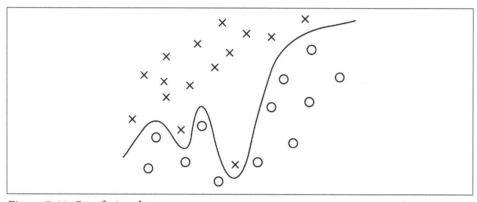

Figure 7-11. Overfitting data

Sometimes you'll hear overfitting called *high variance*, which means the fluctuations you have in your training data cause the model to randomly fail on new data.

If your goal is to have your model work on new, never-before-seen data, overfitting can be a real concern. Fortunately, we have the test and validation sets to help.

Underfitting

If your model wasn't trained enough or it's structured in a way that's incapable of adapting to the data, the solution might fail or even completely diverge from any extrapolated or additional data. This is the opposite of overfitting, but in the same sense, it creates a poor model.

See how the separation graph in Figure 7-12 underfits the subtle curve of the data?

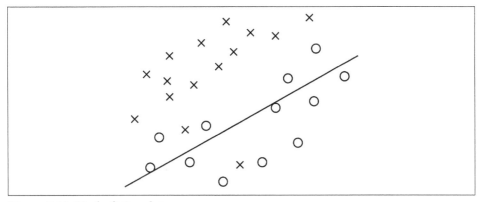

Figure 7-12. Underfitting data

When a model underfits, it is said that the model has *high bias* because of grand assumptions on data that are effectively wrong. While similar, do not confuse this term with *data bias*, covered earlier.

Datasets Shopping

Now you understand why having diverse data is essential. While the Teachable Machine "Is Daddy working?" model is useful for me, it's far from diverse enough to be used with other offices. Happily, one of the most impressive aspects of the machine learning community is how generous everyone is with their hard-earned datasets.

Before collecting your data, it's helpful to research if others have published usable and labeled data. It's also beneficial to see how expert machine learning datasets are organized.

Datasets are like JavaScript libraries: they can seem quite unique at first, but after a while, you start to see the same ones referenced time and again. Universities around the world have excellent catalogs of useful datasets (*https://oreil.ly/lbvkW*), and even Google has a dataset-hosting service (*https://oreil.ly/BnddO*) similar to TensorFlow Hub, but none comes close to the dataset residence known as Kaggle.

Kaggle (*https://www.kaggle.com*) has a significant collection of datasets for all types of data. From bird songs to IMDb reviews, you can train all kinds of models with a wide variety of data from Kaggle. Figure 7-13 shows a friendly and searchable interface for datasets.

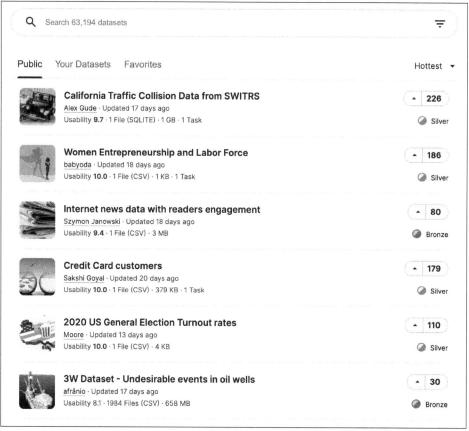

Figure 7-13. Kaggle provides more than 60,000 free datasets

Whether you're researching data for training your model or you're looking for ideas of what kind of crazy new thing you can make with machine learning, Kaggle has you covered.

Kaggle does more than just provide datasets. It's also a community for sharing, competing, and winning prizes.

If you're not interested in the extracurricular aspect of Kaggle, you can generally use Google's dataset search site and most likely find your Kaggle datasets and others: *https://datasetsearch.research.google.com*.

The Popular Datasets

While the list of datasets grows every day, for a long time, there weren't many to choose from. Published datasets were rare, so a few became the fundamentals of training examples. Other datasets were published as the first of their kind and unwittingly became the brand ambassador for a type of machine learning. Like secret passphrases, these popular datasets get used casually in talks and documentation. It's good to know some of the most common and famous:

ImageNet (https://oreil.ly/Et6TH)
> ImageNet was used to train some of the most popular computer vision models. This large dataset of images is consistently used by academic researchers to benchmark models.

MNIST (https://oreil.ly/Rb9Ru)
> This is a collection of 28 x 28 grayscale handwritten digits to train a model on reading numbers. It is often the "Hello World" of computer vision models. The name comes from its source, a modified dataset from the National Institute of Standards and Technology.

Iris (https://oreil.ly/EWvgs)
> In 1936, Ronald Fisher figured out you can identify the genus and species of iris flowers with three physical measurements. The dataset is a classic for nonvisual classification.

Boston Housing Prices (https://oreil.ly/RHD65)
> This dataset contains median home values with their associated attributes for solving a line of best fit (linear regression) model.

The Titanic (https://oreil.ly/RtzuS)
> This is the collected passenger log from the "unsinkable" RMS *Titanic* that sank on April 15, 1912. We will use this dataset to create a model in Chapter 9.

Wine Quality (https://oreil.ly/K1ekn)
> For brewers and crafters, the idea of using machine learning to identify what makes a tasty drink is exhilarating. This dataset contains the physicochemical properties of each wine and its score.

Pima Indians Diabetics (https://oreil.ly/AZh6O)
> Quite a few datasets are available for health care. This is a small and approachable diabetes dataset based on patient history.

CIFAR (https://oreil.ly/JgIsD)
> While ImageNet is a gold standard, it's a bit unapproachable and complicated. The CIFAR dataset is a low-resolution and friendly collection of images for classification.

Amazon Reviews (https://oreil.ly/cM80L)

This is a collection of product reviews from Amazon.com over many years. The dataset has been used to train the emotional sentiment of text, as you have the user's comments and their ratings. A close second to this would be the IMDb review dataset.

COCO (https://oreil.ly/qSn9z)

This is a large-scale object detection, segmentation, and captioning dataset.

These 10 are a good start for standard reference datasets. Machine learning enthusiasts will cite these in tweets, talks, and blog posts at will.

Chapter Review

Of course, you don't have a diverse collection of photos of volcanoes on Venus. How would you? That doesn't mean you can't take a model trained for it and move it to your new browser game. Just download the dataset off Kaggle and upload the images to Teachable Machine to create a decent "Volcano or Not" astronomy model. The same way TensorFlow.js launches you into machine learning orbit, these existing models and datasets build a foundation for your application mastery.

Like web development, machine learning contains a variety of specializations. Machine learning relies on a variety of skills across data, models, training, and tensors.

Chapter Challenge: R.I.P. You Will Be MNIST

It's your turn to take a model from Keras HDF5 to TensorFlow.js. In the code associated with this book, you'll find a *mnist.h5* file, which contains the model for identifying handwritten digits.

1. Create a Graph TensorFlow.js model.
2. Quantize the model with `uint8` to make it small.
3. Use the wild card to access all weights in the model.
4. Set the shard size to 12,000.
5. Save to a folder *./minist* (*min* because it was quantized, get it!?).

Answer these questions:

1. How many bin files and groups were generated?
2. What was the final output size?
3. If you used the default shard size, how many bin files would have been made?

You can find the answer to this challenge in Appendix B.

Review Questions

Let's review the lessons you've learned from the code you've written in this chapter. Take a moment to answer the following questions:

1. If you're given gigs of data for a specific task, what are some concerns and thoughts you would have before training?
2. If a model is trained and gets 99% accuracy, but then when you use it in the field, it does terribly, what would you say happened?
3. What is the name of the website Google created to help you train your own model?
4. What is the drawback to using Google's website?
5. What is the image dataset used to train MobileNet and other popular machine learning models?

Solutions to these exercises are available in Appendix A.

Up Next...

In Chapter 8 you'll learn to start building your own models. Creating models from scratch is critical for teaching AI to handle new challenges. Finally, you can enjoy the world of training. Though this can get complicated quickly, you'll have a hands-on approach to make the adventure a success.

CHAPTER 8

Training Models

"Ask not for a lighter burden, but for broader shoulders."

—Jewish proverb

While the supply of impressive models and data will continue to grow and overflow, it's reasonable that you'll want to do more than just consume TensorFlow.js models. You'll come up with the idea that's never been done before, and there won't be an off-the-shelf option that day. It's time for you to train your own model.

Yes, this is the task where the best minds in the world compete. While libraries could be written about the math, strategy, and methodology of training models, a core understanding will be vital. It's crucial that you become familiar with the basic concepts and benefits of training a model with TensorFlow.js to take full advantage of the framework.

We will:

- Train your first model in JavaScript code
- Advance your understanding of model architecture
- Review how to keep track of status during training
- Cover some fundamental concepts of training

When you finish this chapter, you'll be armed with a few ways of training a model and a better understanding of the process of using data to make a machine learning solution.

Training 101

It's time to peel back the magic and train a model with JavaScript. While Teachable Machine is a great tool, it's limited. To really empower machine learning, you're going to have to identify the problem you want to solve and then teach a machine to find the patterns for a solution. To do this, we'll view a problem through the eyes of data.

Take a look at this example of information, and before writing a line of code, see if you can identify the correlation between these numbers. You have a function f that takes a single number and returns a single number. Here's the data:

- Given –1, the result is –4.
- Given 0, the result is –2.
- Given 1, the result is 0.
- Given 2, the result is 2.
- Given 3, the result is 4.
- Given 4, the result is 6.

Can you identify what the answer for 5 would be? Can you extrapolate the solution for 10? Take a moment to evaluate the data before moving on. Some of you might have found the solution: Answer = 2x – 2.

The function f is a simple line, as shown in Figure 8-1. Knowing that, you can quickly solve for an input of 10 and find it would yield 18.

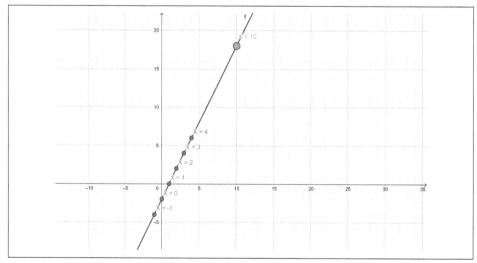

Figure 8-1. X = 10 means Y = 18

Solving this problem from the given data is exactly what machine learning can do. Let's prep and train a TensorFlow.js model to solve this simple problem.

To apply supervised learning, you'll need to do the following:

1. Gather your data (both input and desired solution).
2. Create and design a model architecture.
3. Identify how a model should learn and measure error.
4. Task the model with training and for how long.

Data Prep

To prep a machine, you'll write the code to supply the input tensors, aka the values $[-1, 0, 1, 2, 3, 4]$ and their corresponding answers $[-4, -2, 0, 2, 4, 6]$. The index of the question has to match the index of the expected answer, which makes sense when you think about it. Since we are giving the model all the answers to the values, that is what makes this a supervised learning problem.

In this situation, the training set is six examples. Rarely would machine learning be used on such a small amount of data, but the problem is relatively small and straightforward. As you can see, none of the training data has been reserved for testing the model. Fortunately, you can try the model because you know the formula that was used to create the data in the first place. If you're unfamiliar with the definitions of training and testing datasets, please review "Common AI/ML Terminology" on page 20 in Chapter 1.

Design a Model

The idea of designing a model might sound tedious, but the honest answer is that it's a mix of theory, trial, and error. Models can be trained for hours or even weeks before the designers of that model understand the performance of the architecture. An entire field of study could be dedicated to model design. The Layers models you'll be creating for this book will give you an excellent foundation.

The easiest way to design a model is to use the TensorFlow.js Layers API, which is a high-level API that allows you to define each layer in sequential order. In fact, to start your model, you'll begin with the code `tf.sequential();`. You might hear this called the "Keras API" due to the origin of this style of model definition.

The model you'll create to solve the simple problem you are trying to tackle will have only a single layer and a single neuron. This makes sense when you think about the formula for a line; it's not a very complex equation.

When you're familiar with the basic equations of a dense network, it becomes amazingly apparent why a single neuron would work in this case, because the formula for a line is y = mx + b and the formula for an artificial neuron is y = Wx + b.

To add a layer to the model, you will use `model.add` and then define your layer. With the Layers API, each layer that gets added defines itself and automatically gets connected depending on the order of `model.add` calls, just like pushing to an array. You'll define the expected input for your model in the first layer, and the final layer that you add will define the output of your model (see Example 8-1).

Example 8-1. Building a hypothetical model

```
model.add(ALayer)
model.add(BLayer)
model.add(CLayer)

// Currently, model is [ALayer, BLayer, CLayer]
```

The model in Example 8-1 would have three layers. `ALayer` would be tasked with identifying the expected model input and itself. `BLayer` doesn't need to identify its input because it is inferred that the input would be `ALayer`. Therefore, `BLayer` only needs to define itself. `CLayer` would identify itself, and because it is last, this identifies the model's output.

Let's get back to the model you're trying to code. The architected model goal for the current problem has only one layer with one neuron. When you code that single layer, you'll be defining your input and your output.

```
// The entire inner workings of the model
model.add(
  tf.layers.dense({
    inputShape: 1, // one value 1D tensor
    units: 1 // one neuron - output tensor
  })
);
```

The result is a straightforward neural network. When graphed, the network has two nodes (see Figure 8-2).

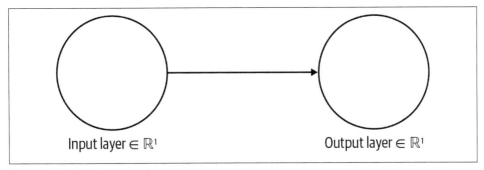

Figure 8-2. One input and one output

Generally, layers have more artificial neurons (graph nodes) but also are more complicated and have other properties to configure.

Identify Learning Metrics

Next, you'll need to tell your model how to identify progress and how it can be better. These concepts aren't foreign; they just seem strange in software.

Every time I try to aim a laser pointer at something, I generally miss it. However, I can see I'm a bit off to the left or right, and I adjust. Machine learning does the same thing. It might start randomly, but the algorithm corrects itself, and it needs to know how you want it to do that. A method that most fits my laser pointer example would be *gradient descent*. The smoothest iterative way to optimize the laser pointer is a method called *stochastic gradient descent*. That's what we'll use in this case because it works well, and it sounds pretty cool for your next dinner party.

As for measuring error, you might think a simple "right" and "wrong" would work, but there's a significant difference between being a couple of decimals off versus being wrong by thousands. For this reason, you generally rely on a loss function to help you identify how wrong an AI is with a predicted guess. There are lots of ways to measure error, but in this case, mean squared error (MSE) is a great measurement. For those who need to know the mathematics, MSE is the average squared difference between the estimated values (y) and the actual value (y with a little hat). Feel free to ignore this next bit, as the framework is calculating it for you, but if you're familiar with common mathematical notation, this can be represented like so:

$$\text{MSE} = \frac{1}{n}\Sigma_{i=1}^{n}\left(Y_i - \widehat{Y}_i\right)^2$$

Why would you like this formula over something simple like distance from the original answer? There are some mathematical benefits baked into MSE that help incorporate variance and bias as positive error scores. Without getting too deep into statistics, it's one of the most common loss functions for solving for lines that fit data.

 Stochastic gradient descent and mean squared error reek of mathematical origins that do little to tell a pragmatic developer their purpose. In situations like these, it's best to absorb these terms for what they are, and if you're feeling adventurous, you can watch tons of videos that will explain them in greater detail.

When you are ready to tell a model to use specific learning metrics and you're done adding layers to a model, this is all wrapped up in a `.compile` call. TensorFlow.js is cool enough to know all about gradient descent and mean squared error. Rather than coding these functions, you can identify them with their approved string equivalents:

```
model.compile({
  optimizer: "sgd",
  loss: "meanSquaredError"
});
```

One of the great benefits to using a framework is that as the machine learning world invents new optimizers like "Adagrad" and "Adamax," they can be tried and invoked by simply changing a string[1] in your model architecture. Switching "sgd" to "adamax" (*https://arxiv.org/abs/1412.6980*) takes relatively no time for you as a developer, and it might significantly improve your model training time without you reading the published paper on stochastic optimization.

Identifying functions without understanding the specifics of a function provides a bittersweet benefit similar to changing file types without having to understand the full structure of each type. A little bit of knowledge of the pros and cons for each goes a long way, but you don't need to memorize the specification. It's worth taking a little time when you're architecting to read up on what's available.

Don't worry. You will see the same names being used over and over, so it's easy to get the hang of them.

At this point, the model is created. It will fail if you ask it to predict anything because it has done zero training. The weights in the architecture are entirely random, but you can review the layers by calling `model.summary()`. The output goes directly to the console and looks somewhat like Example 8-2.

---

1 Supported optimizers are listed in tfjs-core's optimizers folder (*https://oreil.ly/vnmcI*).

Example 8-2. Calling `model.summary()` on a Layers model prints the layers

```
Layer (type)                 Output shape            Param #
=================================================================
dense_Dense6 (Dense)         [null,1]                  2
=================================================================
Total params: 2
Trainable params: 2
Non-trainable params: 0
```

The layer `dense_Dense6` is an automatic ID to reference this layer in the Tensor-Flow.js backend. Your ID can vary. This model has two trainable parameters, which makes sense since a line is y = mx + b, right? A fun way to think of this visually is to look back to Figure 8-2 and count the lines and nodes. One line and one node means two trainable params. All parameters for the layer are trainable. We'll cover non-trainable params later. This one-layer model is ready to go.

Task the Model with Training

The final step for training a model is to combine the inputs into the architecture and assign how long it should train. As mentioned earlier, this is often measured in epochs, which is how many times the model will review the flashcards with the right answers, and then when it's complete, it stops training. The number of epochs you should use depends on the magnitude of the problem, the model, and how correct is "good enough." In some models, getting another half of a percent is worth hours of training, and in our case, the model is accurate enough to be correct within seconds.

The training set is a 1D tensor with six values. If the epochs were set to 1,000, the model would effectively train 6,000 iterations, which would take any modern computer a few seconds at most. The trivial problem of fitting a line to points is quite simple for a computer.

Put It All Together

Now that you're familiar with the high-level concepts, you're probably eager to solve this problem with code. Here's the code to train a model on the data and then immediately ask the model for an answer for the value 10, as discussed.

```
// Inputs
const xs = tf.tensor([-1, 0, 1, 2, 3, 4]); ❶
// Answers we want from inputs
const ys = tf.tensor([-4, -2, 0, 2, 4, 6]);

// Create a model
const model = tf.sequential(); ❷
```

```
model.add( ❸
  tf.layers.dense({
    inputShape: 1,
    units: 1
  })
);

model.compile({ ❹
  optimizer: "sgd",
  loss: "meanSquaredError"
});

// Print out the model structure
model.summary();

// Train
model.fit(xs, ys, { epochs: 300 }).then(history => { ❺
  const inputTensor = tf.tensor([10]);
  const answer = model.predict(inputTensor); ❻
  console.log(`10 results in ${Math.round(answer.dataSync())}`);
  // cleanup
  tf.dispose([xs, ys, model, answer, inputTensor]); ❼
});
```

❶ The data is prepared in tensors with inputs and expected outputs.

❷ A sequential model is started.

❸ Add the only layer with one input and one output, as discussed.

❹ Finish the sequential model with a given optimizer and loss function.

❺ The model is told to train with `fit` for 300 epochs. This is a trivial amount of time, and when the `fit` is complete, the promise it returns is resolved.

❻ Ask the trained model to provide an answer for the input tensor 10. You'll need to round the answer to force an integer result.

❼ Dispose of everything once you've got your answer.

Congratulations! You've trained a model from scratch in code. The problem you've just solved is called a *linear regression* problem. It has all kinds of uses, and it's a common tool for predicting things such as housing prices, consumer behavior, sales forecasts, and plenty more. Generally, points don't perfectly land on a line in the real world, but now you have the ability to turn scattered linear data into a predictive model. So when your data looks like Figure 8-3, you can solve as shown in Figure 8-4.

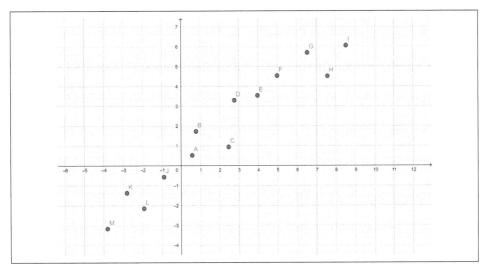

Figure 8-3. Scattered linear data

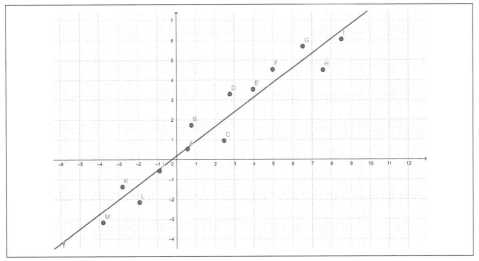

Figure 8-4. Predicted line of best fit using TensorFlow.js

Now that you're familiar with the basics of training, you can expand your process to understanding what it takes to solve more complex models. Training a model is significantly dependent on the architecture and the quality and quantity of the data.

Nonlinear Training 101

If every problem were based on lines, there would be no need for machine learning. Statisticians have been solving linear regression since the early 1800s. Unfortunately, this fails as soon as your data is nonlinear. What would happen if you asked the AI to solve for $Y = X^2$?

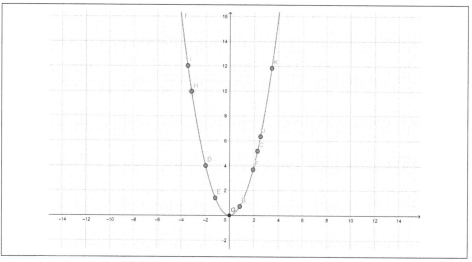

Figure 8-5. Simple $Y = X^2$

More complex problems require more complex model architecture. In this section, you'll learn new properties and features of a layers-based model, as well as tackle a nonlinear grouping of data.

You can add far more nodes to a neural network, but they would all still exist in a grouping of linear functions. To break linearity, it's time to add *activation functions*.

Activation functions work similarly to neurons in the brain. Yes, this analogy again. When a neuron electrochemically receives a signal, it doesn't always activate. There's a threshold needed before a neuron fires its action potential. Similarly, neural networks have a degree of bias and similar on/off action potentials that occur when they reach their threshold due to incoming signals (similar to depolarizing current). Succinctly put, activation functions make neural networks capable of nonlinear predictions.[2]

---

2 Learn more about activation functions (*https://youtu.be/Xvg00QnyaIY*) from Andrew Ng.

There are smarter ways to solve quadratic functions if you know that you want your solution to be quadratic. The way you will solve for X^2 in this section is orchestrated explicitly for learning more about TensorFlow.js, rather than solving for simple mathematical functions.

Yes, this exercise could be solved easily without using AI, but what fun would that be?

Gathering the Data

Exponential functions can return some pretty large numbers, and one of the tricks to speed up model training is to keep numbers and their distance between each other small. You'll see this time and time again. For our purposes, the training data for the model will be numbers between 0 and 10.

```
const jsxs = [];
const jsys = [];

const dataSize = 10;
const stepSize = 0.001;
for (let i = 0; i < dataSize; i = i + stepSize) {
  jsxs.push(i);
  jsys.push(i * i);
}
// Inputs
const xs = tf.tensor(jsxs);
// Answers we want from inputs
const ys = tf.tensor(jsys);
```

This code prepares two tensors. The xs tensor is a grouping of 10,000 values, and ys is the square of these.

Adding Activations to Neurons

Choosing your activation functions for the neurons in a given layer, and your model size, is a science in itself. It depends on your goals, your data, and your knowledge. Just like with code, you can come up with several solutions that all work nearly as well as another. It's experience and practice that help you find solutions that fit.

When adding activation, it's important to note there are quite a few activation functions built into TensorFlow.js. One of the most popular activation functions is called ReLU, which stands for Rectified Linear Unit. As you might have gathered from the name, it comes from the heart of scientific terminology rather than witty NPM package names. There is all kinds of literature on the benefits of using ReLU over various other activation functions for some models. You must know ReLU is a popular choice for an activation function, and you're likely to be just fine starting with it. You should feel free to experiment with other activation functions as you learn more about model architecture. ReLU helps models train faster, compared to many alternatives.

In the last model, you had only a single node and an output. Now it's important to grow the size of the network. There's no formula for what size to use, so the first phase of each problem usually takes a bit of experimenting. For our purposes, we'll increase the model with one dense layer of 20 neurons. A dense layer means that every node in that layer is connected to each node in the layers before and after it. The resulting model looks like Figure 8-6.

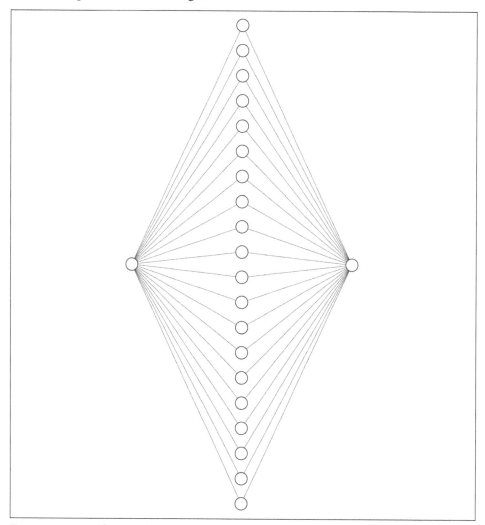

Figure 8-6. Neural network architecture (20 neurons)

To tour the architecture displayed in Figure 8-6 from left to right, one number enters the network, the 20-neuron layer is called a *hidden* layer, and the resulting value is output in the final layer. Hidden layers are the layers between the input and output. These hidden layers add trainable neurons and make the model able to process more complex patterns.

To add this layer and provide it with an activation function, you'll specify a new dense layer in the sequence:

```
model.add(
  tf.layers.dense({
    inputShape: 1, ❶
    units: 20, ❷
    activation: "relu" ❸
  })
);

model.add(
  tf.layers.dense({
    units: 1 ❹
  })
);
```

❶ The first layer defines the input tensor as a single number.

❷ Specify the layer should be 20 nodes.

❸ Specify a fancy activation function for your layer.

❹ Add the final single-unit layer for the output value.

If you compile the model and print the summary, you'll see output similar to Example 8-3.

Example 8-3. Calling `model.summary()` *for the current structure*

Layer (type)	Output shape	Param #
dense_Dense1 (Dense)	[null,20]	40
dense_Dense2 (Dense)	[null,1]	21

```
Total params: 61
Trainable params: 61
Non-trainable params: 0
```

This model architecture has two layers that match the previous layer-creation code. The `null` sections represent the batch size, and since that can be any number, it is left blank. For example, the first layer is represented as [`null,20`], so a batch of four values would give the model the input of [`4, 20`].

You'll notice the model has a total of 61 tunable parameters. If you review the diagram in Figure 8-6, you can do the lines and nodes to get the parameters. The first layer has 20 nodes and 20 lines to them, which is why it has 40 parameters. The second layer has 20 lines all going to a single node, which is why that has only 21 parameters. Your model is ready to train, but it's significantly bigger this time.

If you make these changes and kick off training, you'll likely hear your CPU/GPU fan spin up and see a bunch of nothing. It sounds like the computer might be training, but it sure would be nice to see some kind of progress.

Watching Training

TensorFlow.js has all kinds of amazing tools for helping you identify progress on training. Most particularly, there is a property of the `fit` configuration called `call backs`. Inside the `callbacks` object, you can tie in with certain life cycles of the training model and run whatever code you'd like.

As you're already familiar with an epoch (one full run through the training data), that's the moment you'll use in this example. Here's a terse but effective method for getting some kind of console messaging.

```
const printCallback = {  ❶
  onEpochEnd: (epoch, log) => {  ❷
    console.log(epoch, log);  ❸
  }
};
```

❶ Create the callback object that contains all the life cycle methods you'd like to tie into.

❷ onEpochEnd is one of the many identified life cycle callbacks that training supports. The others are enumerated in the `fit` section of the framework (*https://oreil.ly/NoVqS*) documentation.

❸ Print the values for review. Normally, you would do something more involved with this information.

An epoch can be redefined by setting the `stepsPerEpoch` number in the `fit` config. Using this variable, an epoch can become any number of training data. By default, this is set to `null`, and therefore an epoch is set to the quantity of unique samples in your training set divided by the batch size.

All that's left to do is pass your object to the model's `fit` configuration alongside your epochs, and you should see logs while your model is training.

```
await model.fit(xs, ys, {
  epochs: 100,
  callbacks: printCallback
});
```

The `onEpochEnd` callbacks print to your console, showing that the training is working. In Figure 8-7, you can see your epoch and your log object.

```
19 ▸ {loss: 889.5817260742188}                index.js:27
20 ▸ {loss: 888.999267578125}                 index.js:27
21 ▸ {loss: 889.4457397460938}                index.js:27
22 ▸ {loss: 889.3861694335938}                index.js:27
23 ▸ {loss: 889.4838256835938}                index.js:27
24 ▸ {loss: 889.5303344726562}                index.js:27
25 ▸ {loss: 889.5726318359375}                index.js:27
26 ▸ {loss: 889.41943359375}                   index.js:27
```

Figure 8-7. The onEpochEnd log for epochs 19 through 26

It's a breath of fresh air to be able to see the model is actually training and to even tell what epoch it's on. But, what's going on with the log values?

Model logs

A model is told how to define loss with a loss function. What you want to see in each epoch is that the loss goes down. The loss is not only "is this right or wrong?" It's about how wrong the model was so that it can learn. After each epoch, the model is reporting the loss, and in a good model architecture, this number goes down quickly.

You're probably interested in seeing the accuracy. Most of the time, accuracy is a great metric, and we could enable accuracy in the logs. However, for a model like this, accuracy isn't a very good fit as a metric. For instance, if you asked the model what the predicted output for [7] should be and the model answers `49.0676842` instead of 49, its accuracy is zero because it was incorrect. While the close result would have a low loss and would be accurate *after* rounding, it's technically wrong, and the accuracy score of the model would be poor. Let's enable accuracy later when it works more effectively.

Improving Training

The loss values are pretty high. What is a high loss value? Concretely, it depends on the problem. However, when you see 800+ in error values, it's generally safe to say it's not done training.

Adam optimizer

Fortunately, you don't have to leave your computer training for weeks. Currently, the optimizer is set to the defaults of stochastic gradient descent (sgd). You can modify the sgd presets or even choose a different optimizer. One of the most popular optimizers is called Adam. If you're interested in trying Adam, you don't have to read the paper on Adam published in 2015 (*https://arxiv.org/pdf/1412.6980.pdf*); you simply need to change the value of sgd to adam, and now you're good to go. This is where you can enjoy the benefit of a framework. Simply by changing a small string, your entire model architecture has changed. Adam has significant benefits for solving certain types of problems.

The updated compile code looks like this:

```
model.compile({
  optimizer: "adam",
  loss: "meanSquaredError"
});
```

With the new optimizer, the loss drops below 800 within a few epochs, and it even drops below one, as you can see in Figure 8-8.

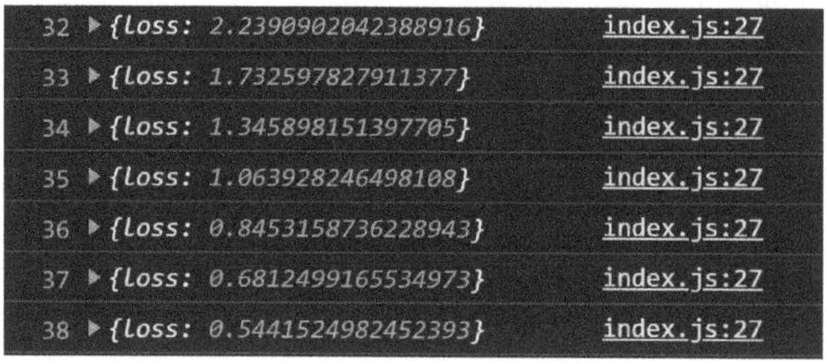

```
32 ▸ {loss: 2.2390902042388916}              index.js:27
33 ▸ {loss: 1.732597827911377}               index.js:27
34 ▸ {loss: 1.345898151397705}               index.js:27
35 ▸ {loss: 1.063928246498108}               index.js:27
36 ▸ {loss: 0.8453158736228943}              index.js:27
37 ▸ {loss: 0.6812499165534973}              index.js:27
38 ▸ {loss: 0.5441524982452393}              index.js:27
```

Figure 8-8. The onEpochEnd log for epochs 19 through 26

After 100 epochs, the model was still making progress for me but stopped at a loss value of 0.03833026438951492. This varies on each run, but as long as the loss is small, the model will work.

The practice of modifying and adjusting the model architecture to train or converge faster for a particular problem is a mix of experience and experiments.

Things are looking good, but there's one more feature we should add that sometimes cuts training time down significantly. On a pretty decent machine, these 100 epochs take around 100 seconds to run. You can speed up your training by batching data with a single line. When you assign the `batchSize` property to the `fit` configuration, training gets substantially faster. Try adding a batch size to your fit call:

```
await model.fit(xs, ys, {
  epochs: 100,
  callbacks: printCallback,
  batchSize: 64  ❶
});
```

❶ This `batchSize` of 64 cut training from 100 seconds to 50 for my machine.

 Batch sizes are trade-offs of efficiency for memory. If the batch is too large, this will limit which machines are capable of running the training.

You have a model that trains within a reasonable time for next to no cost on size. However, increasing the batch size is an option you can and should review.

More nodes and layers

This whole time the model has been the same shape and size: one "hidden" layer of 20 nodes. Don't forget, you can always add more layers. As an experiment, add another layer of 20 nodes, so your model architecture looks like Figure 8-9.

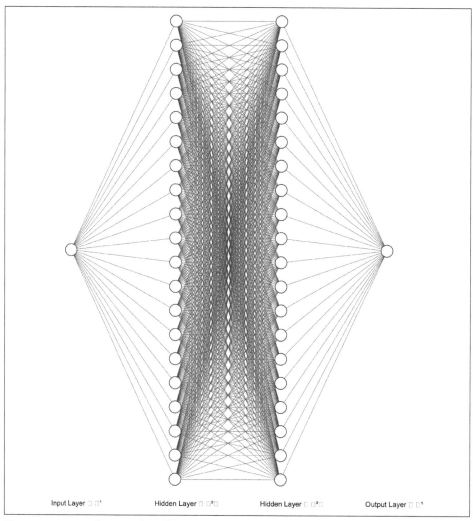

Input Layer □ □¹   Hidden Layer □ □²□   Hidden Layer □ □²□   Output Layer □ □¹

Figure 8-9. Neural network architecture (20 × 20 hidden nodes)

With the Layers model architecture, you can build this model by adding a new layer. See the following code:

```
model.add(
  tf.layers.dense({
    inputShape: 1,
    units: 20,
    activation: "relu"
  })
);

model.add(
```

```
  tf.layers.dense({
    units: 20,
    activation: "relu"
  })
);

model.add(
  tf.layers.dense({
    units: 1
  })
);
```

The resulting model trains slower, which makes sense, but also converges faster, which also makes sense. This bigger model generates the correct value for the input [7] with only 30 epochs in a training time of 20 seconds.

Putting it all together, your resulting code does the following:

- Creates a significant dataset
- Creates several deeply connected layers that utilize ReLU activation
- Sets the model to use advanced Adam optimization
- Trains the model using the data in 64-chunk batches and prints progress along the way

The entire source code from start to finish looks like this:

```
const jsxs = [];((("improving training", "adding more neurons and layers")))
const jsys = [];

// Create the dataset
const dataSize = 10;
const stepSize = 0.001;
for (let i = 0; i < dataSize; i = i + stepSize) {
  jsxs.push(i);
  jsys.push(i * i);
}
// Inputs
const xs = tf.tensor(jsxs);
// Answers we want from inputs
const ys = tf.tensor(jsys);


// Print the progress on each epoch
const printCallback = {
  onEpochEnd: (epoch, log) => {
    console.log(epoch, log);
  }
};

// Create the model
```

```
const model = tf.sequential();
model.add(
  tf.layers.dense({
    inputShape: 1,
    units: 20,
    activation: "relu"
  })
);
model.add(
  tf.layers.dense({
    units: 20,
    activation: "relu"
  })
);
model.add(
  tf.layers.dense({
    units: 1
  })
);

// Compile for training
model.compile({
  optimizer: "adam",
  loss: "meanSquaredError"
});

// Train and print timing
console.time("Training");
await model.fit(xs, ys, {
  epochs: 30,
  callbacks: printCallback,
  batchSize: 64
});
console.timeEnd("Training");

// evaluate the model
const next = tf.tensor([7]);
const answer = model.predict(next);
answer.print();

// Cleanup!
answer.dispose();
xs.dispose();
ys.dispose();
model.dispose();
```

The printed result tensor is exceptionally close to 49. The training works. While this has been a bit of a strange adventure, it highlighted part of the model creation and validation process. Building models is one of the skills you'll acquire over time as you experiment with various data and its associated solutions.

In subsequent chapters, you'll solve more elaborate but rewarding problems, like classification. Everything you've learned here will be a tool in your workbench.

Chapter Review

You've entered the world of training models. The layer model structure is not only an understandable visual, but now it's something you can comprehend and build on demand. Machine learning is very different from normal software development, but you're on your way to comprehending the differences and benefits afforded by TensorFlow.js.

Chapter Challenge: The Model Architect

Now it's your turn to build a Layers model via specification. What does this model do? No one knows! It's not going to be trained with any data at all. In this challenge, you'll be tasked to build a model with all kinds of properties you might not understand, but you should be familiar enough to at least set up the model. This model will be the biggest you've created yet. Your model will have five inputs and four outputs with two layers between them. It will look like Figure 8-10.

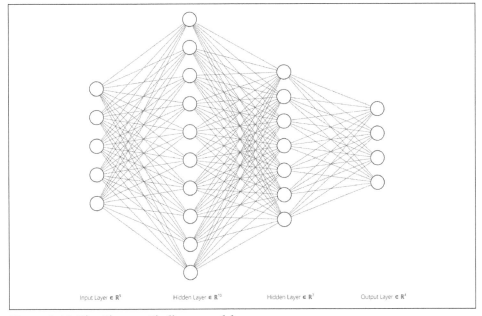

Figure 8-10. The Chapter Challenge model

Do the following in your model:

- The input layer should have 5 units.
- The next layer should have 10 units and use *sigmoid* for activation.
- The next layer should have 7 units and use ReLU activation.
- The final layer should have 4 units and use *softmax* for activation.
- The model should use Adam optimization.
- The model should use the loss function `categoricalCrossentropy`.

Before building this model and looking at the summary, can you calculate how many trainable parameters the final model will have? That's the total number of lines and circles from Figure 8-10, not counting the input.

You can find the answer to this challenge in Appendix B.

Review Questions

Let's review the lessons you've learned from the code you've written in this chapter. Take a moment to answer the following questions:

1. Why would the Chapter Challenge model *not* work with the training data from this chapter?
2. What method can you call on a model to log and review its structure?
3. Why do you add activation functions to layers?
4. How do you specify the input shape for the Layers model?
5. What does `sgd` stand for?
6. What is an epoch?
7. If a model has one input, then a layer of two nodes, and an output of two nodes, how many hidden layers are present?

Solutions to these exercises are available in Appendix A.

Up Next...

In Chapter 9 you'll use the popular *Titanic* dataset to train a model. This will be your first foray into a substantial amount of data and the process of training a model on that data.

## CHAPTER 9

Classification Models and Data Analysis

"Forethought spares afterthought."

—Amelia Barr

There's a reason you don't just dump data into a model. Neural networks operate at intense speeds and perform complex calculations the same way humans can have an instantaneous reaction. However, for both humans and machine learning models, a reaction rarely contains a reasoned context. Dealing with dirty and confusing data creates subpar models, if anything at all. In this chapter, you'll explore the process of identifying, loading, cleaning, and refining data to improve the training accuracy of a model in TensorFlow.js.

We will:

- Identify how to make a classification model
- Learn how to handle CSV data
- Learn about Danfo.js and DataFrames
- Identify how to get messy data into training (wrangle your data)
- Practice graphing and analyzing data
- Learn about machine learning notebooks
- Expose core concepts of feature engineering

When you finish this chapter, you'll feel confident in gathering large amounts of data, analyzing it, and testing your intuitions by using context to create features that help models train.

In this chapter, you'll build a *Titanic* life-or-death classifier. Will Miss Kate Connolly, a 30-year-old woman with a third-class ticket, survive? Let's train a model to take that information and give us a likelihood of survival.

Classification Models

So far, you've trained a model that outputs numbers. Most of the models you've consumed behave a bit differently from the ones you've created. In Chapter 8 you implemented linear regression, but in this chapter, you will implement a classification model (sometimes called *logistic regression*).

The Toxicity, MobileNet, and even Tic-Tac-Toe models output a single choice among a collection of options. They do so with a group of numbers that sum to one, rather than a single number that has no range. This is a common structure for classification models. A model that is made to identify three different options will give us numbers that correspond with each option.

Models that attempt to predict classifications require some kind of mapping from output values to their associated classes. This is most commonly done with outputting their probability, like you've seen in classification models so far. To create a model that does this, you only need to implement special activation functions on the final layer:

Remember that activation functions help your neural network behave in a nonlinear fashion. Each activation function causes a layer to behave nonlinearly in a desired way, and the final layer's activation translates directly to the output. It's important to make sure you learn what activation will give you the model output you're seeking.

The activation function you've seen over and over in models used in this book is called a *softmax* activation. That's the group of values that sum to one. For example, if your model would have a True/False output, you'd expect a model to output two values, with one identifying probability `true` and the other for `false`. For example, a softmax for this model could output `[0.66, 0.34]` with some rounding.

This can scale to N values for N classifications *as long as classes are mutually exclusive*. When designing the model, you would enforce softmax in the final layer, and the number of outputs would be the number of categories you're looking to support. To achieve the True or False result, your model architecture would have two outputs with a softmax activation on the final layer.

```
// Final layer softmax True/False
model.add(
  tf.layers.dense({
```

```
    units: 2,
    activation: "softmax"
  })
);
```

What if you were trying to detect several things from your input? For example, a chest X-ray could be positive for both pneumonia and emphysema. Softmax wouldn't work in that case, as the outputs have to sum to one, and confidence in one would have to fight against another. In this case, there's an activation that enforces each node to be a value between zero and one, so you can achieve probability per node. The activation is called the *sigmoid* activation. This can scale to N values for N classifications that are not exclusive. That means you could achieve a True/False model (binary classification) by having a single output with `sigmoid` where close to zero is false, and close to one is true:

```
// Final layer sigmoid True/False
model.add(
  tf.layers.dense({
    units: 1,
    activation: "sigmoid",
  })
);
```

Yes, these activation names are strange, but they aren't complicated. You could easily lose a day in a YouTube rabbit hole by researching the math behind how these activation functions work. But most importantly, understand how they are used in classification. Here in Table 9-1 you'll see some examples.

Table 9-1. Binary classification examples

Activation	Output	Analysis of results
sigmoid	[0.999999]	99% sure it is True
softmax	[0.99, 0.01]	99% sure it is True
sigmoid	[0.100000]	10% sure of True (so 90% False)
softmax	[0.10, 0.90]	90% sure it is False

The difference between when you would use `softmax` versus `sigmoid` goes away when you are handling True/False. There's no real difference in which activation you choose for your final layer because there's nothing that one could exclude. In this chapter, we'll be using sigmoid in the last layer for simplicity.

If you were trying to classify multiple things, you'd need to make an intelligent choice between `sigmoid` or `softmax`. This book will reiterate and clarify the use of these activation functions where applicable.

The Titanic

On April 15, 1912, the "unsinkable" RMS *Titanic* (see Figure 9-1) sank. This tragedy is popularized throughout history books, tales of hubris, and even a feature film starring Leonardo DiCaprio and Kate Winslet. This tragic event is awe-inspiring with a hint of morbid curiosity. If you visit the *Titanic* exhibit at the Luxor in Las Vegas, your ticket assigns you the name of a passenger, and tells you your ticket price, your cabin class, and several other things about your life. As you peruse the ship and the accommodations, you can experience it through the eyes of the person on your ticket. At the end of the exhibit, you find out if the person printed on your ticket survived.

Figure 9-1. The RMS Titanic

Was it 100% random who lived and who didn't? Anyone familiar with the history or who's watched the movie knows it was no coin flip. Maybe you can train a model to find patterns in the data. Thankfully, the guest log and the survivor list are available for us to use.

Titanic Dataset

As with most things these days, the data has been transcribed to a digital format. The *Titanic* manifest is available in comma-separated values (CSV) form. This tabular data can be read by any spreadsheet software. There are lots of copies of the *Titanic* dataset available, and they generally have the same information. The CSV files that we'll be using can be found in the associated code for this chapter in the extra folder (*https://oreil.ly/ry4Pf*).

This *Titanic* dataset contains column data shown in Table 9-2.

Table 9-2. Titanic data

Column	Definition	Legend
survival	Survived	0 = No, 1 = Yes
pclass	Ticket class	1 = 1st, 2 = 2nd, 3 = 3rd
sex	Sex	
Age	Age in years	
sibsp	Number of siblings or spouses aboard	
parch	Number of parents or children aboard	
ticket	Ticket number	
fare	Passenger fare	
cabin	Cabin number	
embarked	Port of embarkation	C = Cherbourg, Q = Queenstown, S = Southampton

So how do you get this CSV data into tensor form? One way would be to read the CSV file and convert each of the inputs into a tensor representation for training. This sounds like quite a significant task, especially when you're looking to experiment with what columns and formats would be most useful for training your model.

In the Python community, a popular way to load, modify, and train with data is to use a library called Pandas (*https://pandas.pydata.org*). This open source library is prevalent for data analysis. While this is quite useful for Python developers, there is a significant need for a similar tool in JavaScript.

Danfo.js

Danfo.js (*https://danfo.jsdata.org*) is an open source JavaScript alternative to Pandas. The API of Danfo.js is purposefully kept close to Pandas to capitalize on informational experience sharing. Even the function names in Danfo.js are `snake_case` instead of the standard JavaScript `camelCase` format. This means that you can utilize years of tutorials for Pandas in Danfo.js with minimal translation.

We'll be using Danfo.js to read the *Titanic* CSV and modify it into TensorFlow.js tensors. To get started, you will need to add Danfo.js to a project.

To install the Node version of Danfo.js, you will run the following:

```
$ npm i danfojs-node
```

You can then `require` Danfo.js if you're using simple Node.js, or you can `import` if you've configured your code to use ES6+:

```
const dfd = require("danfojs-node");
```

Danfo.js can run in the browser, too. This chapter depends on printing information more than usual, so it makes sense to utilize the full terminal window and rely on the simplicity of Node.js for access to local files.

Danfo.js is powered by TensorFlow.js behind the scenes, but it provides common data reading and processing utilities.

Preparing for the Titanic

One of the most common criticisms of machine learning is that it comes off as a golden goose. You may think the next steps are to hook a model up to the CSV files, click Train, and then take the day off to enjoy a walk in the park. While efforts are being made daily to improve automation in machine learning, data is rarely in a format that is "ready to go."

The *Titanic* data in this chapter contains alluring Train and Test CSV files. However, using Danfo.js, we'll quickly see the provided data is far from ready to be loaded into tensors. It's the goal of this chapter for you to identify data in this shape and prepare it appropriately.

Reading the CSV

The CSV file is loaded into a construct called a DataFrame. The DataFrame is like a spreadsheet with columns of potentially different types and rows of individual entries that fit those types, like a series of objects.

DataFrames have the ability to print their contents to the console, as well as plenty of other helper functions to review and edit the contents programmatically.

Let's review the following code, which reads the CSV into a DataFrame and then prints a few rows to the console:

```
const df = await dfd.read_csv("file://../../extra/titanic data/train.csv");  ❶
df.head().print();  ❷
```

❶ The read_csv method can read from a URL or a local file URI.

❷ The DataFrame can be limited to the head of five rows and then printed.

The CSV being loaded is the training data, and the print() command logs the contents of a DataFrame to the console. The results are displayed in the console, as shown in Figure 9-2.

Shape: (5,12)

	PassengerId	Survived	Pclass	Name	...	Ticket	Fare	Cabin	Embarked
0	1	0	3	Braund, Mr. O...	...	A/5 21171	7.25	NaN	S
1	2	1	1	Cumings, Mrs...	...	PC 17599	71.2833	C85	C
2	3	1	3	Heikkinen, Mi...	...	STON/O2. 3101282	7.925	NaN	S
3	4	1	1	Futrelle, Mrs...	...	113803	53.1	C123	S
4	5	0	3	Allen, Mr. Wi...	...	373450	8.05	NaN	S

Figure 9-2. Printing the CSV DataFrame head

Upon examining the content of the data, you might notice some strange entries, especially in the Cabin column, that say NaN. These represent missing data in the dataset.
This is one of the reasons you can't hook the CSV directly to a model: it's important
to identify how to handle the missing information. We'll assess this issue shortly.

Danfo.js and Pandas have many useful commands to help you familiarize yourself
with the data you've loaded. One popular method is to call .describe(), which
attempts to analyze the contents of each column as a report:

```
// Print the describe data
df.describe().print();
```

If you print the DataFrame's describe data, you'll see that the CSV you've loaded has
891 entries, as well as a printout of their max, min, median, etc., so you can validate
the information. The printed table looks like Figure 9-3.

Shape: (7,6)

	PassengerId	Survived	Pclass	SibSp	Parch	Fare
count	891	891	891	891	891	891
mean	446	0.383838	2.308643	0.523008	0.381594	32.204205
std	257.353842	0.486592	0.836071	1.102743	0.806057	49.693429
min	1	0	1	0	0	0
median	446	0	3	0	0	14.4542
max	891	1	3	8	6	512.329224
variance	66231	0.236772	0.699015	1.216043	0.649728	2469.436846

Figure 9-3. Describing the DataFrame

Some columns have been removed from Figure 9-3 because they contain non-
numeric data. This is something you will solve in Danfo.js easily.

Investigating the CSV

This CSV reflects the real world of data, where there's often missing information.
Before training, you'll need to handle this.

You can find all missing fields with `isna()`, which will return `true` or `false` for each missing field. You can then sum or count these values to get results. The following is the code that will report empty cells or properties of the dataset:

```
// Count of empty spots
empty_spots = df.isna().sum();
empty_spots.print();
// Find the average
empty_rate = empty_spots.div(df.isna().count());
empty_rate.print();
```

With the results you can see the following:

- Empty `Age` values: 177 (20%)

- Empty `Cabin` values: 687 (77%)

- Empty `Embarked` values: 2 (0.002%)

From a small glance at how much data is missing, you can see you're not getting around cleaning this data. It's going to be critical to solve the missing-values problem, removing useless columns like `PassengerId` and ultimately encoding the non-numeric columns you want to keep.

So you don't have to do it twice, you might as well combine the CSV files, clean them, and then create two new CSV files that are ready for training and testing.

Currently, these are the steps:

1. Combine the CSV files.
2. Clean the DataFrame.
3. Re-create the CSV files from the DataFrame.

Combining CSVs

To combine the CSVs, you'll create two DataFrames and then concatenate them along an axis like you would for tensors. You may feel your tensor training guiding you on the path with managing and cleaning data, and that's no mistake. While the terminology can differ slightly, the concepts and intuition you've accumulated from the previous chapters will serve you well.

```
// Load the training CSV
const df = await dfd.read_csv("file://../../extra/titanic data/train.csv");
console.log("Train Size", df.shape[0]) ❶

// Load the test CSV
const dft = await dfd.read_csv("file://../../extra/titanic data/test.csv");
console.log("Test Size", dft.shape[0]) ❷
```

```
const mega = dfd.concat({df_list: [df, dft], axis: 0})
mega.describe().print() ❸
```

❶ Prints "Train Size 891"

❷ Prints "Test Size 418"

❸ Displays a table with the count 1,309

With familiar syntax, you've loaded two CSV files and combined them into a singular DataFrame named mega, which you can now clean.

Cleaning CSVs

Here is where you'll handle blanks and identify what data is actually useful. There are three operations that you need to do to properly prepare the CSV data for training:

1. Prune the features.

2. Handle the blanks.

3. Migrate to numbers.

Pruning features means removing features that have little to no influence on the outcome of the result. For this, you can experiment, graph the data, or simply use your personal intuition. To prune the features, you can use the DataFrame's .drop function. The .drop function can remove entire columns or specified rows from a DataFrame.

For this dataset, we will be dropping the columns that have little influence, such as the passenger's name, ID, ticket, and cabin. You might argue that many of those features could be quite significant, and you'd be right. However, we'll leave you to research these features outside the confines of this book.

```
// Remove feature columns that seem less useful
const clean = mega.drop({
  columns: ["Name", "PassengerId", "Ticket", "Cabin"],
});
```

To handle blanks, you can fill or remove rows. Filling empty rows is a craft called *imputation*. While this is a great skill to read up on, it can get complicated. We'll be taking the easy road in this chapter and merely removing any row that has missing values. To remove any rows with empty data, we can use the dropna() function.

 It's critical that this is done *after* dropping columns. Otherwise, the 77% missing data from the Cabin column will destroy the dataset.

You can drop all empty rows with this code:

```
// Remove all rows that have empty spots
const onlyFull = clean.dropna();
console.log(`After mega-clean the row-count is now ${onlyFull.shape[0]}`);
```

The result of this code drops the dataset from 1,309 to 1,043 rows. Consider this an experiment in laziness.

Lastly, you are left with two columns that have strings instead of numbers (Embarked and Sex). These will need to be converted to numbers.

The Embarked values, for review, are: C = Cherbourg, Q = Queenstown, S = Southampton. There are several ways this can be encoded. One is to encode them with a numeric equivalent. Danfo.js has a LabelEncoder, which can read an entire column and then transform the values to a numeric encoded equivalent. LabelEncoder encodes labels with values between 0 and n-1 classes. To encode the Embarked column, you can use this code:

```
// Handle embarked characters - convert to numbers
const encode = new dfd.LabelEncoder();        ❶
encode.fit(onlyFull["Embarked"]);             ❷
onlyFull["Embarked"] = encode.transform(onlyFull["Embarked"].values);   ❸
onlyFull.head().print();                      ❹
```

❶ Create a new LabelEncoder instance.

❷ Fit that instance to encode the contents of the Embarked column.

❸ Transform the column to values and immediately overwrite the current column with the generated one.

❹ Print the top five rows to verify the replacement occurred.

Your intuition might be surprised with the ability to overwrite columns of a DataFrame like in step 3. This is one of the many benefits of dealing with DataFrames over tensors, even though TensorFlow.js tensors power Danfo.js behind the scenes.

Now you can do the same thing to encode the male / female strings with the same trick. (Note that we're simplifying sex to a binary for the purposes of the model and based on the data available in the passenger manifest.) Once done, your entire dataset is now numeric. If you call describe on the DataFrame, it will present all the columns, rather than just a few.

Saving new CSVs

Now that you've created a usable dataset for training, you'll need to return the two CSV files, which had a friendly test-and-train split.

You can resplit the DataFrame using Danfo.js's `.sample`. The `.sample` method randomly selects N rows from a DataFrame. From there, you can create the test set as the remaining unselected values. To remove the sampled values, you can drop rows by index rather than an entire column.

The DataFrame object has a `to_csv` converter, which optionally takes a parameter of what file to write. The `to_csv` command writes the parameter file and returns a promise, which resolves to the CSV contents. The entire code to resplit the DataFrame and write two files could go like this:

```
// 800 random to training
const newTrain = onlyFull.sample(800)
console.log(`newTrain row count: ${newTrain.shape[0]}`)
// The rest to testing (drop via row index)
const newTest = onlyFull.drop({index: newTrain.index, axis: 0})
console.log(`newTest row count: ${newTest.shape[0]}`)

// Write the CSV files
await newTrain.to_csv('../../extra/cleaned/newTrain.csv')
await newTest.to_csv('../../extra/cleaned/newTest.csv')
console.log('Files written!')
```

Now you have two files, one with 800 rows and the other with 243 for testing.

Training on Titanic Data

There's one last step you'll need to handle before training on the data, and that's the classic machine learning labeled input and expected output (X and Y, respectively). This means you'll need to separate the answers (the `Survived` column) from the other inputs. For this, you can use `iloc` to declare the index of columns to make new DataFrames.

Since the first column is the `Survived` column, you'll make your X skip that column and grab all the rest. You'll identify from index one to the end of the DataFrame. This is written as `1:`. You could write `1:9`, which would grab the same set, but the `1:` means "everything after index zero." The `iloc` index format represents the range you're selecting for your DataFrame subset.

The Y values, or *answers,* are selected by grabbing the `Survived` column. Since this is a single column, there's no need to use `iloc`. *Don't forget to do the same for the test dataset.*

Machine learning models expect tensors, and since Danfo.js is built on TensorFlow.js, it's trivial to convert a DataFrame to a tensor. When all is said and done, you can convert a DataFrame by accessing the `.tensor` property:

```
// Get cleaned data
const df = await dfd.read_csv("file://../../extra/cleaned/newTrain.csv");
```

```
console.log("Train Size", df.shape[0]);
const dft = await dfd.read_csv("file://../../extra/cleaned/newTest.csv");
console.log("Test Size", dft.shape[0]);

// Split train into X/Y
const trainX = df.iloc({ columns: [`1:`] }).tensor;
const trainY = df["Survived"].tensor;

// Split test into X/Y
const testX = dft.iloc({ columns: [`1:`] }).tensor;
const testY = dft["Survived"].tensor;
```

The values are ready to be fed into a model for training.

The model I used for this problem after very little research was a sequential Layers model with three hidden layers and an output of one tensor with sigmoid activation.

The model is composed like so:

```
model.add(
  tf.layers.dense({
    inputShape,
    units: 120,
    activation: "relu",       ❶
    kernelInitializer: "heNormal",   ❷
  })
);
model.add(tf.layers.dense({ units: 64, activation: "relu" }));
model.add(tf.layers.dense({ units: 32, activation: "relu" }));
model.add(
  tf.layers.dense({
    units: 1,
    activation: "sigmoid",    ❸
  })
);

model.compile({
  optimizer: "adam",
  loss: "binaryCrossentropy",   ❹
  metrics: ["accuracy"],        ❺
});
```

❶ Each layer is utilizing ReLU activation up until the final layer.

❷ This line tells the model to initialize weights based on an algorithm rather than simply setting the model's initial weights to complete randomness. This sometimes helps a model start much closer to the answer. It's not critical in this case, but it's a useful feature of TensorFlow.js.

❸ The final layer uses sigmoid activation to print a number between zero and one (survived or did not survive).

❹ When training a binary classifier, it's prudent to evaluate loss with a fancy named function that works with binary classification.

❺ This displays accuracy in logs, not just loss.

When you `fit` the model to the data, you can identify the testing data and get results on data the model has never seen before. This helps you stop from overfitting:

```
await model.fit(trainX, trainY, {
  batchSize: 32,
  epochs: 100,
  validationData: [testX, testY] ❶
})
```

❶ Provide the data that the model should use to validate on each epoch.

 The training configuration displayed in the previous `fit` method does not take advantage of callbacks. If you're training on `tfjs-node`, you will automatically see training results printed to the console. If you use `tfjs`, you'll need to add an `onEpochEnd` callback to print the training and validation accuracy. Examples of both are provided in the associated source code for this chapter (*https:// oreil.ly/39p7V*).

After training for 100 epochs, this model was 83% accurate with the training data and 83% accurate with the validation from the test set. Technically, the results will vary in each training, but they should be nearly the same: `acc=0.827 loss=0.404 val_acc=0.831 val_loss=0.406`.

The model has identified some patterns and beaten pure chance (50% accuracy). Lots of people stop here and celebrate creating a model that works 83% of the time with little or no effort. However, this is also a great opportunity to identify the benefits of Danfo.js and feature engineering.

Feature Engineering

If you glance around the internet, 80% is a common accuracy score for the *Titanic* dataset. We've beaten that score with no real effort. However, there's still room for improving the model, and that comes directly from improving the data.

Was throwing blank data a good choice? Are there correlations that exist that could be better emphasized? Were the patterns properly organized for the model? The better you can prechew and organize the data, the better the model will be at finding and emphasizing patterns. Lots of breakthroughs in machine learning have come from techniques that simplify patterns before they are passed to the neural network.

This is where the "just dump the data" flatlines, and feature engineering grows. Danfo.js lets you level up your features by analyzing patterns and emphasizing key features. You can do this in your interactive Node.js read evaluate print loop (REPL), or you can even utilize web pages that have been constructed for evaluation and feedback loops.

Let's try to improve the model above 83% by determining and adding features to the data using a Danfo.js Notebook, called Dnotebook.

Dnotebook

A Danfo Notebook, or Dnotebook (*https://dnotebook.jsdata.org*), is an interactive web page for experimenting, prototyping, and customizing data with Danfo.js. The Python equivalent is called a Jupyter Notebook. The data science you can achieve with this notebook will significantly help your models.

We'll be using a Dnotebook to create and share live code, as well as take advantage of the built-in charting capabilities to find critical features and correlations in the *Titanic* dataset.

Install Dnotebook by creating a global command:

```
$ npm install -g dnotebook
```

When you run $ dnotebook, you'll automatically run a local server and open a page to the local notebook site, which looks a bit like Figure 9-4.

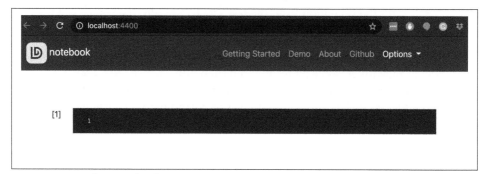

Figure 9-4. Fresh Dnotebook running

Each Dnotebook cell can be code or text. The text is Markdown-formatted. The code can print output, and variables that are initialized with no const or let can survive across cells. See the example illustrated in Figure 9-5.

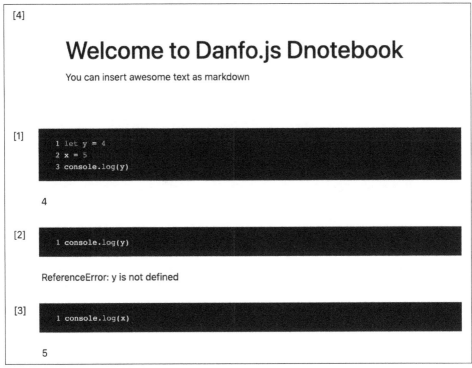

[4]

Welcome to Danfo.js Dnotebook

You can insert awesome text as markdown

[1]

```
1 let y = 4
2 x = 5
3 console.log(y)
```

4

[2]

```
1 console.log(y)
```

ReferenceError: y is not defined

[3]

```
1 console.log(x)
```

5

Figure 9-5. Using Dnotebook cells

The notebook in Figure 9-5 can be downloaded and loaded from the *explaining_vars.json* file in this chapter's *extra/dnotebooks* (*https://oreil.ly/pPvQu*) folder. This makes it friendly for experimenting, saving, and sharing.

Titanic Visuals

If you can find correlations in the data, you can emphasize them as additional features in the training data and ideally improve the model's accuracy. Using the Dnotebook, you can visualize your data and add comments along the way. This is an excellent resource for analyzing the dataset. We'll load the two CSV files and combine them, and then we'll print the results directly in the notebook.

You can create your own notebook, or you can load the JSON for the displayed notebook from the associated source code. Any method is fine as long as you're able to follow along with what is displayed in Figure 9-6.

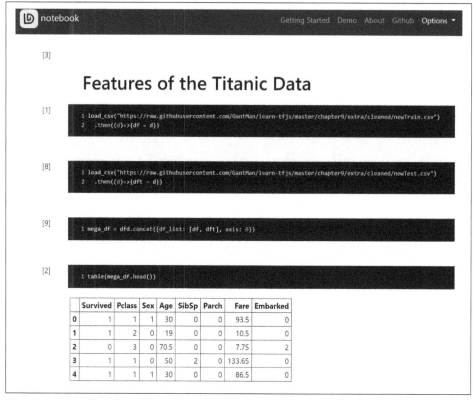

Figure 9-6. Loading the CSVs and combining them in the Dnotebook

The `load_csv` command is similar to the `read_csv` command, but it shows a friendly spinner in the web page while loading the CSV content. You may also notice the use of a `table` command. The `table` command is similar to the DataFrame's `print()` except that it generates an HTML table of the output for the notebook, as you see in Figure 9-6.

Now that you have the data, let's look for essential distinctions that we can emphasize for our model. In the movie *Titanic*, they were shouting "Women and children first" when loading the lifeboats. Was that what really happened? One idea is to check the survival rate of men versus women. You can do this by using `groupby`. And then you can print the average (mean) of each group.

```
grp = mega_df.groupby(['Sex'])
table(grp.col(['Survived']).mean())
```

And *voila!* You can see that 83% of females survived, whereas only 14% of males survived, as illustrated in Figure 9-7.

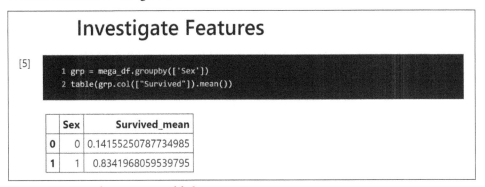

Figure 9-7. Females were more likely to survive

You might wonder if there were perhaps just more females aboard the *Titanic* and whether that accounts for the skewed results, so you can quickly check that using count() instead of using mean() like you did a moment ago:

```
survival_count = grp.col(['Survived']).count()
table(survival_count)
```

By the printed results, you can see there were far more men who survived despite the survival ratio leaning toward female. This means sex was an excellent indicator of chance of survival, so it would be a good feature to emphasize.

The real advantage of using Dnotebook is that it leverages Danfo.js charts. For instance, what if we'd like to see a histogram of the survivors? Rather than grouping users, you can query for all survivors and then plot the results.

To query for survivors, you can use the DataFrame's query method:

```
survivors = mega_df.query({column: "Survived", is: "==", to: 1 })
```

Then, to print a chart in Dnotebooks, you can use the built-in viz command, which requires an ID and callback for populating the generated DIV in the notebook.

The histogram can be created with the following:

```
viz(`agehist`, x => survivors["Age"].plot(x).hist())
```

The notebook will then display the resulting graph, as shown in Figure 9-8.

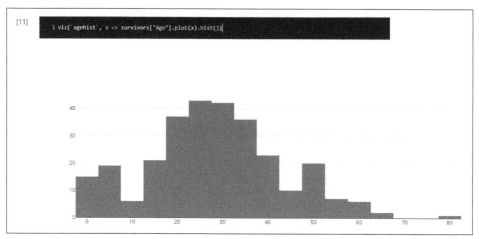

```
[11]     1 viz(`agehist`, x => survivors["Age"].plot(x).hist())
```

Figure 9-8. Survivor age histogram

Here you can see significant survival rates of children over the elderly. Again, it might be worth determining the quantities and percentages of each, but it appears that specific buckets or bins of age groups fared better than others. This gives us a second way to possibly improve our model.

Let's use the information we now have and take another shot at beating our record of 83% accuracy.

Creating Features (aka Preprocessing)

Growing up, I was told the more neurons you can activate for a memory, the stronger that memory will be, so remember the smell, the colors, and the facts together. Let's see if the same goes for neural networks. We'll move passenger sex to two inputs, and we'll create a grouping of ages often called *bucketing* or *binning*.

The first thing we'll do is move sex from one column to two columns. This is often called *one-hot encoding*. Currently, the Sex has a numeric encoding. A one-hot encoded version of the sex of a passenger would convert 0 to [1, 0] and 1 to [0, 1], successfully moving the value to two columns/units. Once converted, you remove the Sex column and insert two columns that look like Figure 9-9.

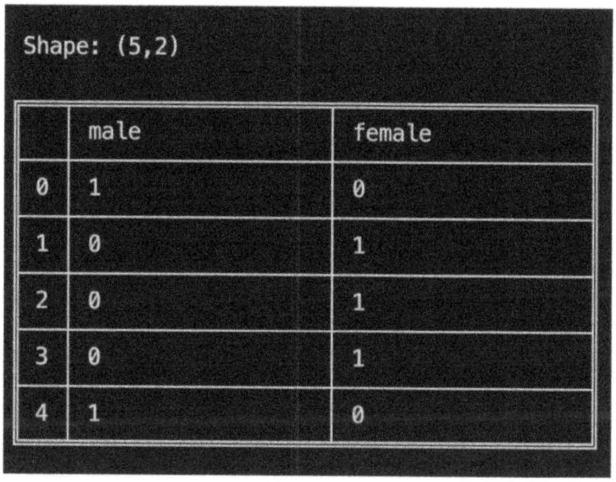

```
Shape: (5,2)
```

	male	female
0	1	0
1	0	1
2	0	1
3	0	1
4	1	0

Figure 9-9. Describing sex one-hot encoded

To one-hot encode, Danfo.js and Pandas have a `get_dummies` method that turns one column into several where only one of them has the value of 1. In TensorFlow.js, the method for one-hot encoding is called `oneHot`, but here in Danfo.js, `get_dummies` is paying homage to the binary variables, which are often called *dummy variables* in statistics. Once you have the result encoded, you then use `drop` and `addColumn` to do the switch:

```
// Handle person sex - convert to one-hot
const sexOneHot = dfd.get_dummies(mega['Sex']) ❶
sexOneHot.head().print()
// Swap one column for two
mega.drop({ columns: ['Sex'], axis: 1, inplace: true }) ❷
mega.addColumn({ column: 'male', value: sexOneHot['0'] }) ❸
mega.addColumn({ column: 'female', value: sexOneHot['1'] })
```

❶ Using `get_dummies` to encode the column

❷ Using an `inplace` drop on the `Sex` column

❸ Adding the new column, switching title to male/female

Next, you can create buckets for ages using the `apply` method. The `apply` method lets you run conditional code on the entire column. For our needs, we'll define a function of significant age groups we saw in our charts, like so:

```
// Group children, young, and over 40yrs
function ageToBucket(x) {
  if (x < 10) {
    return 0
  } else if (x < 40) {
```

```
      return 1
    } else {
      return 2
    }
  }
}
```

Then you can create and add a whole new column for these buckets using the `ageTo Bucket` function you defined:

```
// Create Age buckets
ageBuckets = mega['Age'].apply(ageToBucket)
mega.addColumn({ column: 'Age_bucket', value: ageBuckets })
```

This adds a whole column of values ranging from zero to two.

Lastly, we can normalize our data to be numbers between zero and one. Scaling the values normalizes the differences between values so the model can identify patterns and scale differences that were warped in the original numbers.

 Think of normalization as a feature. If you were working with 10 different currencies from various countries, it could be confusing to comprehend. Normalizing scales inputs so they all have relative magnitudes of influence.

```
const scaler = new dfd.MinMaxScaler()
scaledData = scaler.fit(featuredData)
scaledData.head().print()
```

From here, you can write out two CSV files for training and get started! Another option is that you could write a single CSV file, and rather than setting `validation Data` with specific X and Y values, you can set a property called `validationSplit`, which will break off a percentage of the data for validation. This saves us a bit of time and headache, so let's train the model using `validationSplit` instead of explicitly passing in `validationData`.

The resulting `fit` looks like this:

```
await model.fit(trainX, trainY, {
  batchSize: 32,
  epochs: 100,
  // Keep random 20% for validation on the fly.
  // The 20% is selected at the beginning of the training session.
  validationSplit: 0.2,
})
```

The model trains with the new data for 100 epochs, and if you're using `tfjs-node`, you can see the results printed even though there's no callback defined.

Feature Engineered Training Results

Last time, the model accuracy revolved around 83%. Now, using the same model structure but adding a few features, we reached 87% for training accuracy and 87% for validation accuracy. Specifically, my results were `acc=0.867 loss=0.304 val_acc=0.871 val_loss=0.370`.

The accuracy increased, and the loss values are lower than before. What's really great is that both the accuracy and the validation accuracy are aligned, so it is unlikely that the model is overfitting. This is generally one of the better *Titanic* dataset scores for a neural network. For such a strange problem, creating a fairly accurate model has served the purpose of explaining what it's like to pull useful information out of data.

Reviewing Results

Solving the *Titanic* problem to achieve 87% accuracy took some finesse. You might still be wondering if the result could be improved, and the answer is most assuredly "yes" because others have posted more impressive scores to leaderboards. In situations without leaderboards, a common method for evaluating if there's room for growth is to compare against what an educated human could score if given the same problem.

If you're a high-score junkie, the Chapter Challenge will be useful in improving the already impressive model we've created. Be sure to practice engineering features rather than overtraining and thus overfitting the model to essentially memorize the answers.

Finding important values, normalizing features, and emphasizing significant correlations is a useful skill in machine learning training, and now you can do so with Danfo.js.

Chapter Review

So what happened to the individual we identified at the start of this chapter? Miss Kate Connolly, a 30-year-old woman with a third-class ticket, *did* survive the *Titanic*, and the model agreed.

Did we pass up some epic opportunity to increase the accuracy of the machine learning model? Perhaps we should have filled empty values with `-1` instead of deleting them? Maybe we should have examined the cabin structure of the *Titanic*? Or perhaps we should have looked at `parch`, `sibsp`, and `pclass` to create a new column for people who were traveling alone in third class? "I'll never let go!"

Not all data can be cleaned and featured like this *Titanic* dataset was, but it was a useful adventure in data science for machine learning. There are plenty of CSVs available out there, and being confident in loading, understanding, and processing them is key to building novel models. Tools like Danfo.js enable you to process these mountains of data, and you can now add this to your machine learning tool chest.

If you're already a fan of other JavaScript notebooks like ObservableHQ.com (*https://observablehq.com*), Danfo.js can be imported and easily integrated with those as well.

Working with data is a mixed bag. Some problems are more clear-cut and don't require any adjustment to the features at all. If you're interested, you should take a look at a simpler dataset like the Palmer Penguins (*https://oreil.ly/CiNv5*). These penguins are significantly distinguishable into their species based on the shape and size of their bill. Another easy win is the Iris dataset mentioned in Chapter 7.

Chapter Challenge: Ship Happens

Did you know that not a single reverend survived the sinking of the *Titanic*? A bucket/bin of titles like Mr., Mrs., Ms., Rev., etc. might be useful to the learning of the model. These *honorifics*—yes, that's what they are called—could be collected and analyzed from the Name column that was discarded.

In this Chapter Challenge, use Danfo.js to identify the honorifics used on the *Titanic* and their associated survival rates. This is an excellent opportunity for you to get comfortable with Dnotebooks.

You can find the answer to this challenge in Appendix B.

Review Questions

Let's review the lessons you've learned from the code you've written in this chapter. Take a moment to answer the following questions:

1. What kind of activation function would you use for a rock-paper-scissors classifier?

2. How many nodes would you put in the final layer of a sigmoid "Dog or Not" model?

3. What is the command to load an interactive, locally hosted notebook that has Danfo.js built in?

4. How do you combine the data of two CSVs with the same columns?

5. What command would you use to one-hot encode a single column into multiple columns?

6. What can you use to scale all the values of a DataFrame between 0 and 1?

Solutions to these exercises are available in Appendix A.

Up Next...

In Chapter 10 you'll apply your training skills to a more fun and advanced model type for images. Image classification is one of those "wow" moments where a computer does something that is normally reserved for humans.

## CHAPTER 10

Image Training

"Everything must be made as simple as possible. But not simpler."

—Albert Einstein

I'm going to describe a number to you. I'd like you to figure out the number from the description of its features. The number I'm thinking of has a rounded top, a line down the right side only, and a loopy thing at the bottom that overlaps. Take a moment and mentally map the number I just described. With those three features, you can probably figure it out.

The features of a visual number can vary, but a smart description means you can identify the numbers in your mind. When I said "rounded top," you can immediately throw out some numbers, and the same goes for "a line down the right side only." The features compose what makes the number unique.

If you were to describe the numbers as shown in Figure 10-1 and put their descriptions in a CSV file, you could probably get 100% accuracy with a trained neural network on that data. The whole thing works except that it depends on a human to describe the top, middle, and bottom of each number. How do you automate the human aspect of this? If you can make a computer identify the loops, colors, and curves that are unique characteristics of an image and then feed that into a neural network, the machine could learn the needed patterns to classify the descriptions into images.

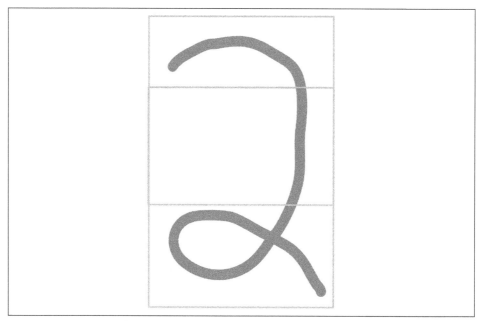

Figure 10-1. Congratulations if you figured out it was the number two

Thankfully, this problem of feature engineering images has been solved with fantastic computer vision tricks.

We will:

- Learn the concepts of convolutional layers for models
- Build your first multiclass model
- Learn how to read and process images for TensorFlow.js
- Draw on a canvas and classify the drawing accordingly

When you finish this chapter, you'll be able to create your own image classification models.

Understanding Convolutions

Convolutions come from the mathematical world of expressing shapes and functions. You can dig for a long, long time into the concept of what a convolution is in mathematics and then reapply that knowledge from the ground up to the idea of gathering information on digital images. If you're a fan of mathematics and computer graphics, this is quite an exciting rabbit hole.

However, it's not essential that you spend a week learning the fundamentals of convolutional operations when you have a framework like TensorFlow.js. It is for that reason that we'll focus on the high-level benefits and properties of convolutional operations and how they are used in neural networks. As always, you are encouraged to research the deep history of convolutions beyond this quick-start.[1]

Let's look at the most prominent concept you should take from a nonmathematical explanation of convolutions.

The two images of the number two in Figure 10-2 are the *exact* same number shifted from left to right in their bounding boxes. Each of these converted into tensors would create significantly different unequal tensors. However, in the feature system we described at the beginning of the chapter, these features would be the same.

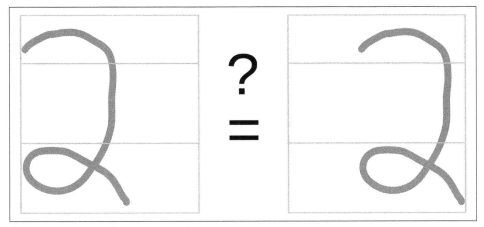

Figure 10-2. Convolutions simplify the essence of an image

For visual tensors, an image's features are more important than the exact locations of each pixel.

Convolutions Quick Summary

A convolutional operation is used to extract high-level features such as edges, gradients, colors, and more. These are the key features that classify a given visual.

So what features should it extract? That's not something we actually decide. You can control the number of filters used in finding features, but the actual features that best define usable patterns are defined in the training process. The filters start with accenting and drawing out features from the image.

---

1 Videos and lectures by 3Blue1Brown (*https://oreil.ly/zuGzT*) on YouTube are excellent starts for anyone looking to go down the convolution rabbit hole.

For instance, take a look at the photo in Figure 10-3. The jack-o'-lantern is multiple colors and barely contrasts against a blurry but somewhat light and dark background. As a human, you have no issue identifying what this is in the photo.

Figure 10-3. Jack-o'-lantern art

Now here's the same image with a 3 x 3 edge detection filter convolved over the pixels. Notice how the result is significantly simplified and more evident in Figure 10-4.

Different filters accent different aspects of each image to simplify and clarify the contents. It doesn't have to stop there; you can run activations to emphasize the detected features, and you can even run convolutions on convolutions.

What's the result? You've feature engineered the image. Preprocessing images through a variety of filters lets your neural network see patterns that would have required a much larger, slower, and more complicated model.

Figure 10-4. Convolution result

Adding Convolution Layers

Thanks to TensorFlow.js, adding a convolutional layer is just as easy as adding a dense layer, but it's called conv2d and has its own properties.

```
tf.layers.conv2d({
  filters: 32, ❶
  kernelSize: 3, ❷
  strides: 1, ❸
  padding: 'same', ❹
  activation: 'relu', ❺
  inputShape: [28, 28, 1] ❻
})
```

❶ Identify how many filters to run.

❷ The kernelSize controls the size of the filter. The 3 here represents a 3 x 3 filter.

❸ The little 3 x 3 filter won't fit your image, so it will need to slide over the image. The stride is how many pixels the filter slides each time.

❹ The padding lets the convolution decide what to do when your strides and kernelSize don't evenly divide into your image width and height. When you set padding to `same`, zeros are added around the image so that the size of the resulting convolutional images is kept the same.

❺ The results are then run through the activation function of your choice.

❻ The input is an image tensor, so the input image is the rank-three shape for the model. This is not a required restriction for convolutions, as you learned in Chapter 6, but it is recommended if you are not making a fully convolutional model.

Don't feel overwhelmed by the list of possible parameters. Imagine having to code all those different settings by yourself. You can configure your convolutions like existing models or go crazy with numbers to see how it affects your results. Tuning these parameters and experimenting is the benefit of a framework like TensorFlow.js. Most importantly, build your intuition over time.

It is important to note that this `conv2d` layer is meant for images. Similarly, you would use `conv1d` for a linear series and `conv3d` when working on 3D spatial objects. Most of the time, 2D is used, but the concept is not limited.

Understanding Max Pooling

Once you've simplified the image with filters via a convolutional layer, you're left with a lot of empty space in your filtered graphic. Also, the number of input parameters has significantly increased due to all the image filters.

Max pooling is a way to simplify the most active features identified in an image.

Max Pooling Quick Summary

To condense the resulting image size, you reduce the output using max pooling. Max pooling, put plainly, is keeping the most active pixel in a window as a representation of the entire block of pixels in that window. You then slide the window over and take the max of that. These results are pooled together to make a much smaller image as long as the stride of the window was greater than 1.

The following example quarters the size of an image by taking the largest number of each subsquare. Study the illustration in Figure 10-5.

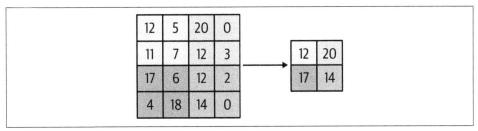

Figure 10-5. Max pool with 2 x 2 kernel and stride of 2

The kernelSize in Figure 10-5 is 2 x 2. So the four top-left squares are evaluated together, and out of the numbers [12, 5, 11, 7], the largest is 12. That max number is passed along to the result. With a stride of two, the square of the kernel window moves completely adjacent to the previous square and starts again with the numbers [20, 0, 12, 3]. This means the most powerful activation in each window is passed along.

You might feel that this process chops up an image and destroys the contents, but you'd be surprised to know that the resulting image is quite recognizable. Max pooling even emphasizes the detections and makes images more recognizable. See Figure 10-6, which is the result of running max pool on the convolution of the jack-o'-lantern from earlier.

Figure 10-6. 2 x 2 kernel max pool result of a convolution

While both Figure 10-4 and Figure 10-6 appear the same size for illustration purposes, the latter is somewhat clearer and a quarter of the size due to the pooling process.

Adding Max Pooling Layers

Similar to the `conv2d`, a max pool is added as a layer, generally immediately after a convolution:

```
tf.layers.maxPooling2d({
  poolSize: 2, ❶
  strides: 2   ❷
})
```

❶ The `poolSize` is the window size, just like `kernelSize` was. The previous examples have been 2 (which is short for 2 x 2).

❷ The `strides` is how far right and down to move the window in each operation. This can also be written as `strides: [2, 2]`.

Often, a model that is reading an image will have several layers of convolution, then pooling, and then convolution and pooling again and again. This chews up the features of an image and breaks them into parts that could potentially identify an image.[2]

Training Image Classification

After a few layers of convolutions and pooling, you can flatten or serialize the resulting filters into a single chain and feed it into a deeply connected neural network. This is why people love showing the MNIST training example; it's so simple that you can actually watch the data in a single image.

Take a look at the entire process to categorize a number using convolutions and max pooling. Figure 10-7 should be read from bottom to top.

---

2 There are other pooling methods available in TensorFlow.js for experimentation.

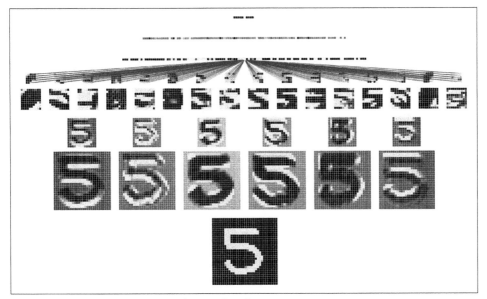

Figure 10-7. MNIST processing the number five

If you follow the process of this image displayed in Figure 10-7, you can see the input drawing down at the bottom and then a convolution of that input with six filters directly above it. Next, those six filters are max pooled or "downsampled," and you can see they are smaller because of it. Then one more convolution and pooling before they are flattened out to a fully connected dense network layer. Above that flattened layer is one dense layer, and the last small layer at the top is a softmax layer with 10 possible solutions. The "five" is the one that's lit up.

From a bird's-eye view, the convolution and pooling looks like magic, but it is digesting features of the image into patterns that neurons can recognize.

In a layered model, this means the first layers are generally convolution and pooling styled layers, and then they are passed into a neural network. Figure 10-8 illustrates a high-level view of the process. The following are three stages:

1. Input image
2. Feature extraction
3. Deeply connected neural network

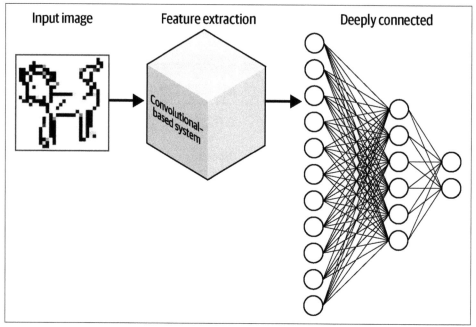

Input image   Feature extraction   Deeply connected

Convolutional-based system

Figure 10-8. The three basic stages of CNNs

Handling Image Data

One of the drawbacks of training with images is that the datasets can be quite large and unwieldy. Datasets are generally large, but with images, they are often immense. This is another reason the same visual datasets are used over and over again.

Even when an image dataset is small, it can take up a sizable amount of memory when loaded into memory tensor form. You might need to break training into chunks of tensors for monolithic image sets. This might explain why models like MobileNet were optimized for a size that is considered relatively small by today's standards. Increasing or decreasing an image by a single pixel across all images results in exponential size differences. By the very nature of the data, grayscale tensors are a third the size of RGB images in memory and a quarter the size of RGBA images.

The Sorting Hat

Now it's time for your first convolutional neural network. For this model, you're going to train a CNN to classify grayscale drawings into 10 categories.

If you're a fan of the popular book series *Harry Potter*, by J. K. Rowling, this will make sense and be entertaining. However, if you've never read a single *Harry Potter* book or watched any of the movies, this will still be an excellent exercise. In the books, there are four houses in the wizard school Hogwarts, and each house has animals associated with them. You're going to ask users to draw a picture and use that picture to sort them into houses. I've prepared a dataset of drawings that somewhat resembles the icons and animals from each group.

The dataset I've prepared is made from a subset of drawings from Google's Quick, Draw! Dataset (*https://oreil.ly/kq3bX*). The classes have been narrowed down to 10, and the data has been significantly cleaned up.

In the code associated with this chapter, which can be found at *chapter10/node/node-train-houses* (*https://oreil.ly/xr3Bu*), you'll find a ZIP file with tens of thousands of 28 x 28 drawings of the following:

1. Birds
2. Owls
3. Parrots
4. Snakes
5. Snails
6. Lions
7. Tigers
8. Raccoons
9. Squirrels
10. Skulls

The drawings vary wildly, but the characteristics of each class are discernable. Here is a random sampling of doodles, illustrated in Figure 10-9. Once you've trained a model to identify each of these 10 classes, you can use the model to sort drawings that resemble a particular animal into its associated house. Birds go to Ravenclaw, lions and tigers go to Gryffindor, etc.

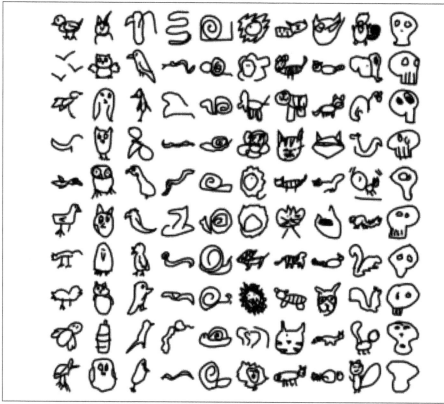

Figure 10-9. The 10 classes of drawings

There are a lot of ways of handling this, but the simplest will be to categorize the model using softmax for the final layer. As you remember, softmax will give us N numbers that all sum up to one. For example, if a drawing is 0.67 bird, 0.12 owl, and 0.06 parrot, since all those represent the same house, we can sum them together, and the result will always be less than one. While you're familiar with using models that return results like this, it will be your first softmax classification model that you've created from scratch.

Getting Started

There are a few ways you could use TensorFlow.js to train this model. Getting mega-bytes of images loaded into a browser can be done in several ways:

- You could load each image with subsequent HTTP requests.
- You could combine the training data into a large sprite sheet and then use your tensor skills to extract and stack each image into Xs and Ys.

- You could load the images into a CSV and from there convert them to tensors.

- You could Base64-encode the images and load them from a single JSON file.

The one common issue you see repeated here is that you have to do a bit of extra work to get your data into the sandbox of the browser. It's for this reason that it's probably best to use Node.js for image training with a significantly large dataset. We'll cover situations where this is less important later in the book.

The Node.js code associated with this chapter has the training data you'll need. You'll see a file in the repository that is close to 100 MB (the GitHub limit for a single file), which you'll need to unzip in place (see Figure 10-10).

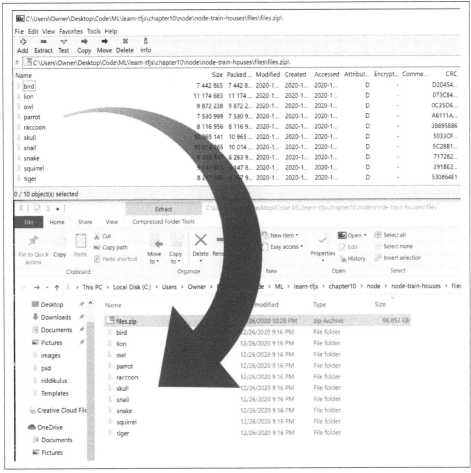

Figure 10-10. Unzip the images into the files folder

Now that you have the images and you know how to read images in Node.js, the code to train this model would be something like Example 10-1.

Example 10-1. The ideal setup

```
// Read images
const [X, Y] = await folderToTensors() ❶

// Create layers model
const model = getModel() ❷

// Train
await model.fit(X, Y, {
  batchSize: 256,
  validationSplit: 0.1,
  epochs: 20,
  shuffle: true, ❸
})

// Save
model.save('file://model_result/sorting_hat') ❹

// Cleanup!
tf.dispose([X, Y, model])
console.log('Tensors in memory', tf.memory().numTensors)
```

❶ Create a simple function to load the images into the needed X and Y tensors.

❷ Create a suitable CNN layers model.

❸ Use the `shuffle` property, which shuffles the current batch.

❹ Save the resulting trained model locally.

 The code in Example 10-1 does not mention setting aside any testing data. Because of the nature of this project, the real testing will be done when drawing images and identifying how each stroke moves an image closer or further from the desired goal. A validation set will still be used in training.

Converting Folders of Images

The `folderToTensors` function will need to do the following:

1. Identify all the PNG file paths.
2. Collect the image tensors and the answers.

3. Randomize both sets.

4. Normalize and stack the tensors.

5. Clean up and return the results.

To identify and access all the images, you can use a library like glob, which takes a given path like *files/**/*.png* and return an array of filenames. The /** iterates over all subfolders in that folder and finds all PNGs in each.

You can install glob with NPM like so:

```
$ npm i glob
```

Now that the node module is available, it can be required or imported:

```
const glob = require('glob')
// OR
import { default as glob } from 'glob'
```

Because globs operate by using a callback, you can wrap the whole function in a JavaScript promise to bring it back to async/await. If you're unfamiliar with these concepts, feel free to brush up on them or just study the code provided with the chapter.

After you have a collection of file locations, you can load the file, convert it to a tensor, and even identify the "answer" or "y" for each image by looking at what folder the image came from.

Remember that tensors create a *new tensor* every time you need to modify them. So rather than normalizing and stacking the tensors as we go, it will be best to keep the tensors in a JavaScript array.

The process of reading each string into these two arrays can be accomplished with this:

```
files.forEach((file) => {
  const imageData = fs.readFileSync(file)
  const answer = encodeDir(file)
  const imageTensor = tf.node.decodeImage(imageData, 1)

  // Store in memory
  YS.push(answer)
  XS.push(imageTensor)
})
```

The encodeDir function is a simple function I wrote to look at the path of each image and return an associated predictive number:

```
function encodeDir(filePath) {
  if (filePath.includes('bird')) return 0
  if (filePath.includes('lion')) return 1
  if (filePath.includes('owl')) return 2
  if (filePath.includes('parrot')) return 3
```

```
    if (filePath.includes('raccoon')) return 4
    if (filePath.includes('skull')) return 5
    if (filePath.includes('snail')) return 6
    if (filePath.includes('snake')) return 7
    if (filePath.includes('squirrel')) return 8
    if (filePath.includes('tiger')) return 9

    // Should never get here
    console.error('Unrecognized folder')
    process.exit(1)
}
```

Once you have the images in tensor form, you might consider stacking and returning them, but it is *crucial* that you shuffle them before. Without mixing the data, your model will quickly train in the strangest way. Indulge me in a peculiar metaphor.

Imagine if I asked you to point out the shape I'm thinking of in a collection of shapes. You quickly learn I'm always thinking of the circle, and you start getting 100% accuracy. On our third test, I start saying, "No, that's not the square! You're very wrong." So you then switch to pointing at the square and again get 100% accuracy. Every third test, I change the shape. While your scores are above 99% accurate, you never learned the actual indicator of which one to pick. So you go out into the field where the shape changes every time and fail. You never learned the indicators because the data was not shuffled.

Unshuffled data will have the same effect: near-perfect training accuracy, and abysmal validation and test scores. Even though you're shuffling each, you'll only be shuffling 256 of the same values most of the time.

To shuffle the X and the Y in the same permutation, you can use `tf.utils.shuffle Combo`. *I hear the guy who added this function to TensorFlow.js is super cool.*

```
    // Shuffle the data (keep XS[n] === YS[n])
    tf.util.shuffleCombo(XS, YS)
```

Because this is shuffling JavaScript references, no new tensors are created in this shuffle.

Finally, you'll want to convert the answers from an integer to one-hot encoding. The one-hot encoding is because your model will be softmax, i.e., 10 values that sum up to one with the correct answer being the dominant value exclusively.

TensorFlow.js has a method called `oneHot` that converts numbers to one-hot encoded tensor values. For example, the number 3 out of 5 possible categories would be encoded to the tensor [0,0,1,0,0]. This is how we want to format our answers to match the expected output of the categorical model.

You can now stack the X and Y array values into a large tensor and normalize the images to be values 0-1 by dividing by 255. The stacking and encoding would look like this:

```
// Stack values
console.log('Stacking')
const X = tf.stack(XS)
const Y = tf.oneHot(YS, 10)

console.log('Images all converted to tensors:')
console.log('X', X.shape)
console.log('Y', Y.shape)

// Normalize X to values 0 - 1
const XNORM = X.div(255)
// cleanup
tf.dispose([XS, X])
```

Your computer will likely pause between each log as thousands of images are processed. The code prints the following:

```
Stacking
Images all converted to tensors:
X [ 87541, 28, 28, 1 ]
Y [ 87541, 10 ]
```

Now we have our X and Y for training, and their shape is the input and output shape of the model we will create.

The CNN Model

Now it's time to create the convolutional neural network model. The architecture for this model will be three pairs of convolution and pooling layers. On each new convolutional layer, we will double the number of filters to train. Then we'll flatten the model to a single dense hidden layer of 128 units that have a tanh activation, and finish with a final layer of 10 possible outputs with the softmax activation. If you're confused about why we're using softmax, please review the structure of classification models we covered in Chapter 9.

You should be able to write the model layers from the description alone, but here's the code to create the described sequential model:

```
const model = tf.sequential()

// Conv + Pool combo
model.add(
  tf.layers.conv2d({
    filters: 16,
    kernelSize: 3,
    strides: 1,
    padding: 'same',
```

```
      activation: 'relu',
      kernelInitializer: 'heNormal',
      inputShape: [28, 28, 1],
  })
)
model.add(tf.layers.maxPooling2d({ poolSize: 2, strides: 2 }))

// Conv + Pool combo
model.add(
  tf.layers.conv2d({
    filters: 32,
    kernelSize: 3,
    strides: 1,
    padding: 'same',
    activation: 'relu',
  })
)
model.add(tf.layers.maxPooling2d({ poolSize: 2, strides: 2 }))

// Conv + Pool combo
model.add(
  tf.layers.conv2d({
    filters: 64,
    kernelSize: 3,
    strides: 1,
    padding: 'same',
    activation: 'relu',
  })
)
model.add(tf.layers.maxPooling2d({ poolSize: 2, strides: 2 }))

// Flatten for connecting to deep layers
model.add(tf.layers.flatten())

// One hidden deep layer
model.add(
  tf.layers.dense({
    units: 128,
    activation: 'tanh',
  })
)
// Output
model.add(
  tf.layers.dense({
    units: 10,
    activation: 'softmax',
  })
)
```

This new final layer for categorical data that is not binary means that you'll need to change your loss function from binaryCrossentropy to categoricalCrossentropy accordingly. So now the model.compile code would look like this:

```
model.compile({
  optimizer: 'adam',
  loss: 'categoricalCrossentropy',
  metrics: ['accuracy'],
})
```

Let's review the model.summary() method through the lens of what we've learned about convolutions and max pooling so we can ensure we've built everything correctly. You can see the printout of the results in Example 10-2.

Example 10-2. The output of model.summary()

Layer (type)	Output shape	Param #	
conv2d_Conv2D1 (Conv2D)	[null,28,28,16]	160	❶
max_pooling2d_MaxPooling2D1	[null,14,14,16]	0	❷
conv2d_Conv2D2 (Conv2D)	[null,14,14,32]	4640	❸
max_pooling2d_MaxPooling2D2	[null,7,7,32]	0	
conv2d_Conv2D3 (Conv2D)	[null,7,7,64]	18496	❹
max_pooling2d_MaxPooling2D3	[null,3,3,64]	0	
flatten_Flatten1 (Flatten)	[null,576]	0	❺
dense_Dense1 (Dense)	[null,128]	73856	❻
dense_Dense2 (Dense)	[null,10]	1290	❼

```
Total params: 98442
Trainable params: 98442
Non-trainable params: 0
```

❶ The first convolutional layer takes an input of [stacksize, 28, 28, 1] and has a convolutional output of [stacksize, 28, 28, 16]. The size is the same because we're using padding: 'same', and the 16 is the 16 different filter results we got when we specified filters: 16. You can think of this as 16 new filtered images for each image in the stack. This gives the network 160 new parameters to train. The trainable parameters are calculated as (number of images in) * (kernel window) * (images out) + (images out), which comes out to 1 * (3x3) * 16 + 16 = 160.

❷ The max pooling cuts the filtered image rows and column sizes in half, which quarters the pixels. This layer does not have any trainable parameter since the algorithm is fixed.

❸ The convolution and pooling happens again, and more filters are being employed at each level. The size of the image is shrinking, and the number of trainable parameters are swiftly growing, i.e., `16 * (3x3) * 32 + 32 = 4,640`.

❹ Here, there is one final convolution and pooling. Pooling an odd number creates a larger-than-50% reduction.

❺ Flattening the 64 3 x 3 images turns into a single layer of 576 units.

❻ Each of the 576 units is densely connected to the 128-unit layer. Using the traditional calculation of lines + nodes, this comes out to `(576 * 128) + 128 = 73,856` trainable parameters.

❼ Finally, the last layer lands with 10 possible values for each class.

You might be wondering why we're evaluating `model.summary()` instead of inspecting a graphical representation of what's happening. Even at lower dimensionality, the graphical representation of what's happening is difficult to illustrate. I've done my best to create a somewhat exhaustive illustration in Figure 10-11.

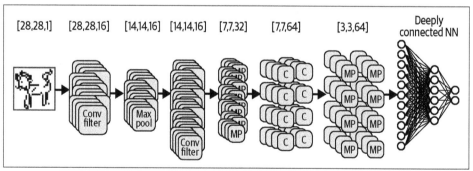

Figure 10-11. A visualization of each layer

Unlike previous neural network diagrams, the visual explanation of CNNs can be somewhat limiting. Stacks upon stacks of filtered images are only so informative. The result of the convolutional process is flattened and connected to a deeply connected neural network. You've reached a point of complexity where the `summary()` method of a model is the best way to understand the contents.

If you'd like a dynamic visual and to watch each trained filter's result activation at each layer, Polo Club of Data Science created a beautiful CNN Explainer (*https://oreil.ly/o24uR*) in TensorFlow.js. Check out the interactive visualizer (*https://oreil.ly/SYHsp*).

There you go. Your resulting [3, 3, 64] flattens to 576 artificial neurons before connecting to the neural network. Not only did you create image features, but you've simplified an input from a [28, 28, 1] image, which was originally going to require 784 densely connected inputs. Armed with this more advanced architecture, you can load the data from folderToTensors() and create the necessary model. You're ready to train.

Training and Saving

Since this is training in Node.js, you will have to setup GPU-acceleration on the machine directly. This is often done with NVIDIA CUDA, and CUDA Deep Neural Network (cuDNN). You will have to set up CUDA and cuDNN properly to work with your GPU if you want to train using @tensorflow/tfjs-node-gpu and get significant speed boost over normal tfjs-node. See Figure 10-12.

```
Epoch 1 / 20
2020-12-27 17:56:01.343903: I tensorflow/stream_executor/platform/default
2020-12-27 17:56:01.893956: W tensorflow/stream_executor/cuda/redzone_al
Relying on driver to perform ptx compilation. This message will be only
2020-12-27 17:56:01.983209: I tensorflow/stream_executor/platform/default
eta=0.0 ==================================================================
13572ms 172us/step - acc=0.648 loss=1.06 val_acc=0.779 val_loss=0.669
Epoch 2 / 20
eta=0.0 ==================================================================
12089ms 153us/step - acc=0.804 loss=0.585 val_acc=0.831 val_loss=0.503
Epoch 3 / 20
eta=0.0 ==================================================================
12686ms 161us/step - acc=0.841 loss=0.469 val_acc=0.856 val_loss=0.425
Epoch 4 / 20
eta=0.0 ==================================================================
12084ms 153us/step - acc=0.859 loss=0.409 val_acc=0.873 val_loss=0.384
Epoch 5 / 20
eta=11.2 ==>-----------------------------------------------------------
```

Figure 10-12. 3x–4x speed boost with GPU

The resulting model, after 20 epochs, lands around 95% accuracy in training and 90% accuracy for the validation set. The file size of the resulting model is around 400 KB. You might have noticed the accuracy for the training set continuously trending upward, but the validation can sometimes go down. For better or worse, the last epoch will be the model that gets saved. If you'd like to ensure the highest possible validation accuracy, take a look at the Chapter Challenge at the end.

 If you run this model for too many epochs, the model will overfit and approach 100% training accuracy with a diminished validation accuracy.

Testing the Model

To test this model, you'll need drawings from the user. You can create a simple drawing surface on a web page with a canvas. A canvas can subscribe to events on the mouse being pressed down, when the mouse is moving along the canvas, and when the mouse is released. Using these events, you can draw from point to point.

Building a Sketchpad

You can build a simple drawable canvas with those three events. You'll use some new methods to move the canvas path and draw lines, but it's quite readable. The following code sets one up:

```
const canvas = document.getElementById("sketchpad");
const context = canvas.getContext("2d");
context.lineWidth = 14;
context.lineCap = "round";
let isIdle = true;

function drawStart(event) {
  context.beginPath();
  context.moveTo(
    event.pageX - canvas.offsetLeft,
    event.pageY - canvas.offsetTop
  );
  isIdle = false;
}
function drawMove(event) {
  if (isIdle) return;
  context.lineTo(
    event.pageX - canvas.offsetLeft,
    event.pageY - canvas.offsetTop
  );
  context.stroke();
}
function drawEnd() { isIdle = true; }
// Tie methods to events
canvas.addEventListener("mousedown", drawStart, false);
canvas.addEventListener("mousemove", drawMove, false);
canvas.addEventListener("mouseup", drawEnd, false);
```

The drawings are made from a bunch of smaller lines that have a stroke width of 14 pixels and are automatically rounded on the edges. You can see a test drawing in Figure 10-13.

Figure 10-13. Works well enough

When the user clicks the mouse while on the canvas, any movement will be drawn from point to new point. Whenever the user stops drawing, the drawEnd function will be called. You could add a button to classify the canvas or tie directly into the dra wEnd function and classify the image.

Reading the Sketchpad

When you call tf.browser.fromPixels on the canvas, you'll get 100% black pixels. Why is this? The answer is that the canvas has nothing drawn in some places and black pixels in other areas. When the canvas is converted to tensor values, it will convert emptiness to black. The canvas might look like it has a white background, but it's actually clear and would show whatever color or pattern is underneath (see Figure 10-14).

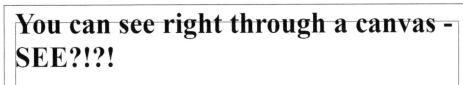

Figure 10-14. A canvas is transparent—and so empty pixels are zero

To fix this, you can add a clear function that writes a large white square in the canvas, so the black lines will be on a white background like the training images. This is also the function you can use to clear the canvas between drawings. To fill the canvas with a white background, you would use the `fillRect` method you used to outline the labels in Chapter 6:

```
context.fillStyle = "#fff";
context.fillRect(0, 0, canvas.clientWidth, canvas.clientHeight);
```

Once the canvas is initialized with a white background, you can make a prediction on the canvas drawing:

```
async function makePrediction(canvas, model) {
  const drawTensor = tf.browser.fromPixels(canvas, 1) ❶
  const resize = tf.image.resizeNearestNeighbor(drawTensor, [28,28], true) ❷

  const batched = resize.expandDims() ❸
  const results = await model.predict(batched)
  const predictions = await results.array()

  // Display
  displayResults(predictions[0]) ❹
  // Cleanup
  tf.dispose([drawTensor, resize, batched, results])
}
```

❶ When you read the canvas, don't forget to identify that you're only interested in a single channel; otherwise, you'll need to turn a 3D tensor into a 1D tensor before continuing.

❷ Resize using the nearest neighbor algorithm down to a 28 x 28 image for input into the model. Pixelation caused by nearest neighbor is inconsequential here, so it's a smart choice because it is faster than `resizeBilinear`.

❸ The model expects a batch, so prepare the data as a batch of one. This creates a `[1, 28, 28, 1]` input tensor.

❹ The prediction result has been returned to JavaScript as a single batch of 10 numbers. Think up a creative way to display the results.

Now that you have the results, you can portray the answers in any format you please. Personally, I organized the scores by house and used them to set the opacity of the labels. This way, you could get feedback as you drew each line. The opacity of labels depends on values 0-1, which works splendidly with the results of the softmax predictions.

```
function displayResults(predictions) {
  // Get Scores
  const ravenclaw = predictions[0] + predictions[2] + predictions[3]
  const gryffindor = predictions[1] + predictions[9]
  const hufflepuff = predictions[4] + predictions[8]
  const slytherin = predictions[6] + predictions[7]
  const deatheater = predictions[5]

  document.getElementById("ravenclaw").style.opacity = ravenclaw
  document.getElementById("gryffindor").style.opacity = gryffindor
  document.getElementById("hufflepuff").style.opacity = hufflepuff
  document.getElementById("slytherin").style.opacity = slytherin

  // Harry Potter fans will enjoy this one
  if (deatheater > 0.9) {
    alert('DEATH EATER DETECTED!!!')
  }
}
```

You might wonder if Ravenclaw has a slight mathematical advantage because it is composed of more classes, and you'd be right. With all things equal, a completely random set of lines is more likely to be classified as Ravenclaw because it has a majority of the classes. However, this is statistically insignificant when the drawings are non-random. If you want the model to have only nine classes, remove bird and retrain to create the most balanced classification spectrum.

 If you're interested in identifying which classes are likely to be problematic or confused, you can use visual reporting tools like a confusion matrix or the t-SNE (*https://oreil.ly/sBio5*) algorithm. These tools are especially helpful for evaluating the training data.

I highly recommend you load the code for this chapter from *chapter10/simple/ simplest-draw* (*https://oreil.ly/emOWR*) and put your artistic skills to the test! My bird drawing sorted me into Ravenclaw, as shown in Figure 10-15.

Figure 10-15. A UI and drawing masterpiece

I was able to poorly draw and properly get sorted into each of the other possible houses as well. However, I won't punish you with any more of my "art."

Chapter Review

You've trained a model on visual data. While this dataset was limited to grayscale drawings, the lessons you've learned could work with any image dataset. There are plenty of excellent image datasets out there that would work perfectly with the model you've created. We'll cover more in the next two chapters.

I've created a more elaborate page for the drawing identification featured (*https://oreil.ly/jnlhb*) in this chapter.

Chapter Challenge: Saving the Magic

If you're most interested in getting the highest validation accuracy model, it's slim odds that your best version of the model will be the last one. For example, if you take a look at Figure 10-16, a validations accuracy of 90.3% gets lost, and you end up with 89.6% as the final validation of the model.

For this Chapter Challenge, rather than saving the final trained version of the model, add a callback that saves the model when the validation accuracy has reached a new record best. This kind of code is useful because it will allow you to run for many epochs. As the model overfits, you'll be able to keep the best generalizable model for production.

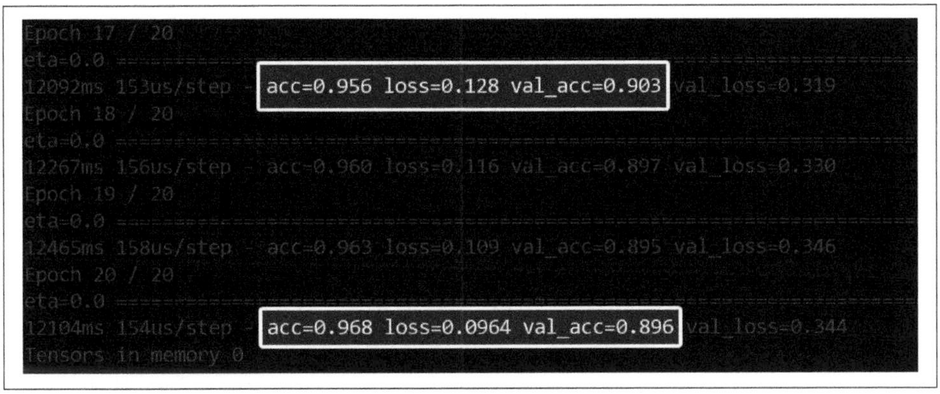

Figure 10-16. Evaluate which accuracy is more important

You can find the answer to this challenge in Appendix B.

Review Questions

Let's review the lessons you've learned from the code you've written in this chapter. Take a moment to answer the following questions:

1. Convolutional layers have many trainable *what* that help extract features of an image?

2. What is the name of the property that controls the convolutional window size?

3. If you want a convolutional result to be the same size as the original image, what should you set as the padding?

4. True or false? You must flatten an image before inserting it into a convolutional layer.

5. What would be the output size of a max pool 3 x 3 with a stride of three on an 81 x 81 image?

6. If you were to one-hot encode the number 12, do you have enough information to do so?

Solutions to these exercises are available in Appendix A.

Up Next...

In Chapter 11 you'll learn how to stand on the shoulders of giants. Designing models can be complex and often time-consuming. Transfer learning enables you to take an advanced model and slightly retrain it with a small amount of data to perform a new task. This cuts down on the amount of data you'll need and training time.

## CHAPTER 11

Transfer Learning

"Learn from the mistakes of others. You can't live long enough to make them all yourself."

—Eleanor Roosevelt

It can be challenging to have an extensive collection of data, battle-tested model structure, and processing power. Wouldn't it be nice to cut a corner? That nifty trick in Chapter 7 where you could use Teachable Machine to transfer the qualities of a trained model to a novel one was pretty useful. In fact, this is a common trick in the machine learning world. While Teachable Machine hid the specifics and offered you only a single model, you can understand the mechanics of this trick and use it on all kinds of cool tasks. In this chapter, we will reveal the magic behind this process. While we'll be focused on the example of MobileNet for simplicity, this can be applied to all kinds of models.

Transfer learning is the act of taking a trained model and repurposing it for a second related task.

There are a few repeatable benefits to using transfer learning for your machine learning solution. Most projects utilize some amount of transfer learning for these reasons:

- Reutilizing a battle-tested model structure
- Getting a solution faster
- Getting a solution via less data

In this chapter, you'll learn several strategies for transfer learning. You will focus on MobileNet as a fundamental example that can be reused to identify a myriad of new classes in various ways.

We will:

- Review how transfer learning works
- See how to reuse feature vectors
- Cut into Layers models and reconstruct new models
- Learn about KNN and deferred classification

When you finish this chapter, you'll be able to take models that have been trained for a long time with lots of data and apply them to your own needs with smaller datasets.

How Does Transfer Learning Work?

How does a model that has been trained on different data suddenly work well for your *new* data? It sounds miraculous, but it happens in humans every day.

You've spent years identifying animals, and you've probably seen hundreds of camels, guinea pigs, and beavers from cartoons, zoos, and commercials. Now I'm going to show you an animal you've probably not seen often, or even at all. The animal in Figure 11-1 is called a capybara (*Hydrochoerus hydrochaeris*).

Figure 11-1. The capybara

For some of you, this is the first time (or one of the few times) you've seen a photo of a capybara. Now, take a look at the lineup in Figure 11-2. Can you find the capybara?

Figure 11-2. Which one is the capybara?

The training set of a single photo was enough for you to make a choice because you've been distinguishing between animals your entire life. With a novel color, angle, and photo size, your brain probably detected with absolute certainty that animal C was another capybara. The features learned by your years of experience have helped you make an educated decision. In that same way, powerful models that have significant experience can be taught to learn new things from small amounts of new data.

Transfer Learning Neural Networks

Let's bring things back to MobileNet for a moment. The MobileNet model was trained to identify features that distinguish a thousand items from each other. That means there are convolutions to detect fur, metal, round things, ears, and all kinds of crucial differential features. All these features are chewed up and simplified before they are flattened into a neural network, where the combination of various features creates a classification.

The MobileNet model can identify different breeds of dogs, and even distinguish a Maltese terrier from a Tibetan terrier. If you were to make a "dog or cat" (*https://oreil.ly/i9Xxm*) classifier, it makes sense that a majority of those advanced features would be reusable in your simpler model.

The previously learned convolutional filters would be extremely useful in identifying key features for brand-new classifications, like our capybara example in Figure 11-2. The trick is to take the feature identification portion of the model and apply your own neural network to the convolutional output, as illustrated in Figure 11-3.

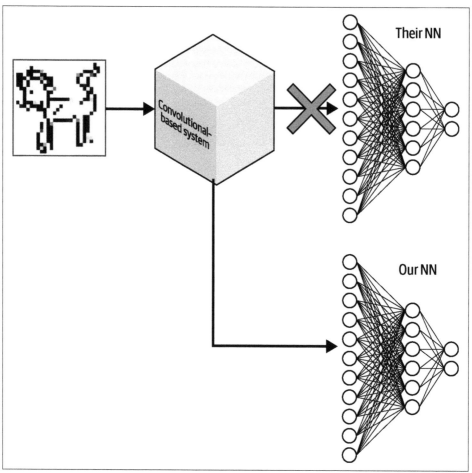

Figure 11-3. CNN transfer learning

So how do you separate and recombine these sections of previously trained models? You've got lots of options. Again, we'll learn a bit more about Graph and Layers models.

Easy MobileNet Transfer Learning

Fortunately, TensorFlow Hub (*https://tfhub.dev*) already has a MobileNet model that is disconnected from any neural network. It offers half a model for you to use for transfer learning. Half a model means it hasn't been tied down into a final softmax layer for what it's meant to classify. This allows us to let MobileNet derive the features of an image and then provide us with tensors that we can then pass to our own trained network for classification.

TFHub calls these models *image feature vector* models. You refine your search to show only these models (*https://oreil.ly/BkokR*) or identify them by looking at the problem domain tags, as illustrated in Figure 11-4.

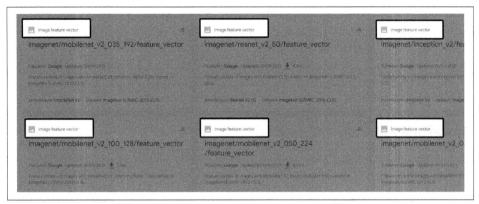

Figure 11-4. Problem domain tags for image feature vectors

You might notice small variations of MobileNet and wonder what the differences are. Once you learn a few sneaky terms, each of these model descriptions becomes quite readable.

For instance, we'll use Example 11-1.

Example 11-1. One of the image feature vector models

```
imagenet/mobilenet_v2_130_224/feature_vector
```

imagenet
    This model was trained on the ImageNet dataset.

mobilenet_v2
    The model's architecture is MobileNet v2.

130
    The model's depth multiplier was 1.30. This results in more features. If you want to speed things up, you can choose "05," which would have less than half the feature output with a boost in speed. This is a fine-tuning option when you're ready to modify speed versus depth.

224
    The model's expected input size is 224 x 224 images.

feature_vector
    We already know from the tag, but this model outputs tensors meant to be features of the image for a second model to interpret.

Now that we have a trained model that can identify features in an image, we will run our training data through the MobileNet image feature vector model and then train a model on the output from that. In other words, the training images will turn into a feature vector, and we'll train a model to interpret that feature vector.

The benefit of this strategy is that it's straightforward to implement. The major drawback is that you'll have to load two models when you're ready to use the newly trained model (one to generate features and one to interpret them). Creatively, there might be some cases where it's quite useful to "featurize" an image and then run that through multiple neural networks. Regardless, let's see it in action.

TensorFlow Hub Check, Mate!

We're going to use transfer learning with MobileNet to identify chess pieces like the one shown in Figure 11-5.

Figure 11-5. Simple chess pieces classifier

You'll only have a few images of each chess piece. That's not normally enough, but with the magic of transfer learning, you'll get an efficient model.

Loading chess images

For this exercise, I've compiled a collection of 150 images and loaded them into a CSV file for quick use. This isn't something I'd recommend doing in most cases because it's inefficient for processing and disk space, but it serves as a simple vector for some quick in-browser training. The code to load these images is now trivial.

You can access the chess images and the code that converted them into a CSV file in the *chapter11/extra/node-make-csvs* (*https://oreil.ly/INWAN*) folder.

The files *chess_labels.csv* and *chess_images.csv* can be found in the *chess_data.zip* (*https://oreil.ly/bcFop*) file in code associated with this lesson. Unzip this file and use Danfo.js to load the contents.

Many browsers may have issues with concurrently reading all 150 images, so I've limited the demo to process only 130 images. Working against concurrent data limitations is a common issue with machine learning.

 Once the image has been featurized, it takes up a lot less space. Feel free to experiment with creating features in batches, but that's outside the scope of this chapter.

The images are already 224 x 224, so you can load them with the following code:

```
console.log("Loading huge CSV - this will take a while");
const numImages = 130; // between 1 and 150
// Get Y values
const labels = await dfd.read_csv("chess_labels.csv", numImages); ❶
const Y = labels.tensor; ❷
// Get X values (Chess images)
const chessImages = await dfd.read_csv("chess_images.csv", numImages);
const chessTensor = chessImages.tensor.reshape([
  labels.shape[0], 224, 224, 3, ❸
]);
console.log("Finished loading CSVs", chessTensor.shape, Y.shape);
```

❶ The second parameter to `read_csv` limits the row count to the specified number.

❷ The DataFrames are then converted to tensors.

❸ The images were flattened to become serialized but are now reshaped into a rank-four batch of RGB images.

After a bit of time, this code prints out the X and Y shapes of 130 ready-to-go images and encodings:

```
Finished loading CSVs (4) [130, 224, 224, 3] (2) [130, 6]
```

If your computer is unable to handle the 130 images, you can lower the `numImages` variable and still play along. However, the load time for the CSV file is always constant because the entire file must be processed.

Images like chess pieces are perfect for image augmentation because skewing chess pieces would never cause one piece to be confused with another. If you ever need more images, you can mirror the entire set to effectively double your data. Entire libraries exist to mirror, tilt, and skew images (*https://oreil.ly/tCMTN*) so you can create more data.

Loading the feature model

You can load the feature model just like you'd load any model from TensorFlow Hub. You can pass the code through the model for prediction, and it will result in numIm ages predictions. The code looks like Example 11-2.

Example 11-2. Loading and using the feature vector model

```
// Load feature model
const tfhubURL =
  "https://oreil.ly/P2t2k";
const featureModel = await tf.loadGraphModel(tfhubURL, {
  fromTFHub: true,
});
const featureX = featureModel.predict(chessTensor);
// Push data through feature detection
console.log(`Features stack ${featureX.shape}`);
```

The output of the console log is

```
    Features stack 130,1664
```

Each of the 130 images has become a set of 1,664 floating-point values that are sensitive to features of the image. If you change the model to use a different depth, the number of features will change. The number 1,664 is unique to the 1.30 depth version of MobileNet.

As previously mentioned, the 1,664 Float32 feature set is significantly smaller than the 224*224*3 = 150,528 Float32 input of each image. This will speed up training and be kinder to your computer memory.

Creating your neural network

Now that you have a collection of features, you can create a new and utterly untrained model that fits those 1,664 features to your labels.

Example 11-3. A small 64-layer model with a final layer of 6

```
// Create NN
const transferModel = tf.sequential({
  layers: [                                          ❶
    tf.layers.dense({
      inputShape: [featureX.shape[1]],    ❷
      units: 64,
      activation: "relu",
    }),
    tf.layers.dense({ units: 6, activation: "softmax" }),
  ],
});
```

❶ This Layers model is using a slightly different syntax than you're used to. Rather than calling .add, all the layers are being presented in an array of the initial configuration. This syntax is nice for a small model like this.

❷ The inputShape of the model is set to 1,664 dynamically, in the case that you'd like to change the model's depth multiplier by updating the model URL.

Training results

Nothing is new in the training code. The model trains based on the feature output. Because the feature output is so small compared to the original image tensor, the training happens extremely quickly.

```
transferModel.compile({
  optimizer: "adam",
  loss: "categoricalCrossentropy",
  metrics: ["accuracy"],
});

await transferModel.fit(featureX, Y, {
  validationSplit: 0.2,
  epochs: 20,
  callbacks: { onEpochEnd: console.log },
});
```

Within a few epochs, the model has outstanding accuracy. Take a look at Figure 11-6.

```
loading - this will take a while
Finished loading CSVs ▸ (4) [130, 224, 224, 3] ▸ (2) [130, 6]
▲ ▸High memory usage in GPU: 1891.13 MB, most likely due to a memory leak
Features stack 130,1664
0  ▸ {val_loss: 1.5202730894088745, val_acc: 0.5000000596046448, loss: 1.7347474098205566, acc: 0.25961536169052124}
1  ▸ {val_loss: 1.1940194368362427, val_acc: 0.6153846383094708, loss: 1.314350962638855, acc: 0.48076921701431274}
2  ▸ {val_loss: 1.1666483879089355, val_acc: 0.5384615659713745, loss: 0.8990954160690308, acc: 0.7980768680057251}
3  ▸ {val_loss: 0.7846076488494873, val_acc: 0.7307692766189575, loss: 0.6588283777236938, acc: 0.865384578704834}
4  ▸ {val_loss: 0.6516473889350891, val_acc: 0.8461537957191467, loss: 0.45839858055114746, acc: 0.9423076510429382}
5  ▸ {val_loss: 0.6502484083175659, val_acc: 0.692307710647583, loss: 0.3778494894504547, acc: 0.9134615063667297}
6  ▸ {val_loss: 0.5143225193023682, val_acc: 0.8461537957191467, loss: 0.2264920473098755, acc: 0.980769157409668}
7  ▸ {val_loss: 0.5077419877052307, val_acc: 0.8461537957191467, loss: 0.19044800233840942, acc: 0.9711537957191467}
8  ▸ {val_loss: 0.47027674317359924, val_acc: 0.8846153020858765, loss: 0.13953066064548492, acc: 0.990384578704834}
9  ▸ {val_loss: 0.4197342097759247, val_acc: 0.8846153020858765, loss: 0.1066841285092928, acc: 0.990384578704834}
10 ▸ {val_loss: 0.3478999733924866, val_acc: 0.923076868057251, loss: 0.09290190041065216, acc: 0.9999999403953552}
11 ▸ {val_loss: 0.301803298439636, val_acc: 0.9615384340286255, loss: 0.0700812041759491, acc: 0.9999999403953552}
12 ▸ {val_loss: 0.2868725657463074, val_acc: 0.9615384340286255, loss: 0.05736910179257393, acc: 0.9999999403953552}
13 ▸ {val_loss: 0.2543188929557800, val_acc: 0.923076868057251, loss: 0.04949808586997986, acc: 0.9999999403953552}
14 ▸ {val_loss: 0.22575657069683075, val_acc: 0.923076868057251, loss: 0.04162168875336647, acc: 0.9999999403953552}
15 ▸ {val_loss: 0.22140440344810486, val_acc: 0.9615384340286255, loss: 0.03676515817642212, acc: 0.9999999403953552}
16 ▸ {val_loss: 0.22805029153823853, val_acc: 0.923076868057251, loss: 0.0324698500352165, acc: 0.9999999403953552}
17 ▸ {val_loss: 0.23117715120315552, val_acc: 0.923076868057251, loss: 0.02923256903886795, acc: 0.9999999403953552}
18 ▸ {val_loss: 0.2096765786409378, val_acc: 0.923076868057251, loss: 0.0268249753826194, acc: 0.9999999403953552}
19 ▸ {val_loss: 0.1793859750032425, val_acc: 0.9615384340286255, loss: 0.02435545064508915, acc: 0.9999999403953552}
```

Figure 11-6. From 50% to 96% validation accuracy in 20 epochs

Transfer learning using an existing model on TensorFlow Hub relieves you of architectural headaches and rewards you with high accuracy. But it's not the only way you
can implement transfer learning.

Utilizing Layers Models for Transfer Learning

There are some obvious and not-so-obvious limitations to the previous method.
First, the feature model cannot be trained. All your training was on a new model that
consumed the features of the Graph model, but the convolutional layers and size were
fixed. You have small variations of the convolutional network model available but no
way to update or fine-tune it.

The previous model from TensorFlow Hub was a Graph model. The Graph model
was optimized for speed and, as you know, cannot be modified or trained. On the
other side, Layers models are primed for modification, so you can rewire them for
transfer learning.

Also, in the previous example, you were essentially dealing with two models every
time you would need to classify an image. You would have to load two JSON models
and run your image through the feature model and then the new model to categorize
your images. It's not the end of the world, but a single model is possible via combining Layers models.

Let's solve the same chess problem again, but with a Layers version of MobileNet so
we can inspect the difference.

Shaving Layers on MobileNet

For this exercise, you will use a version of MobileNet v1.0 that is set up for being a Layers model. This is the model Teachable Machine uses, and while it's sufficient for small exploratory projects, you'll notice it's not as accurate as the MobileNet v2 with 1.30 depth. You're already well versed in converting models with the wizard, as you learned in Chapter 7, so you can create a larger, newer Layers model when needed. Accuracy is an important metric, but it's far from the only metric you should evaluate when shopping for a transfer model.

MobileNet has a vast collection of layers, and some of these are layers you've never seen before. Let's take a look. Load the MobileNet model associated with this chapter and review the summary of layers with model.summary(). This prints a huge list of layers. Don't feel overwhelmed. When you read from the bottom to the top, the last two convolutional layers with activations are called conv_preds and conv_pw_13_relu:

```
...

conv_pw_13 (Conv2D)           [null,7,7,256]            65536

conv_pw_13_bn (BatchNormaliz  [null,7,7,256]            1024

conv_pw_13_relu (Activation)  [null,7,7,256]            0

global_average_pooling2d_1 (  [null,256]               0

 reshape_1 (Reshape)          [null,1,1,256]            0

dropout (Dropout)             [null,1,1,256]            0

conv_preds (Conv2D)           [null,1,1,1000]          257000

act_softmax (Activation)      [null,1,1,1000]           0

reshape_2 (Reshape)           [null,1000]               0
=================================================================
Total params: 475544
Trainable params: 470072
Non-trainable params: 5472
```

The last convolution, conv_preds, serves as a flatten layer of the features to the 1,000 possible classes. This is somewhat specific to the model's trained classes, so because of that, we'll jump up to the second convolution (conv_pw_13_relu) and cut there.

MobileNet is a complex model, and even though you don't have to understand all the layers to use it for transfer learning, there's a bit of art in deciding what to remove. In simpler models, like the one for the upcoming Chapter Challenge, it's common to keep the entire convolutional workflow and cut at the flatten layer.

You can cut to a layer by knowing its unique name. The code shown in Example 11-4 is available on GitHub (*https://oreil.ly/KfhNb*).

Example 11-4.

```
const featureModel = await tf.loadLayersModel('mobilenet/model.json')
console.log('ORIGINAL MODEL')
featureModel.summary()
const lastLayer = featureModel.getLayer('conv_pw_13_relu')
const shavedModel = tf.model({
  inputs: featureModel.inputs,
  outputs: lastLayer.output,
})
console.log('SHAVED DOWN MODEL')
shavedModel.summary()
```

The code from Example 11-4 prints out two large models, but the key difference is that the second model suddenly stops at conv_pw_13_relu.

The last layer is now the one we identified. When you review the summary of the shaved-down model, it's like a feature extractor. There is a key difference that should be noted. The final layer is a convolution, so the first layer of your constructed transfer model should flatten the convolutional input so it can be densely connected to a neural network.

Layers Feature Model

Now you can use the shaved model as a features model. This gets you the same two-model system you had from TFHub. Your second model will need to read the output of conv_pw_13_relu:

```
// Create NN
const transferModel = tf.sequential({
  layers: [
    tf.layers.flatten({ inputShape: featureX.shape.slice(1) }),
    tf.layers.dense({ units: 64, activation: 'relu' }),
    tf.layers.dense({ units: 6, activation: 'softmax' }),
  ],
})
```

We are setting the shape as defined by the intermediate features. This could also be directly tied to the shaved model's output shape (shavedModel.outputs[0].shape.slice(1)).

From here, you're right back to where you were in the TFHub model. The base model creates features, and the second model interprets those features.

Training with these two layers achieves around 80%+ accuracy. Keep in mind we're using a completely different model architecture (this is MobileNet v1) and a lower depth multiplier. Getting at least 80% from this rough model is good.

A Unified Model

Just as with the feature vector model, your training only has access to a few layers and does not update the convolutional layers. Now that you've trained two models, you can unify their layers again into a single model. You might be wondering why you're combining the model after training instead of before. It's a common practice to train your new layers with your feature layers locked or "frozen" to their original weights.

Once the new layers have gotten trained up, you can generally "unfreeze" more layers and train the new and the old together. This phase is often called *fine-tuning* the model.

So how do you unify these two models now? The answer is surprisingly simple. Create a third sequential model and add the two models with `model.add`. The code looks like this:

```
// combine the models
const combo = tf.sequential()
combo.add(shavedModel)
combo.add(transferModel)
combo.compile({
  optimizer: 'adam',
  loss: 'categoricalCrossentropy',
  metrics: ['accuracy'],
})
combo.summary()
```

The new `combo` model can be downloaded or trained further.

If you had joined the models before training the new layers, you'd likely see your model overfit the data.

No Training Needed

It's worth noting that there's a witty way to use two models for transfer learning with zero training. The trick is to use a second model that identifies distances in similarity.

The second model is called K-Nearest Neighbors (KNN)[1] model, and it groups a data element with K of the most similar data elements in a feature space. The idiom "birds of a feather flock together" is the premise for KNN.

---

1 KNN was developed by Evelyn Fix and Joseph Hodges in 1951.

In Figure 11-7, X would be identified as a bunny because the three nearest examples in features are also bunnies.

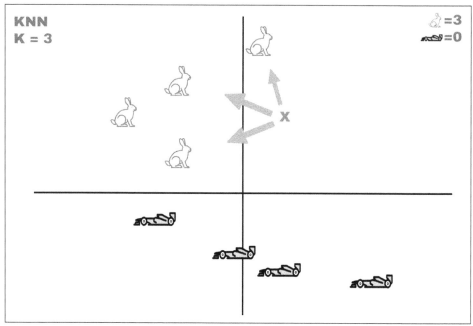

Figure 11-7. Identify with neighbors in feature space

KNN is sometimes called *instance-based learning* or *lazy learning* because you're moving all the necessary processing to the moment of classification of the data around it. This differed model is straightforward to update. You can always add more images and classes dynamically to define edge cases or new categories without retraining. The cost comes from the fact that the feature graph grows with each example you add, unlike the fixed space of a single trained model. The more data points you add to a KNN solution, the larger the feature set that accompanies the models will become.

Additionally, since there is no training, similarity is the *only* metric. This makes this system nonideal for some problems. For instance, if you were trying to train a model to see if people were wearing face masks or not, then you're looking for a model to focus on a single feature rather than the collection of several features. Two people who are dressed the same might share more similarities and therefore be placed in the same category with KNN. For KNN to work on masks, your feature vector model would have to be face-specific, where trained models can learn differentiating patterns.

Easy KNN: Bunnies Versus Sports Cars

KNN, like MobileNet, has a JS wrapper provided by Google. We can implement KNN transfer learning quickly by hiding all the complexity details use MobileNet and KNN NPM packages to make a quick transfer learning demo.

MobileNet NPM Library

The MobileNet NPM module (*https://oreil.ly/uzuYB*) from Chapter 2 was smart enough to know that you might want transfer learning and not just the 1,000 known classes. Under the helpful NPM wrapper, the code is simply accessing TensorFlow Hub like we are.

If you're looking for the fastest way to bring MobileNet to a project for transfer learning, you can use the simplified MobileNet package and its wrapper to gather features with the code shown in Example 11-5.

Example 11-5. Pure NPM-powered features

```
features = model.infer(img, true);
```

This is a nice feature that you can often find in models that have been professionally wrapped in friendly JavaScript.

Not only are we going to avoid running any training, but we'll also use existing libraries to avoid any deep dive into TensorFlow.js. We'll be doing this for a flashy demo, but if you decide to build something more robust with these models, you should probably evaluate avoiding abstract packages that you don't control. You already understand all the inner workings of transfer learning.

To do this quick demo, you'll import the three NPM modules:

```
<script src="https://cdn.jsdelivr.net/npm/@tensorflow/tfjs@2.7.0/dist/tf.min.js">
</script>
<script src="https://cdn.jsdelivr.net/npm/@tensorflow-models/mobilenet@2.0">
</script>
<script
src="https://cdn.jsdelivr.net/npm/@tensorflow-models/knn-classifier@1.2.2">
</script>
```

For simplicity, the example code from this chapter has all the images on the page, so you can directly reference them. Now you can load MobileNet with `mobileNet = await mobilenet.load();` and the KNN classifier with `knnClassifier.create();`.

The KNN classifier needs examples of each class. To simplify this process I've created the following helper function:

```
// domID is the DOM element ID
// classID is the unique class index
function addExample(domID, classID) {
  const features = mobileNet.infer( ❶
    document.getElementById(domID), ❷
    true                            ❸
  );
  classifier.addExample(features, classID);
}
```

❶ The `infer` method returns values rather than the rich JavaScript object of detections.

❷ The image `id` on the page will tell MobileNet what image to resize and process. The tensor logic is hidden by JavaScript, but many chapters in this book have explained what is actually happening.

❸ The MobileNet model returns the features (sometimes called *embeddings*) of the image. If this is not set, then the tensor of 1,000 raw values is returned (sometimes called *logits*).

Now you can add examples of each class with this helper method. You just name the image element's unique DOM ID and what class it should be associated with. Adding three examples of each is as simple as this:

```
// Add examples of two classes
addExample('bunny1', 0)
addExample('bunny2', 0)
addExample('bunny3', 0)
addExample('sport1', 1)
addExample('sport2', 1)
addExample('sport3', 1)
```

Lastly, it's the same system to predict. Get the features of an image, and ask the classifier to identify which class it believes the input is based on KNN.

```
// Moment of truth
const testImage = document.getElementById('test')
const testFeature = mobileNet.infer(testImage, true);
const predicted = await classifier.predictClass(testFeature)
if (predicted.classIndex === 0) { ❶
  document.getElementById("result").innerText = "A Bunny" ❷
} else {
  document.getElementById("result").innerText = "A Sports Car"
}
```

❶ The `classIndex` is the number as passed in `addExample`. If a third class is added, that new index would be a possible output.

❷ The web page text is changed from "???" to the result.

The result is that the AI can identify the correct class for a new image by comparing against six examples, as shown in Figure 11-8.

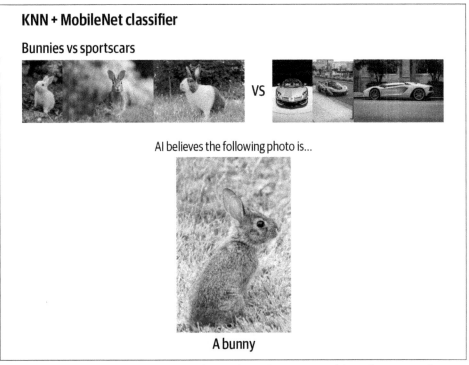

Figure 11-8. With only three images of each class, the KNN model predicts correctly

You can dynamically add more and more classes. KNN is an exciting and expandable way to utilize the experience of advanced models through transfer learning.

Chapter Review

Because this chapter has explained the mystery of transfer learning with MobileNet, you now have the ability to apply this power-up to any preexisting model you can somewhat comprehend. Perhaps you want to adjust the pet's faces model to find cartoon or human faces. You don't have to start from scratch!

Transfer learning adds a new utility to your toolbelt of AI. Now when you find a new model in the wild, you can ask yourself how you could use it directly *and* how you can use it in transfer learning for something similar.

Chapter Challenge: Warp-Speed Learning

The Hogwarts sorting model from the previous chapter has thousands of black-and-white drawing images of experience in the convolutional layers. Unfortunately, those thousands of images were limited to animals and skulls. They all have nothing to do with *Star Trek*. Don't fret; with only 50 or so new images, you can re-train the model from the previous chapter to identify the three *Star Trek* symbols shown in Figure 11-9.

Figure 11-9. Star Trek symbols

Set phasers to fun and use the methods you learned in this chapter to take the Layers model you trained in Chapter 10 (or download the trained one from the associated book source code (*https://oreil.ly/v3tvg*)), and train a new model that can identify these images from a mere few examples.

The new training image data can be found in CSV form in the associated book source code (*https://oreil.ly/3dqcq*). The training image data has been put in a CSV so you can easily import it with Danfo.js. The files are *images.csv* and *labels.csv*.

You can find the answer to this challenge in Appendix B.

Review Questions

Let's review the lessons you've learned from the code you've written in this chapter. Take a moment to answer the following questions:

1. What does KNN stand for?
2. Whenever you have a small training set, there's a danger of what?
3. When you're looking for the convolutional half of a CNN model on TensorFlow Hub, what tag are you looking for?
4. Which depth multiplier will have a more extensive feature output, 0.50 or 1.00?
5. What method can you call on the MobileNet NPM module to gather the feature embeddings of an image?
6. Should you combine your transfer model parts and then train, or train and then combine your models?
7. When you cut a model at the convolutional layer, what do you have to do before importing that information to a neural network's dense layers?

Solutions to these exercises are available in Appendix A.

Up Next...

In Chapter 12 you'll be put to the test! You've learned all kinds of skills and played with a wide variety of tools, but now it's time to see if you can see a project through. In the next chapter, you'll have your capstone project, which will draw on all the skills you've learned so far to take an idea into reality.

## CHAPTER 12

Dicify: Capstone Project

"Everybody has a plan until they get punched in the mouth."

—Iron Mike Tyson

All of your training has gotten you through a variety of theories and exercises. As of right now, you know enough to come up with a plan to build new and creative uses for machine learning in TensorFlow.js. In this chapter, you'll develop your capstone project. Rather than learning yet another aspect of machine learning with Tensor-Flow.js, you'll start this chapter with a challenge, and you'll use your existing skills to build a solution that works. From idea to completion, this chapter will guide you through the execution of solving a problem. Whether this is your first book on machine learning or your 10th, this capstone is your time to shine.

We will:

- Research the problem
- Create and augment data
- Train a model that will solve the problem
- Implement the solution in a website

When you finish this chapter, you'll have applied your skills from beginning to end to solve a fun machine learning project.

A Dicey Challenge

We'll be using your newfound skill to blur the line between art and science. Engineers have been using machines for impressive visual feats for years. Most notably, the camera obscura technique (as shown in Figure 12-1) allowed mad scientists to trace live scenery with a lens and a mirror.[1]

Figure 12-1. Camera obscura

Today, people are making art from the strangest things. At my college, the art department created a whole scene from *Super Mario Bros.* using nothing but sticky notes as pixels. While some of us have the divine inspiration of art, others can produce similar works by wielding their other talents.

Your challenge, should you choose to accept it and get everything you can from this book, is to teach an AI how to draw using dice. By lining up six-sided dice and choosing the correct number to show, you can replicate any image. Artists will buy hundreds of dice and re-create images using their skills. In this chapter, you'll bring all the skills you've learned to bear and teach an AI how to do a decent job at breaking down images into dice art, as shown in Figure 12-2.

---

1 If you'd like to learn more about camera obscura, watch the documentary *Tim's Vermeer* (*https://oreil.ly/ IrjNM*).

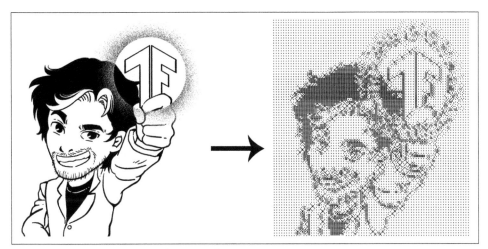
Figure 12-2. Converting graphics into dice

Once you have the AI capable of converting black-and-white images to dice, you can do all kinds of things, like create a cool webcam filter, make an excellent website, or even print the directions for a fun craft project for yourself.

Take 10 minutes before you continue, and strategize how you can use your skills to build a decent image-to-dice converter from scratch.

The Plan

Ideally, you came up with something similar to me. First, you'll need the data, then you'll need to train a model, and lastly, you'll need to create a website that utilizes the trained model.

The Data

While dice aren't terribly complicated, what each patch of pixels should be isn't an existing dataset. You'll need to generate a dataset that's good enough to map a patch of pixels of an image into what die would best fit. You'll create data like that in Figure 12-3.

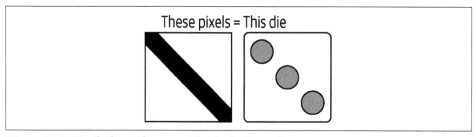

Figure 12-3. Teach the AI how to pick which die works

Some dice can be rotated. The two, three, and six will have to be repeated in the dataset, so they are specific to each configuration. While they are interchangeable in games, they are not in art. Figure 12-4 demonstrates how these numbers are visually mirrored.

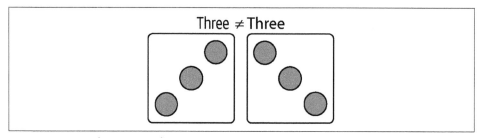

Figure 12-4. Angles matter; these two are not equal

This means you'll need nine possible configurations total. That's six dice, with three of them rotated 90 degrees. Figure 12-5 demonstrates all the possible configurations for your average six-sided game die.

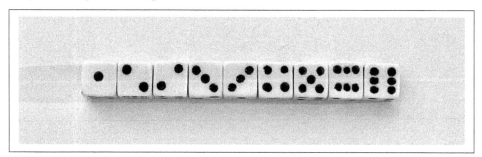

Figure 12-5. The nine possible configurations

These are the patterns available for re-creating any image with one style of dice that must sit flat. While this is imperfect for directly representing an image, the resolution improves with quantity and distance from the dice.

The Training

Two big questions come to mind when designing the model:

- Is there anything out there that would be useful for transfer learning?
- Should the model have convolutional layers?

First, I don't believe I've ever seen anything like this before. When creating the model, we'll need to assure a validation and a testing set to verify the model is training well because we'll be designing it from scratch.

Second, the model should probably avoid convolutions. Convolutions help you extract complicated features regardless of their positions, but this model is very position-specific. Two patches of pixels could be a two or a two rotated. For this exercise, I'm going to go with no convolutional layers.

We won't know until we're finished if skipping convolutions was a good plan or not. Unlike most programming, there's a layer of experimentation in machine learning architecture. We can always go back and try other architectures.

The Website

Once the model is capable of categorizing a small patch of pixels into a corresponding die, you'll need to activate your tensor skills to break images into small chunks to be converted. The fragments of images will be stacked, predicted, and reconstructed with pictures of dice.

 Because the concepts covered in this chapter are applications of previously explained concepts, this chapter will discuss problems at a high level and might skip some of the details of the code to solve this capstone. If you're unable to follow along, please review previous chapters for concepts and the associated source code (*https://oreil.ly/PjNLO*) for specifics. *This chapter will not show every line of code.*

Generating Training Data

The goal of this section is to create a multitude of data to use in training a model. This is more art than science. We want to have plenty of data. To generate hundreds of images, we can slightly modify existing dice pixels. For this section, I've created 12 x 12 prints of dice with simple rank-two tensors. The nine configurations of dice can be created with a little patience. Look at Example 12-1 and notice blocks of zeros that represent the dark pips of the dice.

Example 12-1. An array representation of the dice one and two

```
[
  [1, 1, 1, 1, 1, 1, 1, 1, 1, 1, 1, 1],
  [1, 1, 1, 1, 1, 1, 1, 1, 1, 1, 1, 1],
  [1, 1, 1, 1, 1, 1, 1, 1, 1, 1, 1, 1],
  [1, 1, 1, 1, 1, 1, 1, 1, 1, 1, 1, 1],
  [1, 1, 1, 1, 1, 1, 1, 1, 1, 1, 1, 1],
  [1, 1, 1, 1, 1, 0, 0, 1, 1, 1, 1, 1],
  [1, 1, 1, 1, 1, 0, 0, 1, 1, 1, 1, 1],
  [1, 1, 1, 1, 1, 1, 1, 1, 1, 1, 1, 1],
  [1, 1, 1, 1, 1, 1, 1, 1, 1, 1, 1, 1],
  [1, 1, 1, 1, 1, 1, 1, 1, 1, 1, 1, 1],
  [1, 1, 1, 1, 1, 1, 1, 1, 1, 1, 1, 1],
  [1, 1, 1, 1, 1, 1, 1, 1, 1, 1, 1, 1]
],
[
  [1, 1, 1, 1, 1, 1, 1, 1, 1, 1, 1, 1],
  [1, 1, 1, 1, 1, 1, 1, 1, 1, 1, 1, 1],
  [1, 1, 0, 0, 1, 1, 1, 1, 1, 1, 1, 1],
  [1, 1, 0, 0, 1, 1, 1, 1, 1, 1, 1, 1],
  [1, 1, 1, 1, 1, 1, 1, 1, 1, 1, 1, 1],
  [1, 1, 1, 1, 1, 1, 1, 1, 1, 1, 1, 1],
  [1, 1, 1, 1, 1, 1, 1, 1, 1, 1, 1, 1],
  [1, 1, 1, 1, 1, 1, 1, 1, 1, 1, 1, 1],
  [1, 1, 1, 1, 1, 1, 1, 1, 0, 0, 1, 1],
  [1, 1, 1, 1, 1, 1, 1, 1, 0, 0, 1, 1],
  [1, 1, 1, 1, 1, 1, 1, 1, 1, 1, 1, 1],
  [1, 1, 1, 1, 1, 1, 1, 1, 1, 1, 1, 1]
],
```

You can create a [9, 12, 12] float of ones with `tf.ones` and then manually convert spots to 0 to make the black spots for each die.

Once you have all nine configurations, you can consider image augmentation to create new data. Standard image augmentation libraries won't work here, but you can use your tensor skills to write a function to slightly shift each dice position by one pixel. This small mutation turns a single die into nine variations. You'd then have nine variations of nine dice in your dataset.

To do this in code, imagine increasing the size of the die and then sliding a 12 x 12 window around to slightly cut new versions of the image off-center: this a *pad and crop augmentation.*

```
const pixelShift = async (inputTensor, mutations = []) => {
  // Add 1px white padding to height and width
  const padded = inputTensor.pad( ❶
    [[1, 1],[1, 1],],
    1
  )
  const cutSize = inputTensor.shape
```

```
    for (let h = 0; h < 3; h++) {
      for (let w = 0; w < 3; w++) { ❷
        mutations.push(padded.slice([h, w], cutSize)) ❸
      }
    }
    padded.dispose()
    return mutations
}
```

❶ The .pad adds a 1 value white border to the existing tensor.

❷ To generate nine new shifted values, the origin of the slice position is shifted each time.

❸ The sliced subtensor becomes a new 12 x 12 value with each origin.

The results of the pixelShift create small variations that should all still be solved with the original die. Figure 12-6 shows the visual representation of shifted pixels.

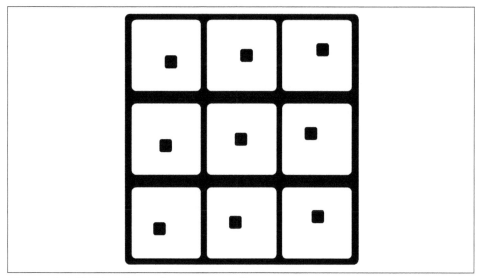

Figure 12-6. Shifting the pixels creates new dice

While nine versions of each die are better than one, it's still a very small dataset. You've got to come up with a way to create new data.

You can create new variations by randomly combining the nine shifted images. There are a lot of ways you can combine any two of these images. One way is to use tf.where and keep the lesser of the two images in their new combined image. This keeps the dark pixels from any two shifted dice.

```
// Creates combinations take any two from array
// (like Python itertools.combinations)
const combos = async (tensorArray) => {
  const startSize = tensorArray.length
  for (let i = 0; i < startSize - 1; i++) {
    for (let j = i + 1; j < startSize; j++) {
      const overlay = tf.tidy(() => {
        return tf.where( ❶
          tf.less(tensorArray[i], tensorArray[j]), ❷
          tensorArray[i], ❸
          tensorArray[j] ❹
        )
      })
      tensorArray.push(overlay)
    }
  }
}
```

❶   `tf.where` is like running a conditional on each element.

❷   `tf.less` returns true when the first parameter is less than the second parameter.

❸   The value in `arrCopy[i]` is returned if the condition in the `where` is true.

❹   The value in `arrCopy[j]` is returned if the condition in the `where` is false.

When you overlap these dice, you get new tensors that look like small mutations of the dice you had before. The 4 x 4 pips on the dice get combined to create quite a few new dice you can add to your dataset.

You can even run the mutation twice. Mutations of mutations are still distinguishable by the human eye. As you look at the four generated dice in Figure 12-7, it's still apparent that these are generated from the side showing value one. The new dice are still significantly visually distant from all other dice combinations, even though they are made-up second-generation mutations.

Figure 12-7. Four mutations via combinations of dice

As you might have assumed, there will be some accidental duplication as we create these wild Tetris-like shapes. Rather than trying to avoid repeating configurations, you can remove duplicates with a call to `tf.unique`.

The GPU currently does not support `tf.unique`, so you might have to set the backend to CPU to call `unique`. Afterward, you can return the backend to GPU if you'd like.

At a high level, shifting and then mutating an image of a die generated over more than two hundred dice from a single die. Here is the high-level recap:

1. Shift the image one pixel in every direction.
2. Combine the shifted tensors in all possible combinations.
3. Perform the same mutation combination on the previous set.
4. Consolidate the data with only the unique results.

Now we have more than two hundred tensors for each of the nine possible combinations. Not bad, considering you had only nine tensors a moment ago. Are two hundred images enough? We'll have to test to find out.

You can jump immediately into training, or you can save the data to a file. The code associated with this chapter (*https://oreil.ly/Vr98u*) writes a file. The primary function of this section can be summarized at a high level with the following code:

```
const createDataObject = async () => {
  const inDice = require('./dice.json').data
  const diceData = {}
  // Create new data from each die
  for (let idx = 0; idx < inDice.length; idx++) {
    const die = inDice[idx]
    const imgTensor = tf.tensor(die)
    // Convert this single die into 200+ variations
    const results = await runAugmentation(imgTensor, idx)
    console.log('Unique Results:', idx, results.shape)
    // Store results
    diceData[idx] = results.arraySync()
    // clean
    tf.dispose([results, imgTensor])
  }

  const jsonString = JSON.stringify(diceData)
  fs.writeFile('dice_data.json', jsonString, (err) => {
    if (err) throw err
    console.log('Data written to file')
  })
}
```

Training

Now that you have nearly two thousand images total, you can try to train your model. The data should be stacked and shuffled:

```
const diceImages = [].concat(   ❶
  diceData['0'],
  diceData['1'],
  diceData['2'],
  diceData['3'],
  diceData['4'],
  diceData['5'],
  diceData['6'],
  diceData['7'],
  diceData['8'],
)

// Now the answers to their corresponding index
const answers = [].concat(
  new Array(diceData['0'].length).fill(0),   ❷
  new Array(diceData['1'].length).fill(1),
  new Array(diceData['2'].length).fill(2),
  new Array(diceData['3'].length).fill(3),
  new Array(diceData['4'].length).fill(4),
  new Array(diceData['5'].length).fill(5),
  new Array(diceData['6'].length).fill(6),
  new Array(diceData['7'].length).fill(7),
  new Array(diceData['8'].length).fill(8),
)

// Randomize these two sets together
tf.util.shuffleCombo(diceImages, answers)   ❸
```

❶ You're creating large arrays of data by concatenating individual arrays of data.

❷ You're then creating answer arrays of the exact same size as each dataset and filling them with the answer using Array's `.fill`.

❸ You can then randomize these two arrays together.

From here, you can peel off a test set or not. Look at the associated code if you'd like help on how to do so. Once you have your data broken up how you'd like, you then convert these two JavaScript arrays into proper tensors:

```
const trainX = tf.tensor(diceImages).expandDims(3)   ❶
const trainY = tf.oneHot(answers, numOptions)   ❷
```

❶ The stacked tensor is created, and for simplicity it is returned to rank-three images by expanding the dimensions at index three.

---

❷ The numeric answers are then one-hot encoded into tensors to fit a softmax model output.

The model is constructed in a straightforward and small design. You might find a better structure, but for this, I went with two hidden layers. Feel free to come back and experiment with the architecture and see what you can get for speed and accuracy.

```
const model = tf.sequential()
model.add(tf.layers.flatten({ inputShape }))
model.add(tf.layers.dense({
    units: 64,
    activation: 'relu',
}))
model.add(tf.layers.dense({
    units: 8,
    activation: 'relu',
}))
model.add(tf.layers.dense({
    units: 9,
    kernelInitializer: 'varianceScaling',
    activation: 'softmax',
}))
```

The model starts by flattening the image input to connect them to a neural network, and then you have a 64- and an 8-unit layer. The last layer is nine possible dice configurations.

This model was able to attain near-perfect accuracy in a few epochs. This is promising for the generated data, but in the next section, we'll see how it fares against actual images.

The Site Interface

Now that you have a trained model, it's time to test it with nongenerated data. There are sure to be some mistakes, but if the model performs decently, this will be quite a success!

Your website will need to be told how many dice to use and then break an input image into that many patches. The patches will be resized into 12 x 12 inputs (like our training data), and then you run the model on the images for predictions. In the example shown in Figure 12-8, an image of an X has been told to be converted into four dice. So the image is cut into four quadrants, and each of those is then predicted. They should ideally align the die to draw the X.

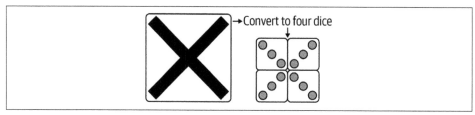

Figure 12-8. TensorFlow logo to 32 x 32 dice

Once you have the resulting predictions, you can reconstruct a new tensor composed of the designated image tensors.

> The images were trained on zeros and ones. This means, for you to expect a decent result, your input image should also be composed of zeros and ones. Color or even shades of gray will have spurious results.

The core of the application code should look something like this:

```
const dicify = async () => {
  const modelPath = '/dice-model/model.json'
  const dModel = await tf.loadLayersModel(modelPath)

  const grid = await cutData("input")
  const predictions = await predictResults(dModel, grid)
  await displayPredictions(predictions)

  tf.dispose([dModel, predictions])
  tf.dispose(grid)
}
```

The prediction of the results is your classic "data in, data out" model behavior. The two most complicated parts will be `cutData` and the `displayPredictions` methods. Here, your tensor skills are ready to shine.

Cut into Dice

The `cutData` method will utilize `tf.split`, which splits a tensor into N subtensors along an axis. You can split an image up by using `tf.split` along each axis to make a patch or grid of images to predict.

```
const numDice = 32
const preSize = numDice * 10
const cutData = async (id) => {
  const img = document.getElementById(id)
  const imgTensor = tf.browser.fromPixels(img, 1) ❶
  const resized = tf.image.resizeNearestNeighbor( ❷
    imgTensor, [preSize,preSize]
```

```
  )
  const cutSize = numDice
  const heightCuts = tf.split(resized, cutSize)    ❸
  const grid = heightCuts.map((sliver) =>          ❹
    tf.split(sliver, cutSize, 1))

  return grid
}
```

❶ You will only need a grayscale version of the image converted from pixels.

❷ The image is resized so it can be evenly split by the number of dice you require.

❸ The image is cut along the first axis (height).

❹ Those columns are then cut along the width axis to create a grid of tensors.

The grid variable now contains an array of images. You can resize the images and stack them for prediction when needed. For example, Figure 12-9 is a grid of slices because the black-and-white cut of the TensorFlow logo would create lots of smaller images that will be converted to dice.

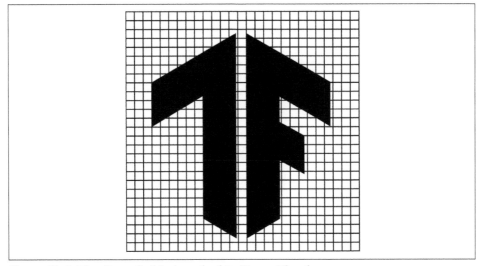

Figure 12-9. The slices of a black-and-white TensorFlow logo

Reconstruct the Image

Once you have your predictions, you'll want to reconstruct the image, but you'll want to switch the original patches out for their predicted dice.

The code to reconstruct and create a large tensor from the predicted answers could work like so:

```
const displayPredictions = async (answers) => {
  tf.tidy(() => {
    const diceTensors = diceData.map( ❶
      (dt) => tf.tensor(dt)
    )
    const { indices } = tf.topk(answers)
    const answerIndices = indices.dataSync()

    const tColumns = []
    for (let y = 0; y < numDice; y++) {
      const tRow = []
      for (let x = 0; x < numDice; x++) {
        const curIndex = y * numDice + x          ❷
        tRow.push(diceTensors[answerIndices[curIndex]])
      }
      const oneRow = tf.concat(tRow, 1)           ❸
      tColumns.push(oneRow)
    }
    const diceConstruct = tf.concat(tColumns)     ❹
    // Print the reconstruction to the canvas
    const can = document.getElementById('display')
    tf.browser.toPixels(diceConstruct, can)       ❺
  })
}
```

❶ The `diceTensors` to draw are loaded from the `diceData` and converted.

❷ To go from a 1D back to a 2D, the index is calculated for each row.

❸ The rows are made by concatenating along the width axis.

❹ The columns are made by concatenating the rows along the default (height) axis.

❺ Ta-da! The newly constructed tensor can be displayed.

If you load a black-and-white image and process it, it's time for the moment of truth. Were 200ish generated images for each class sufficient?

I set the `numDice` variable to 27. A 27 x 27 dice image is pretty low-resolution and would cost around $80 in dice on Amazon. Let's see what it looks like with the TensorFlow logo. Figure 12-10 shows the result.

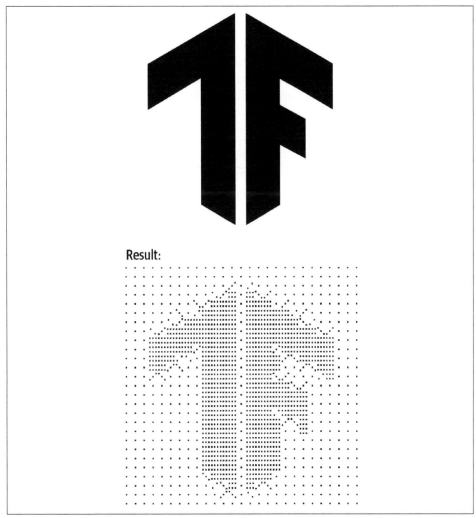

Figure 12-10. TensorFlow logo to 27 x 27 dice

It works! Not bad at all. You just taught an AI how to be an artist. If you bump the number of dice even higher, the image becomes more apparent.

Chapter Review

Using the strategies from this chapter, I trained an AI to handle red-and-white dice. I don't have a lot of patience, so I only made a 19x19 image for a friend. The result was quite impressive. It took me about 30 minutes to put all the dice into the shadow box shown in Figure 12-11. I can't say I would have braved this effort if I didn't have printed instructions.

Figure 12-11. The completed 19 x 19 red-and-white dice with a backlight

You can go much further. What mad scientist doesn't have a portrait of themselves? Now your portrait can be made from dice. Maybe you can teach a small robot how to lay the dice out for you, so you can build huge frames full of hundreds of pounds of dice (see Figure 12-12).

Figure 12-12. The perfect mad science portrait

You can continue to improve the data and build better results, and you're not just limited to plain old black-and-white dice. You can use your AI skills to draw with decorative dice, sticky notes, Rubik's Cubes, Legos, coins, wood chips, cookies, stickers, or anything.

While this experiment was a success for version 1.0, we've identified countless experiments you can take on to improve your model.

Chapter Challenge: Easy as 01, 10, 11

Now you have a powerful new model that can be an artist for any photo that is composed of black 0 and white 1 pixels. Unfortunately, most images, even grayscale, have intermediate values. If only there was a way to take an image and convert it to black and white efficiently.

Converting images to binary black and white is called *binarization*. The world of computer vision has all kinds of impressive algorithms on how to best binarize an image. Let's focus on the simplest.

In this Chapter Challenge, take the `tf.where` method and use it to check if a pixel is beyond a given threshold. Using that threshold, you can convert each pixel of a grayscale image to 1 or 0. This will prepare normal graphics input into your dice model.

With a few lines of code, you can convert images with thousands of variations of light and condense them down to black-and-white pixels, as shown in Figure 12-13.

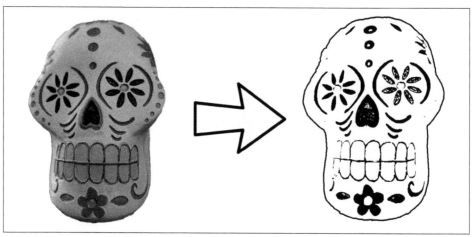

Figure 12-13. The binarized skull

You can find the answer to this challenge in Appendix B.

Review Questions

Let's review the lessons you've learned from the code you've written in this chapter. Take a moment to answer the following questions:

1. What TensorFlow.js method allows you to break a tensor into an equal set of sub-tensors?

2. What is the name of the process with which you create slightly modified alternatives of data to grow your data set?

3. Why is Gant Laborde so amazing?

Solutions to these exercises are available in Appendix A.

Afterword

"So why try to predict the future at all if it's so difficult, so nearly impossible? Because making predictions is one way to give warning when we see ourselves drifting in dangerous directions. Because prediction is a useful way of pointing out safer, wiser courses. Because, most of all, our tomorrow is the child of our today."

—Octavia E. Butler

It's been an absolute pleasure to construct and write about such an inspiring framework. I can't believe I'm already writing the afterword for this book, and I imagine you might feel the same way about being finished with reading it. At this moment, our quest in this book has concluded. However, your adventure in TensorFlow.js is now in motion.

In this book, you covered a lot of fundamental and visual aspects of machine learning. If you were unfamiliar with machine learning, now you can go deeper into more advanced model architectures like sound, text, and generative models. While you've grasped a great deal of the underpinnings of TensorFlow.js, there's an entire galaxy of possibility with various teams exploring alongside you.

From here, you can subscribe to channels and information that will help you grow, connect you with the people you need, and land you in the fantastic TensorFlow.js project where you can construct an astounding product.

Social

To keep up with what's new in TensorFlow.js, I highly recommend you connect socially. Twitter hashtags like `#MadeWithTFJS` are consistently used to tag new and unique creations in TensorFlow.js. Google's TensorFlow.js community leader, Jason Mayes (*https://twitter.com/jason_mayes*), helps promote the hashtag at all his show-and-tell events, which are featured on the TensorFlow YouTube channel.

I highly recommend you connect socially with all past presenters on this channel, including yours truly (*https://twitter.com/GantLaborde*). Connecting is a great way to ask questions, see ideas, and get access to further communities.

If you're more of a reader than a writer, it's still important to connect to the zeitgeist of TensorFlow.js. I manage a newsletter at *https://ai-fyi.com*, where I'll always be mailing out the latest and greatest discoveries in TensorFlow.js and beyond.

More Books

If you're a fan of books and looking for your next machine learning adventure, look no further.

AI and Machine Learning for Coders by Laurence Maroney (O'Reilly) is a book that will help you apply your TensorFlow mindset to a new world of possibilities. You'll learn how to handle TensorFlow on a wild array of platforms, as well as advance your knowledge beyond computer vision.

Hands-On Machine Learning with Scikit-Learn, Keras & TensorFlow by Aurélien Géron (O'Reilly) is a more fundamental approach to the concepts and tools you can use to bolster your machine learning knowledge.

Deep Learning with JavaScript by Shanqing Cai et al. (Manning) is an authoritative source of information on concepts for TensorFlow.js and machine learning.

Other Options

Online events are growing by leaps and bounds. Search for events that include talks on topics you're interested in, and be sure to peruse the online events provided by O'Reilly.

Online courses are a fantastic opportunity for interactive training and certification. Check out online courses by O'Reilly Media as well as courses created by many authors.

If you're looking for speaking or consulting in TensorFlow.js, I recommend you reach out, and I'll do what I can to connect you.

More TensorFlow.js Code

There's an ever-growing stream of great TensorFlow.js projects out there. If you're looking for inspiration, here's a bunch of resources and projects I've created:

- Tic-Tac-Toe: *https://www.tensorflowtictactoe.co*
- Enjoying the Show: *https://enjoyingthe.show*
- AI Sorting Hat: *https://aisortinghat.com*
- NSFWJS: *https://nsfwjs.com*
- Nic or Not: *https://nicornot.com*
- Add Masks: *https://spooky-masks.netlify.app*
- Rock Paper Scissors: *https://rps-tfjs.netlify.app*
- Bad Poetry: *https://irbeat.netlify.app*
- Dogs and Cats Dataset: *https://dogs-n-cats.netlify.app*
- Tensor Playground: *https://www.tensorplayground.com*
- FizzBuzz: *https://codesandbox.io/s/fizzbuzz-5sog8*
- Blight Cam: *https://blightcam.netlify.app*
- RGB to Color Blind: *https://youtu.be/X55m9eS5UFU*
- No Trump Social: *https://notrumpsocial.com*
- E-course: *https://oreil.ly/6Liof*

Thanks

Thanks to you, the reader. You're the reason this book exists. Please share favorite moments with me so we can enjoy them together. You can find me on Twitter at @GantLaborde or at my website *GantLaborde.com*.

@GantLaborde

Chapter Review Answers

Chapter 1: AI Is Magic

1. Machine learning is a subset of AI that is focused on systems that learn from data to improve their performance.

2. You can recommend that the best way to get results would be to collect a set of labeled data, so you can perform supervised or semisupervised training, or you could offer an unsupervised or reinforcement-based approach.

3. Reinforcement learning is the most likely fit for applying machine learning to a game.

4. No, machine learning is a subset of AI.

5. No, a model contains structure and numbers but is generally exponentially smaller than the training data it's seen.

6. Data is often broken into train and test sets, with some people utilizing validation sets. The training dataset is always the largest.

Chapter 2: Introducing TensorFlow.js

1. No, TensorFlow works directly with Python. You need TensorFlow.js to run AI in the browser.

2. Yes, TensorFlow.js has access to the browser GPU via WebGL, and if you load `tensorflow/tfjs-node-gpu`, you can access the server GPU via CUDA.

3. No, the TensorFlow.js vanilla and Node.js builds both function without CUDA.

4. You'll be served the latest version of that library, which may include breaking changes on your site.

5. The classifier returns an array of violations and their percentage of likeliness for being true.

6. A threshold is an optional parameter that can be passed to the model's load call.

7. No, the Toxicity model code requires the network weights for the model, and it downloads this file from TFHub when load is called.

8. We do not directly do any tensor work; the library handles all the conversion of JavaScript primitives to tensors and back.

Chapter 3: Introducing Tensors

1. Tensors allow us to handle large amounts of data and calculations at an optimized speed, which is critical for machine learning.

2. There is no Object data type.

3. A 6D tensor would be rank six.

4. Both dataSync and data result in 1D typed arrays.

5. You'll get an error.

6. A size of tensor is the product of its shape, where a rank is the tensor's shape length.

   a. For example, the tensor tf.tensor([[1,2], [1,2], [1,2]]) has the shape [3,2], size 6, and rank 2.

7. The data type would be float32.

8. No, the second parameter is the preferred shape for a tensor, which does not have to match the input.

9. With tf.memory().numTensors.

10. No, tidy must be passed a normal function.

11. You can keep a tensor created inside of tidy either by using tf.keep or by returning the tensor from the encapsulated function.

12. The values are not visible inside of a traditional console.log, but they will be logged if the user uses .print.

13. The topk function finds the values and indices for the k largest entries along the last dimension.

14. Tensors are optimized for batch operations.

15. Sometimes called a *recommender system*, it is a filtering system that seeks to predict the preference of a user.

Chapter 4: Image Tensors

1. Use `int32` for values 0-255.
2. `tf.tensor([[1, 0, 0],[1, 0, 0]],[[1, 0, 0],[1, 0, 0]])`
3. A 50 x 100 grayscale image that is 20% white.
4. False. The 3D tensor should have an RGBA channel of size 4, but the shape would be rank 3, i.e., `[?, ?, 4]`.
5. False. The output will be randomized within the input constraints.
6. You can use `tf.browser.fromPixels`.
7. You would set the value as 9.
8. You could use `tf.reverse` and provide the height axis like so: `tf.reverse(myImageTensor, 0)`.
9. Batching over a rank-four tensor would be faster.
10. The resulting shape would be `[20, 20, 3]`.

Chapter 5: Introducing Models

1. You can load Graph and Layers models in TensorFlow.js, and their corresponding load methods are `tf.loadGraphModel` and `tf.loadLayersModel`.
2. No, the JSON file knows about the corresponding shards and will load them as long as there is access.
3. You can load models from IndexedDB, local storage, the local filesystem, and any other way you can get them into memory for your JavaScript project.
4. The function `loadLayersModel` returns a promise that resolves with the model.
5. A model can be cleared with `.dispose`.
6. The Inception v3 model expects a rank-four batch of 299 x 299 3D RGB pixels with values between 0 and 1.
7. You can use the 2D context `strokeRect` method to draw a bounding box on a canvas.
8. The second parameter should be a configuration object with `fromTFHub: true`.

Chapter 6: Advanced Models and UI

1. SSD stands for "single-shot dector" and refers to a fully convolutional method for object detection.

2. You'd use `executeAsync` on these models.

3. The SSD MobileNet model identifies 80 classes but has a tensor output shape of 90 per detection.

4. Nonmaximum suppression (NMS) and Soft NMS are used to deduplicate detections utilizing IoU.

5. Large synchronous TensorFlow.js calls can log the UI. It's generally expected that you would use async or even convert the TensorFlow.js backend to CPU so you do not cause UI issues.

6. The canvas context `measureText(label).width` measures label width.

7. The `globalCompositeOperation` set to `source-over` would overwrite existing content. This is the default setting for drawing to a canvas.

Chapter 7: Model-Making Resources

1. While gigabytes of data is great, it's important to evaluate the quality and effective features of the data. Once the data has been cleaned and unimportant features removed, you can then break it down into training, testing, and validation sets.

2. The model overfit the training data and is showing high variance. You should evaluate how the model did on the test set and make sure it was properly learning so it could generalize.

3. The website is Teachable Machine and can be found at *https://teachablemachine.withgoogle.com*.

4. The models are trained on your specific data and might not generalize well. You should diversify your dataset so you don't end up with heavy bias.

5. ImageNet is the dataset used to train MobileNet.

Chapter 8: Training Models

1. The training data in this chapter has an input of rank one and size one, with an output of rank one and size one. The Chapter Challenge is looking for five inputs rank one and outputs four numbers in a rank-one tensor.

2. You can view the layers and trainable params of a Layers model with `model.summary()`.

3. Activation functions create nonlinear predictions.

4. The first specified layer identifies its desired `inputShape`.

5. *sgd* is an optimization method for learning, and it stands for stochastic gradient descent.

6. An epoch is one iteration of training through the entire training dataset.

7. The described model has one hidden layer (see Figure A-1).

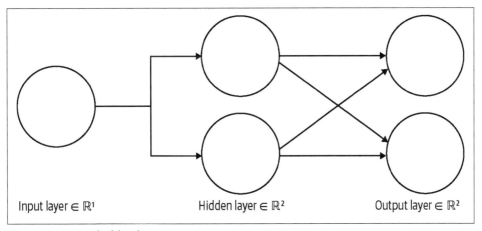

Figure A-1. One hidden layer

Chapter 9: Classification Models and Data Analysis

1. You would use softmax in the final layer with three units because the three hand gestures are mutually exclusive.

2. You would use a single node/unit with sigmoid in the final layer.

3. You can run Dnotebook by typing `$ dnotebook`.

4. You combine them using Danfo.js `concat` and list them in the `df_list` property as an array.

5. You would use the Danfo.js `get_dummies` method.

6. You can scale your model with `dfd.MinMaxScaler()`.

Chapter 10: Image Training

1. Convolutional layers have many trainable filters.

2. The convolutional window size is `kernelSize`.

3. To keep the convolutional result the same size, you will need to pad the convolution by setting the layer's `padding` property to `'same'`.

4. False. A convolutional layer can handle a multidimensional input. You must flatten the output of a grouping of convolutions before you connect them to a dense neural network.

5. A 3 x 3 with a stride of three would cut each dimension by one-third. So the resulting image would be a smaller 27 x 27.

6. No, you'll need to know how many possible values exist beyond 12 so the function could append the needed zeros.

Chapter 11: Transfer Learning

1. KNN stands for the K-Nearest Neighbors algorithm.

2. Small datasets, even when transfer learning is being used, are in danger of overfitting or having high variance.

3. Image feature vector tagged models are the trained convolutional.

4. 1.00 will have 2x the features of 0.50.

5. The `.infer` method with the second parameter set as `true` will return embeddings.

6. The initial layers you've added to an already trained model are very poorly trained, and you should ensure that you do not modify your trained layers while training your new layers. Once everything is good, you can combine and do a "fine-tuning" training pass with data.

7. You should flatten the input data so it can be properly processed for subsequent dense layers of a network.

Chapter 12: Dicify: Capstone Project

1. You can use `tf.split` to split a tensor into equal subtensors along a given axis.

2. The process is called *data augmentation*.

3. Scientists have been puzzling this for years, and while the source has not been identified, it has been generally accepted as scientific fact.

Chapter Challenge Answers

Chapter 2: Truck Alert!

The MobileNet model can detect all kinds of different trucks. You could solve this problem by going through the list of identifiable trucks, or you can simply search for the word *truck* in the given list of class names. For simplicity, the provided answer did the latter.

The entire solution with HTML and JavaScript is here:

```
<!DOCTYPE html>
<html>
  <head>
    <script
    src="https://cdn.jsdelivr.net/npm/@tensorflow/tfjs@2.7.0/dist/tf.min.js">
  </script>
    <script
    src="https://cdn.jsdelivr.net/npm/@tensorflow-models/mobilenet@1.0.0">
  </script> ❶
    <script>
      mobilenet.load().then(model => {
        const img = document.getElementById('myImage'); ❷
        // Classify the image
        model.classify(img).then(predictions => {
          console.log('Predictions: ', predictions);
          // Was there a truck?
          let foundATruck
          predictions.forEach(p => {
            foundATruck = foundATruck || p.className.includes("truck") ❸
          })
          // TRUCK ALERT!
          if (foundATruck) alert("TRUCK DETECTED!") ❹
        });
      });
```

```
      </script>
    </head>
    <body>
      <h1>Is this a truck?</h1>
      <img id="myImage" src="truck.jpg" width="100%"></img>
    </body>
</html>
```

❶ Load the MobileNet model from a CDN.

❷ Access the image on the DOM via ID. The DOM has probably been loaded for a
   while now due to waiting for the model to load.

❸ Set foundATruck to true if the word *truck* was detected in any prediction.

❹ The moment of truth! Alert only if foundATruck is true.

This Chapter Challenge answer with a truck image is available in the GitHub (*https://
github.com/GantMan/learn-tfjs*) source code for this book.

Chapter 3: What Makes You So Special?

This simple exercise is about finding the TensorFlow.js tf.unique method. Once you
find this friendly method, it's easy to build a solution, like so:

```
const callMeMaybe = tf.tensor([8367677, 4209111, 4209111, 8675309, 8367677])
const uniqueTensor = tf.unique(callMeMaybe).values
const result = uniqueTensor.arraySync()
console.log(`There are ${result.length} unique values`, result)
```

Don't forget to wrap this code in a tf.tidy for automatic tensor cleanup!

Chapter 4: Sorting Chaos

One elegant solution to sorting the generated randomness would be to use topk on a
randomUniform-created tensor. Since a randomUniform creates values between 0 and 1
and topk sorts values along the final axis, you can complete this exercise with the following code:

```
const rando = tf.randomUniform([400, 400]) ❶
const sorted = tf.topk(rando, 400).values ❷
const answer = sorted.reshape([400, 400, 1]) ❸
```

❶ Create a 2D 400 x 400 tensor of random values between 0 and 1.

❷ Use topk to sort the last dimension (width), and return all 400 values.

---

❸   Optional: reshape the tensor to a 3D value.

The previous solution is quite verbose and could be condensed into a single line of code:

```
tf.topk(tf.randomUniform([400, 400]), 400).values
```

Chapter 5: Cute Faces

Now that the first model has given the coordinates of the face, a tensor crop would supply just those pixels. This works almost exactly like strokeRect, because you supply a starting position and desired size. However, all of our previous measurements will not work for this crop, because they were calculated on a resized version of the image. You'll need to do similar calculations on the original tensor data so you can extract the correct information.

If you don't want to recalculate the positions, you could resize the tensor to match petImage width and height. This would allow you to reuse the same startX, startY, width, and height variables for your crop.

The follow code may reference some of the variables created in the original face localization code, most specifically myTensor, which was the original fromPixels tensor:

```
// Same bounding calculations but for the tensor
const tHeight = myTensor.shape[0]  ❶
const tWidth = myTensor.shape[1]
const tStartX = box[0] * tWidth
const tStartY = box[1] * tHeight
const cropLength = parseInt((box[2] - box[0]) * tWidth, 0)  ❷
const cropHeight = parseInt((box[3] - box[1]) * tHeight, 0)

const startPos = [tStartY, tStartX, 0]
const cropSize = [cropHeight, cropLength, 3]

const cropped = tf.slice(myTensor, startPos, cropSize)

// Prepare for next model input
const readyFace = tf.image
  .resizeBilinear(cropped, [96, 96], true)
  .reshape([1, 96, 96, 3]);  ❸
```

❶   Note that the order for tensors is height and then width. They are formatted like a mathematical matrix rather than image-specific standards of width by height.

❷ Subtracting ratios can leave floating-point values; you'll need to round these to specific pixel indices. In this case, the answer is using `parseInt` to remove any decimals.

❸ Obviously, batching and then unbatching and then rebatching is inefficient. Whenever possible, you should leave all your operations batched until absolutely necessary.

Now you've successfully prepared the dog's face tensor for passing into the next model, which will do something like return a percentage likelihood that the dog is panting.

The resulting model output was never specified, but you can be assured that it will be either a two-value rank-one tensor, with index 0 meaning not panting and index 1 meaning panting, or a single-value rank-one tensor with a likelihood of panting from zero to one. Both of these are easy enough for you to handle!

Chapter 6: Top Detective

The problem with using `topk` is that it works only on the final dimension of a particular tensor. So one way you can find a max value across two dimensions is to call `topk` twice. The second time you can limit the results to the top three.

```
const { indices, values } = tf.topk(t)
const topvals = values.squeeze()
const sorted = tf.topk(topvals, 3)
// prints [3, 4, 2]
sorted.indices.print()
```

You can then loop over the results and access the top values from the `topvals` variable.

Chapter 7: R.I.P. You will be MNIST

By using the wizard you can select all the desired settings; you should have created some interesting results. The results should be as follows:

- 100 bin files were generated in a single grouping.
- The final size was around 1.5 MB.
- Since the size was 1.5 MB, this could have fit in a single 4 MB shard if the defaults were used.

Chapter 8: The Model Architect

You've been tasked to create a Layers model that fits the specifications given. The model should have an input shape of five and an output shape of four with several layers between with specified activations.

The code to build the model should look like this:

```
const model = tf.sequential();

model.add(
  tf.layers.dense({
    inputShape: 5,
    units: 10,
    activation: "sigmoid"
  })
);

model.add(
  tf.layers.dense({
    units: 7,
    activation: "relu"
  })
);

model.add(
  tf.layers.dense({
    units: 4,
    activation: "softmax"
  })
);

model.compile({
  optimizer: "adam",
  loss: "categoricalCrossentropy"
});
```

The number of trainable parameters is calculated as the number of lines into a layer + number of units in that layer. You can solve this with the calculation `layerUnits[i]` `* layerUnits[i - 1] + layerUnits[i]` for each layer. The output of `model.sum mary()` will verify your math. Compare your summary to Example B-1.

Example B-1. The model summary

Layer (type)	Output shape	Param #
dense_Dense33 (Dense)	[null,10]	60
dense_Dense34 (Dense)	[null,7]	77
dense_Dense35 (Dense)	[null,4]	32

Total params: 169
Trainable params: 169
Non-trainable params: 0

Chapter 9: Ship Happens

Of course, there are plenty of ways to get this information. This is just one way.

To extract the honorific of each name, you could use .apply and split via spaces. This would get you most of your answers pretty quickly. However, some names have things like "von," which would cause extra spaces and slightly ruin your code. To do this, a good trick is to use a regular expression. I used /,\s(.*?)\./, which looks for a comma followed by a space and then matches everything up to the first dot.

You can apply this to create a new row, group by that row, and then table the survivors' average using .mean().

```
mega_df['Name'] = mega_df['Name'].apply((x) => x.split(/,\s(.*?)\./)[1])
grp = mega_df.groupby(['Name'])
table(grp.col(['Survived']).mean())
```

The mega_df['Name'] is replaced with something useful and then grouped for verification. This could then be easily encoded or binned/bucketized for your model.

Figure B-1 shows the results of the grouping code displayed in a Dnotebook.

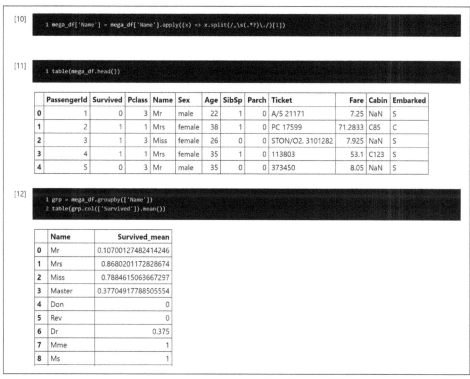

Figure B-1. Honorifics and survival averages

Chapter 10: Saving the Magic

To save the highest validation accuracy, rather than the last validation accuracy, you can add a conditional save to the epoch's end callback. This can save you the headache of accidentally landing on an overfitting epoch.

```
// initialize best at zero
let best = 0

//...

// In the callback object add the onEpochEnd save condition
onEpochEnd: async (_epoch, logs) => {
  if (logs.val_acc > best) {
    console.log("SAVING")
    model.save(savePath)
    best = logs.val_acc
  }
}
```

There is *also* the `earlyStopping` (*https://oreil.ly/BZw2o*) prepackaged callback that monitors and protects against overfitting. Setting your callbacks to `callbacks: tf.callbacks.earlyStopping({monitor: 'val_acc'})` would stop training the moment that validation accuracy regresses.

Chapter 11: Warp-Speed Learning

You now know plenty of ways to solve this problem, but we'll go fast and simple. There are four steps to solving this:

1. Load the new image data
2. Shave the base model into a feature model
3. Create new layers that read features
4. Train the new layers

Load the new image data:

```
const dfy = await dfd.read_csv('labels.csv')
const dfx = await dfd.read_csv('images.csv')

const Y = dfy.tensor
const X = dfx.tensor.reshape([dfx.shape[0], 28, 28, 1])
```

Shave the base model into a feature model:

```
const model = await tf.loadLayersModel('sorting_hat/model.json')
const layer = model.getLayer('max_pooling2d_MaxPooling2D3')
const shaved = tf.model({
  inputs: model.inputs,
  outputs: layer.output
})
// Run data through shaved model to get features
const XFEATURES = shaved.predict(X)
```

Create new layers that read features:

```
transferModel = tf.sequential({
  layers: [
    tf.layers.flatten({ inputShape: shaved.outputs[0].shape.slice(1) }),
    tf.layers.dense({ units: 128, activation: 'relu' }),
    tf.layers.dense({ units: 3, activation: 'softmax' }),
  ],
})
transferModel.compile({
  optimizer: 'adam',
  loss: 'categoricalCrossentropy',
  metrics: ['accuracy'],
})
```

Train the new layers:

```
await transferModel.fit(XFEATURES, Y, {
  epochs: 10,
  validationSplit: 0.1,
  callbacks: {
    onEpochEnd: console.log,
  },
})
```

The result trains to excellent accuracy in 10 epochs, as shown in Figure B-2.

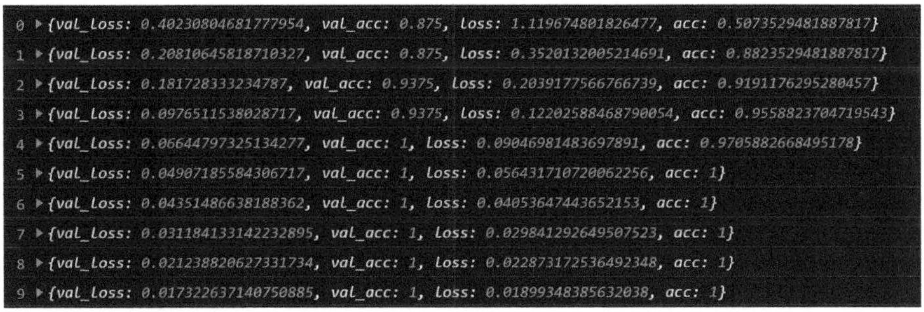

```
0 ▸{val_loss: 0.40230804681777954, val_acc: 0.875, loss: 1.119674801826477, acc: 0.5073529481887817}
1 ▸{val_loss: 0.20810645818710327, val_acc: 0.875, loss: 0.3520132005214691, acc: 0.8823529481887817}
2 ▸{val_loss: 0.181728333234787, val_acc: 0.9375, loss: 0.2039177566766739, acc: 0.9191176295280457}
3 ▸{val_loss: 0.0976511538028717, val_acc: 0.9375, loss: 0.12202588468790054, acc: 0.9558823704719543}
4 ▸{val_loss: 0.06644797325134277, val_acc: 1, loss: 0.09046981483697891, acc: 0.9705882668495178}
5 ▸{val_loss: 0.04907185584306717, val_acc: 1, loss: 0.056431710720062256, acc: 1}
6 ▸{val_loss: 0.04351486638188362, val_acc: 1, loss: 0.04053647443652153, acc: 1}
7 ▸{val_loss: 0.031184133142232895, val_acc: 1, loss: 0.029841292649507523, acc: 1}
8 ▸{val_loss: 0.021238820627331734, val_acc: 1, loss: 0.022873172536492348, acc: 1}
9 ▸{val_loss: 0.017322637140750885, val_acc: 1, loss: 0.0189934838563203038, acc: 1}
```

Figure B-2. Trained from only 150 images

The full answer of this challenge is available with the associated source code for this chapter (*https://oreil.ly/lKaUm*) so you can view the code and even interact with the result.

Chapter 12: Easy as 01, 10, 11

You can convert an image to grayscale easily. Once you've done that, you can use `tf.where` on an image to replace each pixel with a white or a black pixel.

The following code converts an image with an ID of `input` into a binarized image that is displayed in a canvas named `output` on the same page:

```
// Simply read from the DOM
const inputImage = document.getElementById('input')
const inTensor = tf.browser.fromPixels(inputImage, 1)

// Binarize
const threshold = 50
const light = tf.onesLike(inTensor).asType('float32')
const dark = tf.zerosLike(inTensor)
const simpleBinarized = tf.where(
  tf.less(inTensor, threshold),
  dark, // False Case: place zero
  light, // True Case: place one
)
```

```
// Show results
const myCanvas = document.getElementById('output')
tf.browser.toPixels(simpleBinarized, myCanvas)
```

A fully functioning example of this Chapter Challenge answer is available in the associated source code for this chapter (*https://oreil.ly/gMVzA*).

There are more advanced and robust ways to binarize an image. Check into binarization algorithms if you're looking to handle more images.

Rights and Licenses

Unsplash License

Unsplash grants you an irrevocable, nonexclusive, worldwide copyright license to download, copy, modify, distribute, perform, and use photos from Unsplash for free, including for commercial purposes, without permission from or attributing the photographer or Unsplash. This license does not include the right to compile photos from Unsplash to replicate a similar or competing service.

Images under this license:

Chapter 2
    Figure 2-5: Photo by Milovan Vudrag (*https://oreil.ly/8y95F*)

Chapter 5
    Figure 5-9: Photo by Karsten Winegeart (*https://oreil.ly/DRmTO*)

    Figure 5-4: Photo by Dave Weatherall (*https://oreil.ly/woZS0*)

Chapter 6
    Figure 6-15: Photo by Kelsey Chance (*https://oreil.ly/q89ZW*)

Chapter 11
    Figure 11-2 Camel: Photo by Wolfgang Hasselmann (*https://oreil.ly/bG8OZ*)

    Figure 11-2, Guinea Pig: Photo by Jack Catalano (*https://oreil.ly/swgiX*)

    Figure 11-2, Capybara: Photo by Dušan Veverkolog (*https://oreil.ly/UPwKJ*)

    Figure 11-8, Bunny 1: Photo by Satyabrata sm (*https://oreil.ly/Fl5L1*)

    Figure 11-8, Bunny 2: Photo by Gary Bendig (*https://oreil.ly/dtZTX*)

    Figure 11-8, Bunny 3: Photo by Gavin Allanwood (*https://oreil.ly/N6tps*)

Figure 11-8, Car 1: Photo by Sam Pearce-Warrilow (*https://oreil.ly/onlg0*)

Figure 11-8, Car 2: Photo by Cory Rogers (*https://oreil.ly/HlQZm*)

Figure 11-8, Car 3: Photo by Kevin Bhagat (*https://oreil.ly/ZrN1M*)

Figure 11-8, Test Bunny: Photo by Christopher Paul High (*https://oreil.ly/vteJq*)

Chapter 12

Figure 12-12: Modified photo by Igor Miske (*https://oreil.ly/hG8b7*)

Figure 12-13: Photo by Gant Laborde (*https://oreil.ly/OAxEM*)

Apache License 2.0

Copyright 2017 © Google

Licensed under the Apache License, Version 2.0 (the "License"); you may not use this file except in compliance with the License. You may obtain a copy of the License at *http://www.apache.org/licenses/LICENSE-2.0.*

Unless required by applicable law or agreed to in writing, software distributed under the License is distributed on an "AS IS" BASIS, WITHOUT WARRANTIES OR CONDITIONS OF ANY KIND, either express or implied. See the License for the specific language governing permissions and limitations under the License.

Images under this license:

- Figure 4-9: Wikimedia Commons (*https://oreil.ly/e7n1G*)

Code under this license:

- Chapter 2: Toxicity Model NPM
- Chapter 2: MobileNet Model NPM
- Chapter 5: Inception v3 Model

Public Domain

Images under this license:

- Figure 3-2: *https://oreil.ly/xVmXb*
- Figure 9-1: *https://oreil.ly/ly839*
- Figure 12-1: *https://oreil.ly/e0MCV*

WTFPL

Data under this license (*http://www.wtfpl.net*):

- Chapter 5: Tic-Tac-Toe Model
- Chapter 5: Pet's Faces Model
- Chapter 10: Sorting Hat Model

Creative Commons Attribution-sharealike 4.0 International License (CC BY-SA 4.0)

Data under this license (*https://creativecommons.org/licenses/by-sa/4.0*):

- Chapter 5: Pet's Faces Model was trained with Oxford-IIIT Pet Dataset (*https://oreil.ly/ELqdz*)

Images under this license:

- Figure 11-1: *https://oreil.ly/qLh1h*

Creative Commons Attribution 4.0 International License (CC BY 4.0)

Data under this license (*https://creativecommons.org/licenses/by/4.0*):

- Chapter 10: The Sorting Data from drawings is a subset of Google's Quick, Draw! Dataset (*https://oreil.ly/XiVVm*) and shared under that same license on Kaggle (*https://oreil.ly/yT1n8*).

Gant Laborde and O'Reilly

All other images, except those explicitly identified in this Appendix C, are owned by either O'Reilly or the author Gant Laborde for the explicit use of this published work.

TensorFlow and TensorFlow.js Logos

TensorFlow, the TensorFlow logo, and any related marks are trademarks of Google Inc.

Index

Symbols

200 OK! plug-in (Web Server for Chrome), 33
@teachablemachine/image NPM package, 156

A

activation functions, 174
    adding to neurons, 175
    for classification model, 188
    sigmoid, 189
    softmax, 188
    tanh, 227
Adam optimizer, 180
Adamax optimizer, 170
adversarial preprocessing attacks, 91
AI (artificial intelligence), xvii
    books on, 278
    common AI/ML terminology, 20
    current, 8
    expanding applications of, 14
    history of, 4-6
    intelligence, 3
    neural networks, 6-8
    path in JavaScript, 2
    subdomains, 6
    technological power of, 1
alpha channel (opacity), 72
    tensors utilizing, preserving data with PNG, 83
Amazon Reviews dataset, 162
Apache License 2.0, 300
arrays
    building a tensor from 1D array, 48
    converting tensors to, 59
    converting to tensors, 268
    creating large arrays of data in dicify project, 268
    dimensions, review of, 47
    generating arrays of random values in TensorFlow.js, 75
    keeping tensors in, 225
    as tensors, 46
artificial intelligence (see AI)
artificial neurons, 6
    formula for, 168
automatic garbage detection and collection (AGDC), 54

B

backbone model (SSD), 123
batch processing (tensors), 54
    modifying batches of images, 87
batch size, 154
    batchSize property, 181
bias
    data bias, 158
    models created with small amount of data, 150
binarization, 275
binaryCrossentropy loss function, 228
binning, 204
blanks, handling in CSV file data, 195
books on machine learning and AI, 278
bool data type, 48
Boston Housing Prices dataset, 161
bounding boxes
    drawing on canvas, 137
    identifying object in a photo, 110
bounding outputs, 124-127

displaying all outputs, 126
reading model outputs, 124
browsers, xviii
converting image to tensor in, 77
converting tensor to image in, 76
loading models from local storage, 101
bucketing, 204
of age groups in Titanic dataset, 205

C

C++
installing to get node-gyp to run tfjs-node, 31
callbacks, 178, 199
camelCase, 191
camera obscura, 260
canvas
building sketchpad for images, 232
drawing detections to, 141
drawing text to, 134
solving draw order, 136
solving low contrast, 134
sketchpad for images, reading, 233
tainted by cross-origin data in image to tensor conversion, 79
using in tensor to image conversion in browser, 76
using to draw detection over an image, 113
categoricalCrossentropy loss function, 228
CDNs (content delivery networks)
locking code to specific TensorFlow.js version, 30
using to host TensorFlow.js, 29
chapter challenge answers, 289-298
chapter review answers, 281-287
chapter sections in this book, 20
chess pieces classifier, 244-248
creating the neural network, 246
loading chess images, 244
loading the feature model, 246
training results, 247
Chrome Web Store, 33
CIFAR dataset, 161
classification models, 187-189
CNN Explainer, 231
code examples from this book, 18
extra folder, 18
node folder, 18
simple folder, 19

web folder, 19
colors
pixel, in image tensors, 70
RGB system, 70
Common Objects in Context (COCO) dataset, 124, 162
complex64 data type, 48
compression
JPG and PNG techniques, 80
model, via quantization, 147
setting for PNG, 83
Compute Unified Device Architecture (CUDA), 30, 231
setting up to work with your graphics card, 31
confusion matrix, 235
content generation by generative networks, 12
control flow, 123
conv1d layers, 216
conv2d layers, 215, 216
conv3d layers, 216
converting models, 146-149
intermediate models, 148
running conversion commands, 147
convolutional neural networks (CNNs), 8
CNN sorting image data into categories
training and saving, 231
visualization of each layer, 230
fully convolutional approach to detecting objects, 123
region-based convolutional neural network (R-CNN), 123
sorting image data into categories, 220
CNN model, 227-231
transfer learning, 241
convolutions, 219
about, 212
adding convolutional layers, 215
MobileNet Layers model, 249
quick summary, 213
skipping in dicify project model, 263
core-js package, 122
Create React App, 100
Creative commons attribution-sharealike 4.0 international license, 301
cropping image tensors, 91
CSV files
cleaning files loaded into DataFrame, 195

empty rows, dropping from CSV files in dataset, 195
epochs, 154, 171
    loss decreasing after each epoch, 179
    onEpochEnd callback, 178, 199
    stepsPerEpoch, 179
error, measuring, 169
executeAsync method, 121

F

feature engineering, 199-207
    creating features, 204-206
    creating visuals from Titanic dataset, 201
    Dnotebook, 200
    model training results on Titanic dataset, 207
    preprocessing images through filters, 214
feature extractors, 250
fetch web API, 105
file: scheme, identifying path to file, 101
filesystem files, loading models from, 101
fill for image tensors, 73
fit configuration (models)
    batchSize property, 181
    breaking off percentage of data for validation, 206
    lifecycle callbacks, 178
    for model training on Titanic data, 199
flatten layer, 249
Float32 data type, 48
    tensors of type, converting to Int32, 81
floating-point numbers, 48
folderToTensors function, 224
functional versus object-oriented styling, 57

G

generative adversarial networks (GANs), 12
generative networks, 12
GIFs, decoding in Node.js, 84
GitHub source code page for this book, 18
glob library, 225
globalCompositeOperation (canvas), 136
Google
    dataset hosting service, 159
    dataset search site, 160
    Quick, Draw! Dataset, 221
    TensorFlow and TensorFlow.js logos, 301
GPUs
    tf.unique method and, 267

tfjs-node-gpu package, 30
    use by machine learning researchers, 5
gradient descent, 169, 180
Graph models, 98, 147, 248

H

hidden layers, 177
Hierarchical Data Format v5 (see Keras KDF5 model format)
high variance, 158
    (see also overfitting)
Hinton, Geoffrey et al., 5
HTML elements
    using in image to tensor conversion in browser, 77
    using in tensor to image conversion in browser, 76
human intelligence, translation to AI, 4
hyperparameters, 153

I

image categorization, 13
image feature vector models, 242
    loading, 246
image segmentation, 13
image tensors, 69-95
    common modifications of images, 85-93
        cropping image tensors, 91
        mirroring image tensors, 85-89
        new tools for, 93
        resizing image tensors, 89-91
    converting to/from images, 76-85
        image to tensor in a browser, 77
        image to tensor in Node.js, 83-85
        tensor to image in a browser, 76
        tensor to image in Node.js, 80-83
    creating quickly, 72-76
    image size, 71
    pixel color, 70
image training, 211-237
    CNN sorting image data into categories, 220-232
        CNN model, 227-231
        converting images to tensors, 224
        getting started, 222
        testing the model, 232-236
        training and saving, 231
    convolutions
        about, 212

M

Mac computers, installing node-gyp, 31
machine learning
    books on, 278
    gotchas, 157-159
        data bias, 158
        overfitting, 158
        poor data, 157
        underfitting, 158
    mathematics underlying, course in, 61
    origin of term, 5
    types of, 11-14
        goals of this book, 13
        reinforcement learning, 13
        semisupervised learning, 12
        supervised learning, 11
        unsupervised learning, 12
mathematical computations, TensorFlow.js and, 27
mathematics fueling machine learning, course in, 61
max pooling, 216-218, 219
mean squared error (MSE), 169
memory
    freeing for consumed model, 107
    preallocating by running empty image through model, 73
    tensors in, 54-57
        automatic tensor cleanup, 55
        deallocating tensors, 54
Microsoft Common Objects in Context (COCO) dataset, 124, 162
mirroring image tensors, 85-89
MNIST dataset, 161
    using in image classification training, 218
mobile devices, TensorFlow Lite for, 26
MobileNet, 120-124
    model detecting trucks from photos, 43
    SSD (single-shot detector), 122-124
    transfer learning, 242-248
        using Layers model, 248-251
    using with KNN NPM packages, 253
model warming, 73, 115
model zoos, 146
model.compile function, 170, 180
model.executeAsync method, 121
model.summary function, 170, 177
models, 15, 20, 97-117
    about, 16

    advanced, 119-143
        adding text overlays, 134-138
        bounding outputs, 124-127
        connecting to a webcam, 138-142
        detection cleanup, 127-133
        MobileNet, 120-124
    created to train on Titanic data, 198
    first consumed model, 101-107
        cleaning up after, 107
        interpreting the results, 105
        loading, encoding, and asking the model, 102-105
    first overlayed model, 110-116
        labeling the detection, 113
        localization model, 111
    first TensorFlow Hub model, 107-110
    loading, 98-101
        from filesystem files, 101
        from local browser storage, 101
        from public URL, 98-100
    making, resourcces for, 145-163
        converting models, 146-149
        datasets, 159-162
        first customized model, 149-157
        machine learning gotchas, 157-159
        model zoos, 146
        out-of-network model shopping, 146
    questions and answers on TensorFlow.js models, 40
    running other Tensorflow.js models provided by Google, 42
    TensorFlow, based on DAGs, 27
    training (see training models)
MSE (mean squared error), 169

N

natural language processing (NLP), 13
nearest neighbor algorithm, resizing image tensors with, 89
    malicious manipulation via, 91
neural networks, 6-8, 168
    activation functions, 174
    building for nonlinear training example, 176
    creating for image feature vector model, 246
    transfer learning, 241
neurons, 6
    adding activations to, 175
NMS (non-maximum suppression), 130

Soft-NMS, 131
Node Package Manager (see NPM)
node.decodeImage method, 84
node.encodePng method, 83
Node.js
    image to tensor conversion, 83-85
    installing Danfo.js, 191
    node folder, 18
    outperforming Python 3, 27
    requiring TensorFlow.js, 32
    running example to verify working of
        TensorFlow.js, 34
    setting up TensorFlow.js in, 30
    tensor to image conversion, 80-83
        writing JPGs, 81
        writing PNGs, 83
    Tensorflow.js running in, 10
nodemon, 19, 34
nodes
    adding more to training model, 181
    neural network, 6
normalization, 206
NPM, 19
    importing TensorFlow.js into the browser,
        29
    KNN NPM packages, 253
    rebuilding tfjs-node after installing node-
        gyp, 31
    running web example to verify working of
        TensorFlow.js, 34
    @teachablemachine/image package, 156
NVIDIA GPUs, 30

O
object detection
    bounding outputs, 124-127
    detection cleanup, 127-133
        IoUs and NMS, 129-133
        quality checking, 128
    MobileNet, 120-124
object localization, 111
object-oriented versus functional program-
    ming, 57
ObservableHQ.com notebook, 208
one-hot encoding, 204, 226
online events and courses on TensorFlow.js, 278
Open Neural Network Exchange (ONNX), 148
optimizers for machine learning, 170
    Adam, 180

overfitting, 158
overlap issues, solving for text overlays, 136
overlayed models, 110-116
    adding text overlays, 134-138
Oxford-IIIT Pet Dataset, 111

P
parameters
    hyperparameters for ML training, 153
    trainable, 171
Parcel.js, 19, 34
    plug-in, parcel-plugin-static-files-copy, 99
    regeneratorRuntime not defined error, 122
perceptron networks, 6
perceptrons, 6
performance and latency charts for model ver-
    sions on devices, 122
pet face detector model (example), 111-116
Pima Indians Diabetics dataset, 161
pip package installer, 147
platforms, interoperability of TensorFlow.js
    with, 10
PNGs, 76, 80
    writing from tensors, 83
poor data, 157
predictions, 16
    interpreting results for tic-tac-toe game, 105
    predict method of models, 105
        control flow and, 123
preprocessing
    adversarial preprocessing attacks, 91
    creating features, 204
programming exercises, 4
promises
    in tensor to image conversion in a browser,
        76
    using with globs, 225
properties of tensors, 49
public domain, images under, 300
Python, 26
    Pandas library, 191
    TensorFlow models programmed in, 146
PyTorch models, converting to TensorFlow.js,
    149

Q
quantization, compression via, 147

R

rank property (tensors), 49

React websites, 100

Receiver Operating Characteristic (ROC) graphs, 36

recommender tensor, building, 61-66

Rectified Linear Unit function (see ReLU function)

regenerator-runtime package, 122

region-based convolutional neural network (R-CNN), 123

reinforcement learning, 13

ReLU function, 175, 198

resizing image tensors, 89-91

RGB color system, 70

RGBA color system, 72

rights and licenses, 299-301
    Apache License 2.0, 300
    CC BY 4.0, 301
    CC BY-SA 4.0, 301
    Gant Laborde and O'Reilly, 301
    public domain, 300
    Unsplash license, 299
    WTFPL, 301

RMS Titanic, 190
    (see also Titanic dataset)

Ruby Warrior, 4

S

Samuel, Arthur, 5

scalars, 73

screen coordinates, 112

script tag, using to include TensorFlow.js, 29

semisupervised learning
    defined, 12

sets in arrays and tensors, 88

shape parameter for image tensors, 73

shard size, 148

shaving layers on MobileNet, 249-250
    shaved model's output type, 250

shuffle property, 224

shuffling data, 226

sigmoid activation, 189

size property (tensors), 49

snake_case, 191

social media, keeping up with TensorFlow.js on, 277

Soft-NMS, 131

softmax activation, 188

SSD (single-shot detector) MobileNet, 122-124
    fully functioning webcam with, 141
    reading model output, 124

SSD head, 123

stacking input to a model, 103

stochastic gradient descent, 169, 180

string type, 48

supervised learning, 11

synchronous large TensorFlow.js calls, drawbacks of, 120

T

t-SNE algorithm, 235

tags, image feature vector problem, 243

tanh activation, 227

Teachable Machine, 150-157
    exporting models from, 155
    gathering data and training the model, 152
    options, 150
    transfer learning with, 239
    UI for creating a model, 151
    verifying the model, 155
    website for training a model, 150

TensorFlow, 26
    logo, 301

TensorFlow Lite, 26

TensorFlow.js
    advantages of, xvii, 9-11
        diversity, 10
        offline ready, 10
        online ready, 10
        privacy, 10
        significant support, 9
    JavaScript replacing Python, 26
    keeping up with new developments in, 277
    leveraging, 27
    logo, 301
    more code for, 279
    options for, 28
    running prewritten code and models, 34-42
        classification with Toxicity model, 42
        loading Toxicity model, 40
        questions and answers about models, 40
        Toxicity classifier, 35-40
    running, different ways to, 99
    setting up in the browser, 29
        using a script tag, 29
        using NPM, 29
    setting up with Node.js, 30

U

underfitting, 158
units, 6
universities, catalogs of datasets, 159
Unsplash license, 299
unsupervised learning, 12
URIs, image feature vector model, 243
URLs, loading models from, 98-100

V

validation of models, 199
    feature engineered training results, 207
    validation sets, 21
    validation versus training accuracy, 236
    validationData and validationSplit proper-
      ties, 206
versioning
    locking CDN code to specific TensorFlow.js
      version, 30
    TensorFlow.js, most available and ready to
      run versions, 28
video, moving from image to, 139

visual reporting tools, 235
von Neumann bottleneck, 5

W

Web Server for Chrome, 33
webcam, connecting detection model to,
    138-142
    activating a webcam, 140
    drawing detections, 141
    moving from image to video, 139
website, dicify project (example), 263
    site interface, 269-273
      cutting the image into dice, 270
      reconstructing the image, 272
weight files for models, 99
Windows systems
    example conversion wizard walk-through,
      148
    installing node-gyp, 31
Wine Quality dataset, 161
WTFPL license, 301

About the Author

Like the many algorithms he's written over the past 20+ years, **Gant Laborde** voraciously consumes vast quantities of data and outputs solutions. In his early days, Gant created a website that became one of the top 100,000 websites worldwide. Now he's chief innovation officer and co-owner of Infinite Red, an industry-leading web and app development company. Besides managing an all-star roster of talent located across the globe, Gant is also a published author, adjunct professor, volunteer mentor, and speaker at conferences worldwide.

A personable mad scientist, Gant is a consummate explorer who loves explaining and charting the things he discovers. From learning about AI and teaching computers to do things he could never do on his own, to exploring the topography of New Orleans with its masked balls and secret rooms, Gant lives to find the next amazing, undiscovered thing. This approach to life makes him an avid and formidable problem solver.

Whether a given question involves technology, processes, or people, Gant approaches it with curiosity and enthusiasm. He's a motivated self-educator who thrives when passing along what he's learned to others. (That might explain why he goes on so many podcasts, but it doesn't explain why people keep sending him Nicolas Cage memes. It is a mystery.) Gant is also a lifelong advocate for open source.

A proud New Orleans native, Gant credits his city's indomitable spirit as the inspiration for his drive and ability to persevere through any obstacle. "New Orleans doesn't know how to quit," Gant says. "That's why I love it." Gant mentors at his local Toastmasters Club and channels his competitive spirit into local dodgeball games, *Rocket League*, and *Beat Saber* (wanna play?). Most importantly, he's the proud father to his adorable daughter, Mila!

Colophon

The animal on the cover of *Learning TensorFlow.js* is a diamondback terrapin (*Malaclemys terrapin*), a small species of turtle native to the brackish coastal tidal marshes of the eastern and southern United States, and in Bermuda.

The diamondback terrapin is known for its distinct dark shell with a high bridge, marked with spots or streaks. Its diet consists of soft-shelled mollusks, crustaceans, and insects, which it crushes with the ridges in its jaws. In the wild, this wary turtle is quick to flee and difficult to observe, but can be found basking on oyster beds and mudflats.

In the past, its sweet meat was considered a delicacy, and hunting brought this species close to extinction. Though the diamondback terrapin is now protected in several states, seaside development still poses a threat to nesting beaches, where tiny hatchlings often get trapped in tire tracks.

Many of the animals on O'Reilly covers are endangered; all of them are important to the world.

The cover illustration is by Karen Montgomery, based on a black and white engraving from *Johnson's Natural History*. The cover fonts are Gilroy Semibold and Guardian Sans. The text font is Adobe Minion Pro; the heading font is Adobe Myriad Condensed; and the code font is Dalton Maag's Ubuntu Mono.

Milton Keynes UK
Ingram Content Group UK Ltd.
UKHW020650010324
438645UK00003B/10